FACING EVIL

FACING EVIL

Light at the Core of Darkness

Edited by   Paul Woodruff and Harry A. Wilmer

Open ✳ Court
LaSalle, Illinois 61301

For permission to use the selections printed in this book, the authors are grateful to the following: Chiron Publications, for excerpts from *Practical Jung* by Harry Wilmer; Chatto and Windus, for the excerpt from *A Walk with a White Bushman* by Laurens van der Post; Dodd Mead and Co., for the excerpt from 'Masks' by Paul Laurens Dunbar; Doubleday, for the excerpts from *Man and his Symbols* by C. G. Jung; Hackett, for the excerpt from Epictetus by Nicholas White; Harper and Row, for the excerpts from *The Knowledge of Man* by Martin Buber, for 'Conscientious Objector' by Edna St. Vincent Millay, for the excerpt from *Gulag* by Solzhenitsyn, for the excerpt from 'Between the World and Me' by Richard Wright; Holt Rinehart Winston, for 'West-Running Brook' by Robert Frost; Macmillan, for the excerpt from *What are Years?* by Mariane Moore; Penguin, for the excerpts from Saint Augustine, *Confessions*, trans. R. S. Pine-Coffin; Princeton, for the excerpts from these works by C. G. Jung, *Collected Works*, *Letters of C. G. Jung*, *Psychological Reflections*, and *C. G. Jung*, ed. Maguire and Hill; Public Affairs TV, Inc., for permission to quote from their broadcast of 'Facing Evil, with Bill Moyers'. The painting on the cover of this book, entitled *The Shadow: Light at the Core of Darkness*, is by C. G. Jung and is used with the permission of the heirs of C. G. Jung and Princeton University Press.

First printing 1988

Printed and bound in the United States of America.

Library of Congress Cataloging-in-Publication Data

Facing evil : light at the core of darkness / edited by Paul Woodruff and Harry A. Wilmer
    p. cm.
    Papers from the Symposium on Understanding Evil, held Oct. 1987 in Salado, Tex.
    Bibliography: p.
    Includes index.
    ISBN 0-8126-9078-8 : $19.95. ISBN 0-8126-9079-6 (pbk.) : $9.95
    1. Good and evil—Congresses. I. Woodruff, Paul, 1943–
II. Wilmer, Harry A., 1917–   . III. Symposium on Understanding
Evil (1987 : Salado, Tex.)
BJ1401.F36 1988
111'.84—dc19

                                             88-22056
                                                   CIP

To Lee Marvin

February 19, 1924–August 29, 1987

Lee Marvin was an actor who had a deep and very human understanding of evil. He was scheduled to speak at the Symposium but did not live to speak there. The Symposium was dedicated to his memory. Those of us who knew him or his work will not forget him. When he visited Salado in 1983, we asked him how he felt when he saw himself on the screen.

How do I feel when I see myself on the screen? I found it very unpleasant recently when I saw a film of mine called *Point Blank,* which was a violent film. I remember; we made it for the violence. I was shocked at how violent it was. Of course, that was ten, fifteen, eighteen years ago. When I saw the film I literally almost could not stand up, I was so weak. I did *that?* I am capable of that kind of violence? See, *there* is the fright; and this is why I think guys back off eventually. They say, "No, I'm not going to put myself to those demons again." The demon being the self.

—Lee Marvin
(From an interview at Salado, September 18, 1983)

The force which threatens to blow the world asunder resides not in the clouds or mountains but in the invisible heart of the atom. The inner force, too, which, like the power of the atom, can either remake or shatter civilization resides in the smallest unit of society, the individual. The individual is the secret advance base from which the power sets out to invade committee rooms, mothers' meetings, county councils, parliaments, continents and nations.

—LAURENS VAN DER POST
The Dark Eye in Africa

CONTENTS

NOTE TO THE READER

The materials in this book do not presuppose a special knowledge of the scholarly literature on evil. Your reading of the book will be enriched however, if you know something about what has been written on evil. The editors have supplied an Appendix, 'Thinking About Evil', which consists of texts from famous authors on the subject. The recent literature on evil is treated in an annotated bibliography prepared by Jeffrey Burton Russell.

The Symposium at which these papers were presented was recorded on audiotape. These are available from AVW Audio Visual Incorporated, 2254 Valdina, Suite 100, Dallas, Texas 75207. Portions of the Symposium were used in a Bill Moyers television special, 'Facing Evil,' made by Public Affairs Television, Inc. and KERA/Dallas/Fort Worth/Denton. For transcripts of this show, write to Journal Graphics, Inc., 267 Broadway, New York, NY 10007; for performance rights or copies of the videotape, contact Public Affairs Television, Inc., 356 West 58th Street, New York, NY 10009.

PREFACE

The papers presented in this volume contain everything of substance that was said at the Symposium on Understanding Evil convened in October, 1987, by the Institute for the Humanities at Salado, Texas. In most cases, we have printed the speeches exactly as they were given by vigorous speakers to live audiences. We have not imposed on them a standard or academic style, for these speeches are mostly personal expressions of the people who gave them. The subject is one we must face squarely without any of the defenses of academic life. Although many of these speeches were made by scholars, none of them is meant for a scholarly audience; and although they contain frequent allusions to history and to literature, that is not what they are about. They are about the facing of evil that we have done and must do and what others have done and must do. Part of this process is trying to understand evil; but the deepest evil defies our understanding. This book reflects the personal honesty and courage that are essential to the facing of evil. It is also about the paradoxical hope that good can be brought out of evil.

The subject is a dangerous one in many ways and on many levels. The first danger is that we see only the shadows cast by other people. Americans generally associate evil with Europe, especially with the activities of Nazis. Early in the symposium, Maya Angelou reacted to the addresses of Rollo May and Gregory Curtis, and admonished us all to be courageous enough to look at our personal histories:

> I feel as though I'm really in danger, because while I may agree with many of the things you both have said . . . I find it interesting that in 1987 we are able to talk about the evil in Europe and ignore in a kind of blithe and marvelous way the evil with which we are all engaged and have been engaged for three hundred years in this

country, and that is slavery. It is a particular evil. That, then, to me, is evil personified. To know and not to do is in fact not to know.

So here we are, in a marvelous group of brilliant and intelligent people, blithely talking about evil. We have begun this intrigue that will take us through three days of evoking and invoking forces of which we have no consideration, no understanding. And we must at least come to grips early on with this issue plaguing us and that shall plague us until we work with it or we don't. This is why our country is in such trouble: we have not dealt with it as thinkers. At some point, the thinker must think.

Courage is the most important of all the virtues, because without it we can't practice any other virtue. I wish I had said that first. Aristotle said it. But if we could be courageous about our own histories, our individual personal histories—mine, Maya; yours, Gregory Curtis; yours, Rollo May—if we could be courageous enough to think about it, we might question whether in fact there may be more than a dualism of good and evil. There may be many other things. I think so.

A second danger is that we fail to think about the evils that we—not other people—are engaged in. The effect of ignoring evils all around us is a way of being engaged in them. But of course we also need to be thinking of evils that other people do, about how to prevent them or contain them. Philip Hallie speaks with anguish about this. Although he admired the pacifist people of a French village that defied Hitler to save Jews during World War II, he resented them as well:

> They didn't stop Hitler. They did nothing to stop Hitler. A thousand Le Chambons would not have stopped Hitler. It took decent murderers like me to do it. Murderers who had compunctions, but murderers nonetheless. The cruelty that I perpetrated willingly was the only way to stop the cruel march that I and others like me were facing. (Below, p. 127.)

It is not enough to look at the evil within. At times we feel the need to take arms against external evils, and this at an enormous moral price to ourselves. "Today what life demands of us most urgently is to find a means of overcoming evil without becoming another form of evil in its place," writes Sir Laurens van der Post and he adds the thought that "one culture after another is still running amok and men are still murdering one another in the belief that it is not they but their neighbors who are evil."

The ultimate evil could be the atomic destruction of civilization and the world by design or by inadvertance, as Herbert Abrams tells us in his chapter.

A third danger is overlooking the price of repaying evil with evil. Hallie speaks of his guilt over the killing of young German soldiers in World War II. He remembers beautiful heads severed, and he remembers people running with bits of flaming white phosphorous embedded in their living bodies. He does not want to forget:

> If I did not keep aware of the conflict in my mind about being a decent killer, then I would be more immoral than I am . . . Because I deserve that agony; I want to believe in the preciousness of life and be a killer too. And because I feel this way, I have to pay a price morally.[1]

Not forgetting what others have done carries its own danger as well. An evil you cannot forget or forgive lives on in your heart, and continues to affect you and those around you in countless ways. The more you think about particular evils done to you, the greater the risk that you will do evil yourself, and the less able you will be to see that this is evil. Understanding can perhaps bring forgiveness, but not every evil can be understood, and many cannot be forgiven. Al Huang offers the promise of an attitude towards evil beyond understanding and beyond forgiveness, a centered and harmonious way of living, moving, and being after facing evil, without being torn apart by our passions of anger and guilt.

A further danger in looking at evil is that we come to imitate it. We do this not merely because we tend to mimic what we look at, but for other more powerful reasons. When we look at evil, we find it terrifyingly attractive. This was a theme common to several speakers. Jeffrey Russell highlights this. Gregory Curtis explores it in his chapter:

> We must search for the good, while evil finds us out. In Eden, Eve did not go looking for the serpent; rather, it came to her. Evil accepts us. It does not require us to improve. No matter how great our

faults, evil will embrace us. Evil validates our weaknesses and our secret appetites. It tells us we're all right. Evil does not ask us to feel guilty. You are what you are, evil says. In fact, if you want to, you can get worse. (Below, p. 94.)

You can, also, get better, and perhaps help others along the same road. This is the hope in different ways of Scott Peck, Samuel Proctor, and Maya Angelou who show how the good men do *can* live after them, and be passed from generation to generation. The danger here, of course, is that we congratulate ourselves on the small good that we do, and so lose sight of the greater evils in which we are implicated. Who could reasonably hope to escape the battle between good and evil? We will always be a part of it.

PAUL WOODRUFF AND HARRY WILMER

NOTE

[1] From the transcript of 'Facing Evil, with Bill Moyers', New York: Journal Graphics, 1988, p. 8.

ACKNOWLEDGMENTS

We are grateful to the Texas Committee for the Humanities, a state program of the National Endowment for the Humanities; the Rockwell Fund, Inc., Houston, especially Joe M. Green Jr.; The Kempner Fund, Galveston; The Harris Foundation, Chicago, especially Irving B. Harris; The John D. and Catherine T. MacArthur Foundation, Chicago; The Brown Foundation, Inc., Houston; The Potts and Sibley Foundation, Midland; Jane Blaffer Owen, Houston; D.J. Sibley, Austin; members and staff of the Institute for the Humanities at Salado; heirs of C.G. Jung for permission to use the painting by Jung on the jacket; Lonnie Edwards, Salado; Bill Moyers and PBS for their documentary 'Facing Evil'; KERA-TV, Dallas; Norma Maedgen and Nancy Lefler for secretarial help; Louise Mahdi and the editorial and production staff of Open Court Publishing Company; Polly Miller; Jack Knox; Jane Wilmer; Elizabeth Silverthorne; Liz Carpenter; Stewart Smith; David Grubin; David Steward, Director, International Activities, the Corporation for Public Broadcasting, Washington, D.C.; and to members of the Institute who matched the challenge grant from the Texas Committee for the Humanities: Wayne Baden, Dianne Delisi, Grace Jones, Keifer Marshall, Susan Negley, Jane Owen, Bernard Rapoport, Gretchen Lara Shartle, D.J. Sibley, Steward Smith, Erroll and Barbara Jean Wendland, Lorch Folz, Polly Miller, Jane and Harry Wilmer.

Particular appreciation is given to Joe M. Green Jr., president of the Rockwell Fund, Inc., whose support made it possible to create the Institute for the Humanities at Salado.

INTRODUCTION

Harry A. Wilmer

It was from out the rind of one apple tasted, that the knowledge of good and evil, as two twins cleaving together, leaped forth into the world. And perhaps this is that doom which Adam fell into of knowing good and evil: that is to say, of knowing good by evil.

As therefore the state of man now is; what wisdom can there be to choose, what continence to forebear, without the knowledge of evil?

—JOHN MILTON[1]

This book is devoted to the exploration of ideas, feelings, experiences, and perceptions of Evil. Without attempting to define Evil, we report on its present state of being in our culture and our lives.

The Institute for the Humanities at Salado invited world-renowned students of humanity to come and talk about Evil with each other and with members of this Institute for a weekend in the fall of 1987. Every chair in the auditorium was taken. The experience of the event was spellbinding. No dull or boring speeches. There was an unflagging attentiveness of both speakers and audience for two-and-a-half days as one person followed another. There was a rhythmic flow of emotions: hope, despair, sadness, tears, pleasure, laughter, anger, and pain. Small luncheon discussion groups of ten participants were held in various homes in Salado led by a member of the resource faculty or a speaker. There was only one event happening at a time; everyone shared a common moving group experience, a ritual without dogma. Eventually it was a personal experience.

The success of this symposium on evil is testimony to a public receptivity to candid examination of the dark side of humanity. This could happen because there is a better recognition of the shadow side of life now than in past times, and a willingness to forego happy-mindedness, sentimental illusions, and sham. We gathered together to listen and to contemplate the principle of evil without attempting to explain away the dark side of life.

The Institute for the Humanities at Salado is an autonomous non-profit corporation for the presentation of public programs in the humanities. Its membership is limited and there is a long waiting list. At first the capacity of local facilities was a determining factor but soon smallness became our deliberate policy. Successful smallness is actually big news in Texas. Productive smallness is important anywhere.

Salado is a tiny village just north of Austin. Such issues as evil are best examined in a small town atmosphere because they offer better opportunities for interaction and mutual understanding. No one is lost. In this village there is a refreshing attentiveness and courtesy which is more characteristic of a small town than a city. Almost everything and every place in Salado is accessible within ten minutes. There are no traffic hassles, no smog and no congestion of people. Philip Geyelin, newspaper correspondent and speaker at an earlier symposium on Vietnam, wrote a column for the editorial page of the Washington Post headlined "From Saigon To Salado" in which he said "Salado is a far piece from where policy is made. But it might not be a bad place for policy-makers of the moment to repair from time to time to contemplate their handiwork."[2]

The symposium on evil grew out of our earlier conference on Vietnam, in which the shadow of humanity and elemental evil were evident. This was recorded on audiotape and published in a book entitled *Vietnam in Remission*.[3] Well, Vietnam may be in remission, but evil is not.

The word 'evil' itself frightens some people. There is consequently a widespread reluctance to even talk seriously about evil as if ignoring it would diminish its power or deny its actual being. Or perhaps we try to convince ourselves that evil belong to ages past. But evil has always been, and is, and always will be.

Evil is the central problem of our times. The iniquitous roster of evil all around us is an unending list of dark powers that are proliferating: racism, genocide, monstrous crimes, drug gang wars, merciless and random slaughter of innocent civilians, gas bombing of cities, pestilence, famine and war, governmental policies of racial cruelty, death squads, violent or insidious suppression of human rights, forms of slavery, abuse of children, bestial military action against civilians, callousness to the homeless, the AIDS victims and the poor, abuse of the elderly, sexism, rape, wanton murder, cults, terrorism, torture, the unremitting aftermath of past holy and unholy wars, the Holocaust, heinous cruelty and hatred, and the seven deadly sins: wrath, pride, envy, sloth, gluttony, lust, and avarice.

We go on polluting the air, the soil, and the water. We think the unthinkable: atomic destruction of civilization and the earth itself. We trash outer and inner space. We literally are in danger of running amok. All the while we feed an unbridled and insatiable appetite for horror; demonic projections are made on enemies as "Evil Empire", and "The Great Satan"; governments conspire with organized crime, assassinate and massacre, destroy the souls of people for power and money, arm nations and individuals, and as a consequence human beings are now exploding in every corner of the globe. Such things as these are often nourished and cunningly abetted by the media: television, film, newspapers, and even art, literature, and music.

The manifestations of personal evil multiply and the outbreak of collective evil occurs on a scale never before known in world history. Laurens van der Post asks the great question: "Has there been another age that, knowing so clearly the right things to do, has so consistently done the wrong ones?" And he answers, "I doubt it; and because I doubt it, I feel it is important as never before to get our private contributions to the split clear in our minds, and as far as possible to close the gap in ourselves in every detail of our lives."[4]

Darkness is there, always there somewhere. It is ultimate hubris to think that evil is ever defeated or that we conquer the enemies of life. We should enjoy the wonder of that knowledge were it not for the pain in realizing it. Each celebration carries a shadow portending evil as each high carries a low. Each sunrise carries the realization of coming night. And yet, there is the luminous moon at night and the radiant sun in the day. There is no light without darkness, no good without evil; we know one by the other.

There is a dire necessity to try to understand and face evil. To the extent that we are successful in doing this we unleash tensions between those evils whose origins are personal and those evils which are absolute and whose origins are inborn in the human psyche.

Personal evils are manifestations of the dark side of our individual human life, the negative and destructive elements of our unconscious. These are the consequences of our own life-experiences which are repressed and are projected onto others. Thus we see evil in others and not in ourselves.

This personal shadow side is in everyone. While all of it is not evil, the reprehensible parts are evil. Hence there is a subjective judgement which is influenced by time and culture. This evil is manifest in our personal lives, institutions, organizations, groups of people, and nations. We can do something about this personal and institutionalized evil. We can become conscious of it, aware that we project it, and heal the split within each of us.

But there is a deeper evil which is neither personal nor organizational. It is Absolute Evil. This is conceptualized as the archetype of Evil. There is nothing that we as individuals can do to eradicate Absolute Evil. We can, however, strive for good, and try to become aware that evil is deep within each of us. Armed with this understanding of evil we can work to prevent its destructive manifestations.

There is a tension between the personal and the archetypal evil. We can do something to eradicate the former, but we can only cope with the latter. The tension between what is possible to change and what is impossible to change is both foreboding and enlightening. In facing evil the energy from darkness can become a force for light. The speakers at this symposium look at this question.

The cover of this book is a painting by C. G. Jung which he called *The Shadow: Light at the Core of Darkness*.[5] There is light at the core of darkness: Cambridge University physicist Stephen Hawking observes that the black hole appears to emit particles despite the fact that nothing can escape from within what is called its event horizon. Perhaps gravitational collapse, the final Shadow, is not so final and irreversible as we once thought. To explain this Hawking says that at the event horizon at the boundary of the black hole—at the edge of the shadow of impending doom— there are rays of light which do not approach each other.[6]

NOTES

[1] John Milton, *Areopagitica*. J. Max Patrick, (ed.), *The Prose of John Milton*. (New York: New York University Press, 1968), p. 287.

[2] *Washington Post*. November 6, 1982.

[3] James F. Veninga and Harry A. Wilmer (eds.), *Vietnam in Remission* (College Station: Texas A&M University Press, 1985).

[4] Laurens van der Post, *Venture to the Interior* (New York: Penguin, 1978), p. 163.

[5] Aniela Jaffe (ed.), *C. G. Jung: Word and Image* (Princeton: Princeton University Press, 1979), pp. 66–75.

[6] Stephen W. Hawking, *A Brief History of Time: From the Big Bang to Black Holes* (New York: Bantam Books, 1988), pp. 99, 105.

PART I

UNDERSTANDING EVIL

THE DARK EYE IN THE WORLD[1]

Laurens van der Post

Sir Laurens van der Post is
an author, film-maker, diplomat, and soldier. He is godparent
to Prince William of Wales and a close friend of the royal family.
His films include 'The Kalahari Bushmen', 'The Story of C. G.
Jung', 'All Africa Within Us', and 'A Region of Shadow'. Van
der Post was born in South Africa. His great-grandfather led the
Great Trek of the South African Boers away from British rule in
the Cape of Good Hope to the Interior. These Boers were
massacred by the Zulu in 1835. His grandmother, her sister, and
little brother, and a nurse were the only survivors. His father
was a statesman, writer, philosopher, and soldier. He was the
thirteenth of 15 children. When the Japanese attacked Pearl
Harbor, van der Post was assigned by the British to Burma and
then Sumatra. While organizing resistance in Java, he was
captured by the Japanese and spent four years as a prisoner of
war. This experience was made into a motion picture, *Merry
Christmas, Mr. Lawrence,* starring David Bowie. Van der Post was
later on the staff of Lord Mountbatten and was knighted in 1980.
His books include *In a Province, Venture to the Interior, The Face
Beside the Fire, The Lost World of the Kalahari, A Portrait of All the
Russians, A Portrait of Japan, The Heart of the Hunter, The Seed and
the Sower, A View of All the Russians, The Hunter and the Whale, The
Prisoner and the Bomb, A Story Like the Wind, A Far-Off Place, And
Yet Another,* and *A Mantis Carol.*

My title is based on a film I made many years ago called 'A
Region of Shadow' from a book, *The Dark Eye in Africa,*[2] which I
had written not long after the last world war. The book was an
exploration I had undertaken in my own mind, through an

evaluation of my lifelong experience of racial and color prejudice of all kinds in the human spirit. It was an exploration to discover what I thought was the origin of these extraordinary violent and damaging prejudices in the modern world. I had been driven to this very largely by my own experience of racial and color prejudice at the hands of the Japanese when I was a prisoner of war in Java.

I chose the title *The Dark Eye in Africa* then because of a phenomenon that occurs in those islands, which the Malaysians call *amok* and the Javanese call *mata kelap*. It is a phenomenon where a human being who has behaved respectably in the collective sense, obeying all the mores and the collective ethos of a particular culture and people, suddenly at the age of about thirty-five or forty finds all this respectability too much—and takes a dagger and murders everyone around before being overpowered. I wonder if you would feel as I did when I first heard the dreaded cry of "Amok!" going up in Malaya. When this happens, when someone runs amok in this way, there is an extraordinary feeling of panic that seizes the observer.

The same thing happened in Java, whose people are also Malaysian. Here they also call the phenomenon *mata kelap*, 'the dark eye', implying that when a human being does this the human eye has darkened. I called the phenomenon of racial prejudice in South Africa an example of the darkening of the human eye because I suddenly realized that prejudice was caused by the shadow of the darkness in the human spirit, where the human eye—as a symbol of human conscious illumination and penetration—does not enter. Suddenly the human spirit is overpowered by internal forces waiting for recognition, who have grown angry, as it were, by their lack of recognition. They rise up and extinguish the light in that person's eye and the person runs amok. The person wants to kill and destroy.

If there is one thing the human spirit cannot endure, it is the state of meaninglessness that occurs when conscious recognition of what it is and what it needs is denied to itself. This state seems to me to be the whole area in which not only racial and color prejudice arise, but also in which all the dangers confronting us in the modern world have their origins.

You are going on to the much larger question of Evil, and I do not want to equate this area I have called "the Shadow" with Evil.

I just want to say this to you: In my long experience of violence and meaninglessness in the modern world, of tension in modern societies, and of all the disorder accumulating and growing within societies and between cultures, never in the history of humankind has the world been so totally involved in a state of crisis as it is today. This statement does not apply only to the Western world, but also to the great civilizations of the Far East. It applies to all countries, primitive as well as sophisticated, democratic as well as totalitarian. We are all confronted with a strange kind of disorder and sense of meaninglessness that afflicts us.

I think, therefore, the greatest problem of our time is not only to understand evil, but also to recognize the fact that evil is not merely an absence of good. It is also a deep and fundamental part of human and spiritual reality.

How evil came about, and what it precisely is, needs all our attention and understanding. What we can say for certain about it is that three things seem to have happened simultaneously—the evolution of human consciousness, the awareness of good, and the awareness of evil. The moment that consciousness became a part of the spirit of humankind—the more conscious people became of themselves—the more real became their confrontation with the problem of good and evil. These three things seem to have arisen simultaneously in response to a need of life and evolution of creation that we do not adequately understand. Today what life demands of us most urgently is to find a means of overcoming evil without another form of evil taking its place.

We see it going on all over the world, where we find this ancient phenomenon to which the Greek philosopher Heraclitus drew attention. He called it *enantiodromia*, the tendency of life perpetually to go over into its opposites. This problem has us by the throat as never before, and this has been largely due to a darkening of the eye—that is, to a diminution, a decrease, or diminishing of consciousness.

Ever since the Renaissance, the evolution of the Western spirit has tended to be extroverted. After a long medieval age of introspection, it has tended to go over into its opposite—to be utterly extroverted, to be more and more exclusively focused on the outer world—on matter, substance, and material things

—and to be indifferent to the other great objective world, the other great objective spirit that people have within themselves. The tendency has been to equate consciousness more and more with reason, to regard consciousness as merely a kind of rationalism. Of course, consciousness is infinitely more than that. As the light of reason has become sharper, more clearly focused and more highly supported and validated by the immense inventions of technology and science that are so useful to humankind, there has been a rejection and elimination of awareness of this other area from which humans derive their meaning. Therefore, as the shadow in the human spirit has increased, there has been a massing all the other neglected aspects of the feeling and caring values of humans —waiting to play their legitimate role in life.

This is really what it is all about, because in a strange way, with this profound contraction of consciousness, the power of evil has increased. Carl Jung performed a great service for humankind in showing this, which you will have to consider very seriously in your deliberations on the role of the shadow. The shadow is not necessarily evil. One must always remember an old French proverb that says that human beings tend to become that which they oppose. One must remember Christ's prayer, "Deliver us from evil." He did not say, "Oppose evil." He said, "Deliver us from evil." He also said to his disciples a very strange thing, "Resist ye not evil."

We must search for another approach to deal with this problem of evil, to prevent what I call "darkening of the eye", because this led to the dreadful outburst of amok in two world wars in my generation, to the horrors of Vietnam and Korea, and to all the horrors that are afflicting civilizations all over the world where one culture after another is still running amok and people are still murdering one another in the belief that it is not they but their neighbors who are evil.

All this has a connection with what I call the shadow, because as I said, the shadow in itself is not evil. There is almost a sense in which evil is not evil! Evil is a fact. Evil is really a challenge of life for us to transform the thing that evil represents. While the shadow is not evil, it can be a source of evil. But it can and must also be a source of enlargement and enrichment of the human personality.

The human contribution to life depends not on reducing consciousness to a narrow state of reason, but rather on allowing all the naturally instinctive things that are at the disposal of the shadow to become part of our consciousness, expanded into something I prefer to call *awareness*. We must understand the role in which the shadow can be an instrument either of evil or—not merely the opposite of evil, which is good—but *wholeness*.

It is in this form of enlargement that we have to look for an understanding of evil and for a state of mind and spirit in which the human being will be able to contain these tremendous tensions set up by the responsibility of consciousness. It is here also that we hope to deal with the painful choice that consciousness has thrust on the human individual—that is, to choose between good and evil, between truth and error.

That leads not only to the concept of individuation and the necessity for the individual to withdraw the collective shadow from the external world into oneself, but also to take upon oneself as the greatest task the transformation of this shadow—this area of neglect in the human spirit—into a source of light in darkness. Through this vision of wholeness and seeking of wholeness we must win out because we have what St. Paul called *caritas*, a love not only of ourselves and of human beings, but a love of the other, a love even of this darkness that causes the dreadful darkening of the human eye—and through the power of this love to enlarge our consciousness. I suggest you have to examine this problem that confronts you, from now until the end of this significant symposium, with this element of elements as your compass. Let it quicken you as it quickened Paul of Damascus in that great chapter of Corinthians, remembering that *caritas* is Latin for 'charity' in the King James translation of the Bible, and for 'love' in both the English and the American Revised Standard Versions. There Paul says:

> If I speak in the tongues of men and of angels, but have not love, I am a noisy gong or a clanging cymbal. And if I have prophetic powers, and understand all mysteries and all knowledge, and if I have all faith, so as to remove mountains, but have not love, I am nothing. If I give away all I have, and if I deliver my body to be burned, but have not love, I gain nothing.
> Love is patient and kind; love is not jealous or boastful; it is not

arrogant or rude. Love does not insist on its own way; it is not irritable or resentful; it does not rejoice at wrong, but rejoices in the right. Love bears all things, believes all things, hopes all things, endures all things.

Love never ends; as for prophecies, they will pass away; as for tongues, they will cease; as for knowledge, it will pass away. For our knowledge is imperfect and our prophecy is imperfect; but when the perfect comes, the imperfect will pass away.

When I was a child, I spoke like a child, I thought like a child, I reasoned like a child; when I became a man, I gave up childish ways. For now we see in a mirror dimly [through a glass darkly], but then face to face. Now I know in part, then I shall understand fully, even as I have been fully understood. So faith, hope, love abide, these three; but the greatest of these is love. (1 Cor. 13:1–13)

And we, who owe so much to Jung, could complete the meaning with the recollection of how, at the end of his long journey, Jung came to the same conclusion, stressing that these words say all there is to be said and that nothing can really be added to them:

For we are, in the deepest sense, the victims and the instruments of cosmogonic "love" . . . Man can try to name love, showering upon it all the names of his command, and still he will involve himself in endless self-deceptions. If he possesses a grain of wisdom he will lay down his arms and name the unknown by the more unknown, that is by the name of God. This is a confession of his subjection, his imperfection and his dependence; but at the same time a testimony of his freedom to choose between truth and error.[3]

NOTES

[1] This text is an edited transcript of a film of Sir Laurens van der Post, which opened the symposium on "Understanding Evil". This film was directed by Brian Huberman, professor of film at Rice University in Houston, Texas, while he was working with the National Film and Television School in London. Arrangements for this production were made by David Stewart, International

Activities director of the Corporation for Public Broadcasting in Washington, D.C.

² Laurens van der Post, *The Dark Eye in Africa* (London: Hogarth Press, 1955).

³ C. G. Jung, *Memories, Dreams, Reflections* (New York: Pantheon Books, 1963), p. 354.

CLEARING THE SPRING

Liz Carpenter

Liz Carpenter, who lives in Austin, Texas, is a senior consultant to Hill and Knowlton International Public Relations, for which she was formerly corporate vice-president. She has been executive assistant to President Lyndon Johnson, staff director and press secretary to Lady Bird Johnson, a member of the International Women's Year Commission appointed by President Gerald Ford, and assistant secretary of education for public affairs under President Jimmy Carter. Liz has been a member of the Board of Trustees of the Institute for the Humanities at Salado from its beginning. She is a member of the Texas Philosophical Society, and serves on the board of the George W. Peabody Awards. She was a founding member of the National Women's Political Caucus and chair of ERAmerica. She was named Distinguished Alumna of the University of Texas. She received the National Headliners Award from Women in Communication and has been president of the National Women's Press Club. Carpenter was consultant to the Lyndon Baines Johnson Library. She is author of articles in *Redbook, Family Circle,* and the *Washington Post.* Her books are *Ruffles and Flourishes* and *Getting Better All the Time.*

We are here not just to understand why evil happens in one place or in one condition on the face of this anxious planet, but why, in the larger question, it occurs at all—anywhere—in any one of us.

I have to give a word about Salado, for it is my own Lake Wobegon. I was born here under great oaks, and grew up playing along the limestone streams. Every so often, it was necessary for us to go down and clean the spring, pulling out weeds and debris that choked the source, making it flow clear. I think that's what we are doing this time, this weekend.

For me, who thinks of this town in the tenderest of terms, it's hard to reconcile evil with Salado. Yet Evil dwelt here along with goodness. My gentle great-grandfather, who came here first, had slaves. He never called them that, but servants. One went with him to war, but they were humans held by him in the practice of the times. He was the same man who, as a humanitarian, gave the land and the leadership for the first college right up there on the hill. You can still see the skeleton of its chimney there. And there the classics were taught. My mother had six years of Latin on that hill where Salado College tried to live up to the challenge of the great Mirabeau B. Lamar that education is the guardian genius of democracy. He gave the church where we sang the hymns about evil: "I was sinking deep in sin," "Bring them in from the fields of sin." And the commanding words of the "Mighty Fortress": "And though this world, with devils filled, should threaten to undo us, we will not fear, for God hath willed, His truth to triumph through us."

Truth also visited Salado and it was listened to, even in this backwater village on the frontier. Before the Civil War, Sam Houston stood on that balcony of Stagecoach Inn to plead against secession. A hundred and ten years ago my Great Aunt Luella at age eighteen stood on Salado Hill. The year was 1877. At an alumni reunion, she delivered a brilliant essay on the mental capabilities of Woman and a plea for her higher education.

"Fathers, if by one feeble word of mine I could disperse the myths which hang like an incubus around you," she said in that embroidered language of the time, "if I could cause you to view more plainly the necessity of education for your daughters as thoroughly as your sons, I would not feel this essay was in vain."

'Evil' is a strong word for me. I shrink from it on the wide screen. The Holocaust I cannot bear to think about. I turn the remote control from films of violence and my eyes from headlines of horror. But on the scale of my own life, I am familiar with the flaws and frailties of the human condition. Evil as the suppression of the spirit, the denial of joy, the starvation of a child's curiosity, the freezing of a friend's or a mate's love (which, in the words of Rollo May, makes life meaningless)—how many of these acts are evil, an evil perhaps embedded deeply in us and practiced by a teacher, an employer, a husband, a spouse? How much of this destroys imagination and creativity, and renders life meaningless?

I think back to my own Washington and to Allen Drury's marvelous definition of that great marble capitol stretching along the Potomac, "a city where good men do evil and evil men do good in a way so complex that only Americans can understand it and often they are baffled." As a reporter I felt deeply a special reverence for the First Amendment, and yet I felt also and continue to feel a special indignation for the reporters and the publications that prefer blood to ink. The darker side of human nature is never the whole truth, yet we give awards to people for committing printed harassment.

There is no way to cover news really honestly, we feel, without invoking unlimited torture—or is the alternative worse? We cannot concentrate on individual evils, although they come to mind within our human experience. But we can seek the source. We can begin to clear out the spring. And today, we have two brilliant women to help us do that: Maya Angelou and Barbara Jordan. Maya Angelou has told us about growing up in Stamps, Arkansas, where she was both terribly hurt and vastly loved. She took the evil that evoked her rage and anger and translated it into a very basic truth about human resilience. We already understand more because she pulled back the curtain and let us see and, it is to be hoped, act.

THAT WHICH LIVES AFTER US

Maya Angelou

Maya Angelou is a poet, author, historian, educator, editor, actress, singer, and dancer. She has risen to brilliant heights with a formal education limited to high school, and has received many honorary doctorates and the Chubb Fellowship from Yale. In the 1960s, at the request of Martin Luther King, Jr., she became the northern coordinator for the Southern Christian Leadership Conference. In 1981, she was appointed the first Reynolds professor of American Studies at Wake Forest University. Her first autobiographical book, *I Know Why The Caged Bird Sings*, was made into a two-hour TV special for CBS in 1979. Other titles include *Gather Together in My Name*, *Singin' and Swingin' and Gettin' Merry Like Christmas*, *The Heart of a Woman*, and *All God's Children Need Traveling Shoes*. Her books of poetry include *Just Give Me a Cool Drink of Water 'fore I Die*, *Oh Pray My Wings Are Gonna Fit Me Well*, *Shaker, Why Don't You Sing?*, and *Now Sheba Sings the Song*. She wrote the stage play *On A Southern Journey* and was both author and producer of *Sisters, Sisters*, a full-length film for 20th Century Fox. She was also author and executive producer of the CBS miniseries *Three Way Choice* and of the PBS program *Afro-American in the Arts*, for which she received the Golden Eagle Award.

In an interview during the Symposium Maya Angelou recounted this experience:[1]
"When I was seven and a half, I was raped. I won't say severely raped, all rape is severe. The rapist was a person very well known to my family. I was hospitalized. The rapist was let out of jail and was found dead that night, and the police suggested that the rapist had been kicked to death.

"I was seven and a half. I thought that I had caused the man's death,

because I had spoken his name. That was my 7 seven-and-a-half-year-old logic. So I stopped talking, for five years.

"Now, to show you how out of evil there can come good, in those five years I read every book in the Black school library; I read all the books I could get from the White school library; I memorized James Weldon Johnson, Paul Laurence Dunbar, Countee Cullen and Langston Hughes; I memorized Shakespeare, whole plays, 50 sonnets; I memorized Edgar Allan Poe, all the poetry—never having heard it, I memorized it. I had Longfellow, I had Guy de Maupassant, I had Balzac, Rudyard Kipling—it was a catholic kind of reading.

"When I decided to speak, I had a lot to say, and many ways in which to say what I had to say. I listened to the Black minister, I listened to the melody of the preachers, and I could tell when they meant to take our souls straight to heaven, or whether they meant to dash us straight to hell. I understood it.

"This was a dire kind of evil, because rape on the body of a young person more often than not introduces cynicism, and there is nothing quite so tragic as a young cynic, because it means the person has gone from knowing nothing to believing nothing. In my case I was saved in that muteness. And out of this evil I was able to draw from human thought, human disappointments and triumphs, enough to triumph myself."

This is a poem written by Richard Wright in the thirties. It is called 'Between the World and Me'.[2]

And one morning while in the woods I stumbled
    suddenly upon the thing,
Stumbled upon it in a grassy clearing guarded by scaly
    oaks and elms.
And the sooty details of the scene rose, thrusting
    themselves between the world and me . . .

There was a design of white bones slumbering forgottenly
    upon a cushion of ashes.
There was a charred stump of a sapling pointing a blunt
    finger accusingly at the sky.
There were torn tree limbs, tiny veins of burnt leaves, and
    a scorched coil of greasy hemp;
A vacant shoe, an empty tie, a ripped shirt, a lonely hat,
    and a pair of trousers stiff with black blood.

And upon the trampled grass were buttons, dead matches,
  butt-ends of cigars and cigarettes, peanut shells, a
  drained gin-flask, and a whore's lipstick;
Scattered traces of tar, restless arrays of feathers, and the
  lingering smell of gasoline.
And through the morning air the sun poured yellow
  surprise into the eye sockets of a stony skull . . .
And while I stood my mind was frozen with a cold pity
  for the life that was gone.
The ground gripped my feet and my heart was circled by
  icy walls of fear—
The sun died in the sky; a night wind muttered in the
  grass and fumbled the leaves in the trees; the woods
  poured forth the hungry yelping of hounds; the
  darkness screamed with thirsty voices; and the
  witnesses rose and lived:
The dry bones stirred, rattled, lifted, melting themselves
  into my bones.
The grey ashes formed flesh firm and black, entering into
  my flesh.
The gin-flask passed from mouth to mouth; cigars and
  cigarettes glowed, the whore smeared the lipstick red
  upon her lips,
And a thousand faces swirled around me, clamoring that
  my life be burned . . .
And then they had me, stripped me, battering my teeth
  into my throat till I swallowed my own blood.
My voice was drowned in the roar of their voices, and my
  black wet body slipped and rolled in their hands as
  they bound me to the sapling.
And my skin clung to the bubbling hot tar, falling from
  me in limp patches.
And the down and quills of the white feathers sank into
  my raw flesh, and I moaned in my agony.
Then my blood was cooled mercifully, cooled by a
  baptism of gasoline.
And in a blaze of red I leaped to the sky as pain rose like
  water, boiling my limbs.
Panting, begging I clutched childlike, clutched to the hot
  sides of death.
Now I am dry bones and my face a stony skull staring in
  yellow surprise at the sun . . .

To understand Evil, it is necessary to understand what human beings mean by good. In a recent play of mine, entitled *And Still I Rise*,[3] a woman and a man who had died meet a gatekeeper at the portal of that "undiscover'd country from whose bourn no traveller returns". The couple assume that the gatekeeper's charge is to conduct them to Heaven or Hell. He smiles at their questions and responds, "I am always amused at human naiveté, which can only imagine Heaven and Hell." He turns to the man and says, "Why, in your category alone, there is a possibility of five hundred different destinations."

When we use the word 'evil', do we agree with Webster's Dictionary's definition? Or with the idea that the person who causes or adds to human misery is evil? Or does that person use the power of evil? Is good a power separate from mankind existing in a dimension that we cannot even imagine yet? Do Evil and Good exist? (Maybe 'exist' is not the proper word, but I don't know what is. I can find none better.) Do Good and Evil exist as powers in some dimension which we cannot imagine? Are those two forces engaged in a struggle older than the stars? And are we, mankind, on this piddling orb of spit and sand, imitating our makers in a shadowy toy battle endangering our species and forfeiting our chances for true evolution? If it is true that we are the stuff of which dreams are made, I wonder who dreamt us. One, or the other, or both?

From primitive man and ancient Stone Age societies to primitive man in modern, electronic, nuclear, technological society, we find those questions asked and superlatively answered. I do not mean to suggest that the answers have been or now are, or will ever be correct. But it is to man's credit that—faced with bafflement at his own smallness in this expanding vast universe, at his inability to control the rain, drought, earthquakes, or his fears—he has, as Thomas Wilkes said, "gazed upon the senseless stars and written his own meaning into them." When Mark Antony declares to an angry mob that "the evil that men do lives after them, the good is oft interred with their bones", I'm certain that neither Mark Antony nor Shakespeare meant us to believe that facile statement. Rather, it was employed with the same sardonic imperative which Mark Antony used in the often repeated "Brutus is an honourable man; so are they all, all honourable men" (*Julius Caesar*, III. 2).

I'm convinced that the evil we do lives after us, but then I believe the good we do lives after us. To what end, other than matter of relief, I cannot swear. We wrestle as best we can with these concepts, which are larger than our present capacity to embrace them. Our poets, preachers, priests, imams, rabbis, scholars, and honest folk inform us, in the words of the great Black poet, James Weldon Johnson, "Son, your arm's too short to box with God."

That we meet here today testifies to our belief, obviously, that our arms have lengthened somehow. We are capable of engaging a force that, in our brief period on earth, has helped to form and inform our best and our worst actions. Somehow, in the wrestling with the idea of that which lives after us being good, I'm obliged to tell you about an uncle of mine, Uncle Willie.

In a little Arkansas town not far from this site, about as large as this side of the room, my uncle raised me. He was crippled. He left the town of Stamps, Arkansas, twice in his life. He went once to Hope, Arkansas, which is thirty miles away, and once to Los Angeles to visit my father in the thirties. Other than that, he stayed in the town. I was sent to him from California when I was three years old. He and my grandmother owned the only Black-owned store in the town. He was obliged to work in the store, but he was severely crippled, so he needed me to help, and my brother.

So when we were about four, he started us to learn to read and write and do our times tables. In order to get me to do my times tables, he would take me behind my neck, grasp my clothes, and stand me in front of a pot-bellied stove. He would say, "Now sister, do your sixes." I did my sixes. I did sevens. Even now, after an evening of copious libations, I can be awakened at eleven o'clock at night and asked "Will you do your elevens?" I do my elevens with alacrity. I was certain that because my uncle was crippled and strange looking that, had I not obeyed and obeyed quickly, he would have thrown me into the stove.

All children are afraid of that person who looks broken. That is, I'm sure, because children are so recently off the potter's wheel. They are frightened at the prospect that they, too, might have been a broken pot. I, of course, later found that my uncle was so tenderhearted that he wouldn't allow a moth to be killed in the store. But I was forced to learn my times tables.

A few years ago, my uncle died and I went to Little Rock and was met by Miss Daisy Bates, who, you know, is an important American treasure.[4]

She told me, "Girl, there is somebody who wants to meet you."

I said that I'd be glad to meet whoever.

She said, "A good looking man," and I said, "Indeed, yes, certainly."

So that evening, she brought a man over to the hotel. He said, "I don't want to shake your hand. I want to hug you."

And I agreed.

He said, "You know, Willie has died in Stamps."

Well now, Stamps is very near to Texas. And Little Rock, when I was growing up, was as exotic as Cairo, Egypt, Buda, and Pest. I mean, I couldn't—this man knew where Stamps was and my crippled uncle?

He said, "Because of your Uncle Willie, I'm who I am today. In the twenties, I was the only child of a blind mother. Your uncle gave me a job in your store, made me love to learn, and taught me my times tables."

I asked him, "How did he do that?"

He said, "He used to grab me right here" [gesturing to her neck].

He said, "I guess you want to know who I am today."

I said, "Yes, sir."

He said, "I'm Bussey. I'm the vice-mayor of Little Rock, Arkansas." He went on to become the first Black mayor of Little Rock, Arkansas. He said, "Now, when you get down to Stamps, look up—" (and he gave the name of a lawyer). "He's a good ole boy. He'll look after your property."

I went down expecting a middle-aged Black man. A young white man leaped to his feet.

He said, "Ms. Angelou, I'm just delighted to meet you. Why, don't you understand, Mr. Bussey called me today. Mr. Bussey is the most powerful Black man in the state of Arkansas. But more important that that he's a noble man. Because of Mr. Bussey, I am who I am today."

I said, "Let me sit down first."

He said, "I was an only child of a blind mother. When I was eleven years old, Mr. Bussey got hold of me and made me love to learn. And I'm now in the state legislature."

That which lives after us . . . I look back at Uncle Willie—crippled, Black, poor, unexposed to the world's great ideas—who left for our generation and generations to come a legacy so rich. So I wrote a song for Miss Roberta Flack. You may have heard it.[5]

WILLIE

Willie was a man without fame
Hardly anybody knew his name.
Crippled and limping, always walking lame,
He said, "I keep on movin'
Movin' just the same."

Solitude was the climate in his head
Emptiness was the partner in his bed,
Pain echoed in the steps of his tread,
He said, "But I keep on followin'
Where the leaders led."

I may cry and I will die,
But my spirit is the soul of every spring.
Watch for me and you will see
That I'm present in the songs that children sing.

People called him "Uncle," "Boy" and "Hey,"
Said, "You can't live through this another day."
Then, they waited to hear what he would say.
He said, "But I'm living
In the games that children play.

"You may enter my sleep, people my dreams,
Threaten my early morning's ease,
But I keep comin', I'm followin', I'm laughin', I'm cryin',
I'm certain as a summer breeze.

"Look for me, ask for me.
My spirit is the surge of open seas.
Call for me, sing for me
I'm the rustle in the autumn leaves.

"When the sun rises
I am the time.
When the children sing
I am the Rhyme."

Just look for me.

Throughout our nervous history as sentient beings, we have constructed pyramidic towers of evil, oftentimes in the name of good. Our greed, fear, and lasciviousness have enabled us to murder our poets, who are ourselves—to castigate our priests, who are ourselves. We have often surrendered our consciousness in order to placate the surge of Evil in the world and in ourselves.

The lists of our subversions of the good stretch from before recorded history to this moment. We drop our eyes at the mention of the bloody, torturous Inquisition. Our shoulders sag at the thoughts of African slaves lying spoon fashion in the filthy hatches of slave ships, and the subsequent auction blocks upon which were built great fortunes in our country. We turn our heads in bitter shame at the remembrance of Dachau and the other gas ovens where millions of ourselves were murdered by millions of ourselves.

As soon as we are reminded of our actions, more often than not we spend incredible energy trying to forget what we've just been reminded of. Not only do we want to forget that we have perpetuated evil; sadly, we act to forget that we are capable of exquisite good. The poet reminds us that we come from the creator, each of us trailing wisps of glory. To quote the brilliant poet, Tony K. Bombara, "I ask, 'Why are we pretending we have forgotten?' "

If Evil, as I suspect, is a torrential force separate from mankind and Good is a torrential force separate from mankind, then with or without our presence that terrible turmoil will continue on the cosmic level. Martin Buber suggests that negatives and positives, Good and Evil, Masculine and Feminine are merely extremes, which must be engaged for there to be balance in the universe. That awful and wonderful moiling, I mean, full of wonder, *moiling*, is beyond my human comprehension. I do, however, agree with the lyrics of a Bob Dylan song that says, "You got to serve somebody."[6]

If I admit with Richard Wright in that poem 'Between the World and Me' that evil goes into me as does the good, then I'm obliged to study myself, to center myself and make a choice. For I must know that the battles I wage are within myself. The wars I fight are in my mind. They are struggles to prevent the negative from overtaking the positive, and to prevent the good from eradicating all the negative and rendering me into an apathetic, useless organism, which has no struggle, no dynamic, and no life.

David Gruben, the TV producer [of the PBS documentary 'Facing Evil'], told me of an encounter he had with a local young man here in Salado. He asked the young man if he was concerned over the nature of this conference, all this talking about Evil. And the young man's answer was, "No, I'm a Christian. I'm all right."

My first reaction was to smile at that sweet response, and then later I became alarmed. I thought of the many times that I've heard this statement, "I am a Christian. I am a Jew. I am a Buddhist, Shintoist, Muslim." The statements are given with the firm assurance that a condition has been reached and beyond that achievement, nothing extends. There is no more action needed. There is a poignancy in the belief that merely meeting good and identifying good as good, that this alone ensures protection from the threat of being overwhelmed by evil.

We must remember the great struggle between majestic forces—that that struggle introduces a dynamic into our intellect and into our souls. We are required to develop courage to care. Rollo May has shown us that we are obliged to develop the courage to create not only externally, but internally also. We need the courage to create ourselves daily, to be bodacious enough to create ourselves daily as Christians, as Jews, as Muslims, as thinking, caring, laughing, loving human beings.

There is a poem by Edna St. Vincent Millay, which just must be read at this moment. You have to see Ms. Millay to picture her at that time in the twenties and thirties—frail, rather *distingué*, certainly regarded highly as a poet, about to become that recluse that she did become. She wrote:[7]

> I shall die, but that is all that I shall do for Death.
>
> I hear him leading his horse out of the stall; I hear the
>   clatter on the barn-floor.

He is in haste; he has business in Cuba, business in the
    Balkans, many calls to make this morning.
But I will not hold the bridle while he cinches the girth.
And he may mount by himself: I will not give him a leg up.
Though he flick my shoulders with his whip, I will not tell
    him which way the fox ran.
With his hoof on my breast, I will not tell him where the
    black boy hides in the swamp.
I shall die, but that is all that I shall do for Death; I
    am not on his pay-roll.

I will not tell him the whereabouts of my friends nor of my
    enemies either.
Though he promise me much, I will not map him the route to
    any man's door.
Am I a spy in the land of the living, that I should deliver
    men to Death?
Brother, the password and the plans of our city are safe
    with me; never through me
Shall you be overcome.

I am pleased with the Black American spiritual and gospel
tradition, which admits the presence of the Other. In fact, it does
not suggest that the Other should not be here as much as the
One. In one gospel song which emerged in this century, the poet
admits to the topographical difficulty, physical difficulty, but the
singer does not ask God's good to eradicate evil, the obstacle. As
was pointed out to us previously in this symposium, we are
encouraged in the Christian religion to ask God to deliver us from
Evil. It doesn't say *erase* all the evil.

The gospel song says, "Lord, don't move your mountain.
Give me strength to climb it. You don't have to move that
stumbling block, but lead me, Lord, around it." That is profound to me. It encourages us to accept the world, the dualism,
if you will. I'm not all that sure of the dualism, but then I'm
not sure there is only Good and Evil either. But it does
encourage us, if we must deal with the Good and Evil only, to
know that they are there to be dealt with. We have to ally
ourselves with something and work to project our allegiances,
to have the courage to do so.

For centuries, Black people, as you know, in this country were
obliged to laugh when they weren't tickled, and to scratch when

they didn't itch. Those gestures have come down to us as Uncle Tommy. Well, I don't know if we often enough stop to wonder how that Black man's throat must have been closing on him each time he felt he was obliged to say, "Yessa, boss, you're sure right. I sure must be stupid, yes sir." So he could make enough money so he could go home and feed someone. Or that Black woman who said, "No ma'am, Miss Ann, you didn't hurt me when you slapped me. I ain't tenderhearted, sure ain't." So she could make enough money so she could go home and send someone to Fisk or Howard or Atlanta University or Hampton Institute or Texas Southern.

I think that the courage to confront evil and turn it by dint of will into something applicable to the development of our evolution individually and collectively is exciting, honorable. I have written a poem for a woman who rides a bus in New York City. She's a maid. She has two shopping bags. When the bus stops abruptly, she laughs. If the bus stops slowly, she laughs. If the bus picks up someone, she laughs. If the bus misses someone, she goes "ahahaha". So I watched her for about nine months. I thought, "hmm, uh huh." Now if you don't know Black features, you may think she's laughing, but she wasn't laughing. She was simply extending her lips and making a sound, "ahahaha".

"Oh," I said, "I see." That's that survival apparatus. Now let me write about that to honor this woman who helps us to survive. By her very survival, Miss Rosy, through your destruction, I stand up. So I used the poem with Mr. Paul Laurence Dunbar's poem 'Masks', written in 1892, and my own poem 'For Old Black Men'.

WE WEAR THE MASK[8]

We wear the mask that grins and lies,
It hides our cheeks and shades our eyes,—
This debt we pay to human guile;
With torn and bleeding hearts we smile,
And mouth with myriad subtleties.

Why should the world be overwise,
In counting all our tears and sighs?
Nay, let them only see us, while
   We wear the mask.

We smile, but, oh my Christ, our cries
  To thee from tortured souls arrive.
And we sing, [*she sings, snapping fingers*
'Hey baby, bye, hmm we sing, hey.']
We sing, but oh the clay is vile
Beneath our feet, and long the mile;
But let the world think otherwise;
We wear the mask!

When I Think About Myself[9]

When I think about myself,
I almost laugh myself to death,
My life has been one great big joke,
A dance that's walked
A song that's spoke,
I laugh so hard I almost choke
When I think about myself.

Seventy years in these folks' world
The child I works for calls me girl
I say "Yes ma'am" for working's sake.
Too proud to bend
Too poor to break,
I laugh until my stomach ache,
When I think about myself.

My folks can make me split my side,
I laughed so hard I nearly died,
The tales they tell, sound just like lying,
They grow the fruit,
But eat the rind,
I laugh until I start to crying,
When I think about my folks.
And the little children.

Song For The Old Ones[10]

My Fathers sit on benches
  their flesh count every plank
  the slats leave dents of darkness
deep in their withered flanks.

They nod like broken candles
  all waxed and burnt profound,
  they say "But Sugar, it was our submission
that made your world go round."

There in those pleated faces
   I see the auction block
   the chains and slavery's coffles
the whip and lash and stock.

My Fathers speak in voices
   that shred my fact and sound
   they say "But Sugar, it was our submission
that made your world go round."

They've laughed to shield their crying
   then shuffled through their dreams
   and stepped 'n fetched a country
to write the blues with screams.

I understand their meaning
   it could and did derive
   from living on the edge of death
They kept my race alive.
   . . . By wearing the Mask.
[*Three tormented laughs and then a gasp.*]

How we deal with evil, how we confront it and turn it into something good! Confessing to an incredible ego, it may be courage, but certainly it is amazing. Is it insouciance? I was so afraid on the plane coming to Salado. I prayed, "Lord, you remember me. You are sending me. I'm on your side. If this struggle continues and I'm lost, you're going to lose a big speaker." You have to speak sometimes directly to God, you know; you don't play around.

But out of this coming together in this conference, I hope we are able to be honest, honest. I don't mean brutally frank. I've never trusted anyone who says, "I'm brutally frank." Why be brutal? That's stupid. But to be honest and to use that gentleness with which we are all endowed to say to each other things that we are questioning inside ourselves, then the conference will be such a success. I think we ought to laugh as well, I hope.

I wanted to tell you a story about faith. This is a Black story. I don't want to talk about black as a color either, because I thought about it last night and I thought about it this morning—the darkness. Poor Black child who hears 'black lie', 'black heart', and so forth. 'White lie' is okay. But poor child sees the snow in the North falling like a cotton rain covering chairs and streets and people and cars and buildings, and hears his teacher look out at this white world and say, "My God, it is a black day." It is very confusing, you can understand, for a Black child.

But this story is a slave-time story. This slave had great faith in the power of good and his owner decided to deride, humiliate, ridicule the slave.

So he asked him, "John, do you really believe God has power?"

And John said, "Yes, yes sir, I do."

He said, "Well, in that case, why don't you ask God for a hundred dollars."

John said, "But I have never asked God for any tangible thing, anything that I can touch."

He said, "Well, if you ask God for a hundred dollars and God gives it to you, I will free you."

So he said, "Well, I have to do it." He went down to his old praying place under a particular tree and he started to pray.

In the meantime, this slave owner got 99 dollars, put the money into a sack, and got up in the tree over where John was praying.

And John said, "God, now hear this. You will have to give me a hundred dollars. Now, I understand that you own everything. I never asked you before, but these circumstances are too pressing. You must give me a hundred dollars and right now."

Just then the slave owner dropped the bag.

The slave began to praise God: "Thank you for it. You said you would do it. I counted on your word," and so forth.

The slave owner then surreptitiously stepped up and said, "John, what is that you got?"

He said, "I've got my hundred dollars."

The slave owner said, "Count it."

They counted it: ninety-six, ninety-seven, ninety-eight, ninety-nine.

The slave owner said, "John, your God is not all that powerful or else it doesn't care for you, because you asked it for a hundred dollars and it gave you ninety-nine."

John said, "He gave me a hundred dollars. He just charged me a dollar for the sack."

There is that in us which allows us to laugh when we are full of sadness, allows us to be good when we are immersed in the

Evil. There is that which allows us to be courageous in fearful, brutish times. Those elements are natural to us, I believe, as natural as the others are to us, and we can claim those properties. I believe that it is imperative that we ally ourselves with Life, with Love, with Courage, with our brothers and sisters. I believe so, if we are to have, as my grandmother used to say, "starch in our backbone".

Since life is our most precious gift and since, as far as we can be absolutely certain, it is given to us to live but once, let us so live that we will not regret years of useless virtue and inertia and cowardice. Then, dying, each of us can say, "All my conscious life and energies have been dedicated to the most noble cause in the world, the liberation of the human mind and soul to Good, that liberation beginning with me."

Each person in this room has gone to bed with fear or loss or pain or distress—grief—at some night or another. And yet each of us has awakened, arisen, made whatever ablutions we chose to make or could make. Then, seeing other human beings, we said, "Good morning, how are ya?"

"Fine, thanks, and you?"

Now wherever that lives in us—whether it's in the bend of the elbow, behind the kneecap—wherever that lives, there dwells the nobleness in the human spirit. Not nobility. I don't trust the word. I think it's pompous. But the *nobleness* is in the human spirit. It is seen in the fact that we rise to good, we do rise.

STILL I RISE[11]

You may write me down in history
With your bitter, twisted lies,
You may trod me in the very dirt
But still, like dust, I'll rise.

Does my sassiness upset you?
Why are you beset with gloom?
'Cause I walk like I've got oil wells
Pumping in my living room.

Just like moons and like suns,
With the certainty of tides,
Just like hopes springing high,
Still I'll rise.

Did you want to see me broken?
Bowed head and lowered eyes?
Shoulders falling down like teardrops,
Weakened by my soulful cries.

Does my haughtiness offend you?
Don't you take it awful hard
'Cause I laugh like I've got gold mines
Diggin' in my own back yard.

You may shoot me with your words,
You may cut me with your eyes,
You may kill me with your hatefulness,
But just like Life, I'll rise.

Does my sassiness upset you?
My sensuality put you on edge?
Just because I dance as if I had diamonds
At the meeting of my thighs?

Out of the huts of history's shame
I rise
Up from a past that's rooted in pain
I rise
I'm a black ocean, leaping and wide,
Welling and swelling I bear in the tide.

Leaving behind nights of terror and fear
I rise
Into a daybreak miraculously clear
I rise
Bringing the gifts that my ancestors gave,
I am the dream and the hope of the slave.

. . . And so [*one clap*] there I go.

DIALOGUE WITH MAYA ANGELOU

Barbara Jordan

Barbara Jordan holds the Lyndon B. Johnson Centennial Chair in National Policy at the LBJ School of Public Affairs, the University of Texas at Austin. She was the first Black woman to serve in the Texas Senate, of which she was elected president *pro tempore*. From 1972 to 1978, she was a member of the United States House of Representatives. She has served on the United Nations panel to conduct hearings on the role of transnational corporations in South Africa and Namibia. She has been a member of the Presidential Advisory Board on Ambassadorial Appointments and of the Board of Directors of the Public Broadcasting System. She has hosted a series of PBS TV programs called 'Crisis to Crisis with Barbara Jordan'. In 1987, she received the Charles Evans Hughes Gold Medal of the National Conference of Christians and Jews for "courageous leadership in governmental, civic, and humanitarian affairs". In 1976, *Time* magazine chose her as one of "The Ten Women of the Year". That same year, she delivered the keynote address at the National Democratic Convention. In 1984 she was voted "Best Living Orator" by the International Platform Association. The *World Almanac for 1986* selected her for the twelfth consecutive year as "One of the 25 Most Influential Women in America". She is the author of *Barbara Jordan: A Self-Portrait*.

BARBARA JORDAN: We've had an incredible presentation by Maya Angelou. I hope you listened with great care to the themes she sounded for this conference. The overriding theme is that each of us has within us the power of evil and the power of good, and that which lives after us is reflected by the way we have lived our lives. Can we deal with these two powerful forces—evil and good—within us and not succumb, be seduced by evil? Maya, how are we to deal with two such powerful forces in our bodies and try to guarantee that the evil gets suppressed and the good remains dominant? How are we going to do it?

Maya Angelou: I think there is a kind of activity in the evil. There is an energy in the evil. I think we have to call upon the good. We do not have to call upon the evil. I believe that when we look at the two forces, if we use any energy at all we have to use a dual energy, and that is a little like riding a bicycle. We have to press down the one and haul up the other, and be aware that that's what we're doing and try to balance it out.

Jordan: That's it. Well, that balance is what we ought to be about. But there seems to be such an overriding presence of evil in the world. It just seems like we are going to be overcome by it. It takes an extraordinary amount of strength to prevail. You know, I think politically all the time.

Angelou: I don't know why [laughing].

Jordan: I would never say that the political leadership of this country is overcome by evil. I would not say that because everybody tells me that is not the case [laughing]. But, Maya, you see these policies, which are promulgated by these administrations, and you see the devastation that these policies cause in people. For instance, we have a new crop of poor people rising up in the world, the children. The new poor are the children. There are some policies back here that led to this new crop of poor people—children—the most defenseless, the weakest among us. I cannot help but think that those kinds of policies must be spawned by something evil.

Angelou: I agree.

Jordan: You agree?

Angelou: Yes, I'm sorry to say. I wish I could disagree. We are, of course, much too sophisticated even to know that these things exist, but the fundamentalists in churches say that the Devil is walking the land. I have no argument.

Jordan: So, they are all Nipsey Russells: "The Devil made me do it."

ANGELOU: [Laughing] Yes, Shakespeare said that sooner or later they will blame it on the stars, and we see that already. I do think that is why we meet in groups like this, that is why Harry Wilmer would have the idea—that it would come to him. Now I believe that it was in the air and it could have easily come to me [laughing]. I do. I believe the idea is put out there by these forces, one or the other, and it came to him and he was clear enough to see it and act upon it. He brought together this group of thinking human beings to try to look at something frightening.

JORDAN: To sort it out.

ANGELOU: That's right. So that's a positive. What we then try to do as a result of what we learn here in our varying lives, in our own worlds, will depend, of course, upon how much in a state of grace each of us insists upon being. You can't be in a state of grace just by accident.

JORDAN: I was wondering, Maya, do you think that there is one of these forces dominant in our nature in an original way? Do we have some instinctive dominance of good? I was thinking about that little kid who fell into the well in Midland, Texas, and everybody in the country was concerned about whether Jessica McClure would get rescued. And they hung onto every report about how she was doing. When her foot turned a little pink, everybody said, "Her foot's pink. Her foot's pink." That to me said there is something instinctive in us, and maybe that instinctive nature is good.

ANGELOU: Well, I don't know. I wish I could find good in that. I think that is an indication of a soft and lazy mind. I think people would rather worry about that little child in the pit, in the hole, than concern themselves with the children you just mentioned—the children in our own neighborhoods. In Washington D.C.: the fourteen-year-old prostitutes, thirteen-year-old prostitutes—male and female. The drug-dependent children. The hungry. These are our children, too.

JORDAN: Right.

ANGELOU: And they are in pits. Nobody gives a damn because it takes courage and energy to do so. This caring about one child in a well is romantic, and an indication of a lazy and slothful and cowardly mind. That's my feeling. [Clapping]

JORDAN: I tell you, I wish you weren't so clear about things [uproarious laughter]. There's really just no doubt there, and it's wonderful [laughing]. When you speak of the fundamentalists—you know, we've got some fundamentalist people who are seeking public office. They seem to have a corner, or at least they pretend they have a corner, on good and evil. We've got Pat Robertson with the Republicans; we've got Jesse Jackson with the Democrats—and these are men of the cloth, men of God, let us say (at least they say they are). Now I wonder, can we respond to the bad stuff that happens as a result of these policies by placing in leadership positions men (they're both men—that's why I say men; there's no woman now running) who claim to have a mandate from heaven, so to speak? Is that what we need?

ANGELOU: Well, I don't know. I never trust people who . . .

JORDAN: Preachers.

ANGELOU: Well [laughing], people who tell me they have mandates. I mean people born as I am born, of woman, people who are juggling as I juggle these forces and dance so, tip on such point, on such a rare and thin wire. I doubt. There is an African saying, 'The struggle for the thief is not how to steal the chief's bugle, but where to blow it.' [Laughing] I think the person who feels sincerely that she, he, has a mandate from one force or the other will show us in her actions, in his actions, so that people then will say, 'Oh, you must be a child of God.' Or the Other [laughing]. And I do really mean it. I think that of all the other differences between human beings—yet we are more alike than we are unalike—we are either blessings or curses. And we choose those differences, so that you can hear as soon as one person's name is mentioned, somebody says "Oh, Hell," and the curses just begin. Another person is mentioned and people's faces are wreathed in smiles. They say, "Oh, bless her heart, she's so sweet." Well, I think that is the way we should look upon our leaders. They speak by their actions much more than by their rhetoric, who they really are and whether they dare to love us.

JORDAN: Maya, do we dare to love each other? Love is such a powerful emotion. Love can really help us to understand evil. Love can help us to overcome all of the bad stuff we do to each other. Do you think we have it within us to love each of us?

ANGELOU: Yes. Oh, I love that question! I use the word 'love' and I believe that this is how you mean it, not meaning mush nor sentimentality but that condition in the human spirit so profound that it encourages us to develop courage.

JORDAN: Yes.

ANGELOU: And the courage to build bridges, and then the courage to trust those bridges, and to use those bridges in attempts to reach other human beings and better their lives for our movement. That's it. Yes, we have it. It takes a great deal of energy and one has got to admit (I think I should have included this—I know others will make this point) that one will die. It is the one promise we can be sure will not be reneged upon. This will happen to us.

I went to a doctor recently because of something. The doctor was retired, old, about eight-five, white, Southern. He gave me all the examinations and I went back to hear him read them to me. He was a very famous old man, and he said, "Ms. Angelou, what you thought you had you don't have."

I said, "Well."

He said, "Now for a woman of your age you're doing pretty good. But I'll tell you this, that no matter what you do, something will take you away from here."

I swear, I had to laugh. He's so retired that there isn't even a secretary. I just laughed. I said, "Bill me, thank you, thank you." Now that is so.

When we honestly, each of us, honestly comes face to face with that and says, 'I will die, that I know'—then if that big bugaboo can be faced, we can face anything else, because anything else is less than that. I think that we too often decide that if I can just step on someone else's head, I will live a little longer. If I can just become supercilious and act superciliously to this group of people all those short people over there, I will live longer. If I can have two more degrees, I will live longer. If I can just have three more cars and an oil well, I'm sure I will live longer. No. No matter what you do, something will take you away from here. And when we understand that, then we can be free enough to develop the courage to love somebody and have, in fact, the unmitigated gall to accept love in return.

JORDAN: Wow! [Clapping]

ANGELOU: I thank you.

JORDAN: When you first began to speak, Maya, you made the statement that to understand evil you must also understand good. Could you tell me why it is important to have the understanding move on two tracks in order to be complete?

ANGELOU: Thank you. I see in nature, balance. And I see rhythm. Interestingly, for years when Whites would say to Blacks, 'All you people have rhythm', a number of Blacks thought that was a pejorative because it was meant as a pejorative. Years passed, and I found and find myself saying 'Thank you so much', because everything in the world and this universe has rhythm. The sun rises; it sets. The tides come in; they go out. There is winter, and spring, and summer, and fall, and rhythm, and rhythm. So, in the universe as I see it (not being a pure scientist as my brother is here—hard scientist I think they call it—just a poet, mmm hmmmmmmm), I see that balance. I notice that nature abhors imbalance and does not deal with it. I don't mean that nature deals with it grudgingly. Nature just doesn't deal with it. I've been told, as we all have, that 98 percent of all the species that have lived on this little blob of spit and sand are now extinct because they got out of balance. As we are presently constituted, as our brains have been so far awakened, we can only really see the duality. There may be seventy-eight thousand more dimensions—we have no idea right now. If we could live long enough, we might learn something. But at this present time there is the duality that we can see, and so we must, in order to understand one and recognize the other.

JORDAN: I think that to deal with both forces, to understand both forces, the one helps to clarify the other. If we really do want to understand evil, which is the overriding theme of this conference, we must first understand good. That would help clarify our understanding of evil, recognizing that we'll never get rid of it—just as you've said in your talk and was said last night. We're not in the business to try to eliminate evil from the world but to deliver us from evil. Now I wonder, Maya, given our Blackness and what we have experienced from the majority community, do you think that you and I can ever cut through that experience and find this reconciliation and love, which we talked about earlier? Is our perception going to be forever clouded by the Black experience, or is it possible to cut through it?

ANGELOU: I think there is no need to cut through it, as it were. I think the energy must be directed to understanding that we speak and act and live through—with—the Black experience. We're always talking about the human condition—what it is like to be a human being, what makes us weep. If I were Chinese, I would be weeping as a Chinese, as a human being, finally. If I were Asian or on a kibbutz in Israel or in a Palestinian concentration camp—no matter where I were—I would have to speak through my own experiences, always pressing toward that statement of Terence: *homo sum, humani nihil a me alienum puto:* I am a human being; nothing human can be alien to me. I would have to understand, speaking from my position where I stand on this little rock, you know, with all these years and my hopes dashed and my dreams deferred and the triumphs. I would not release or relinquish one iota of my experience. I want to come through it and see myself and all human beings as my brothers and sisters. Some not quite savory. [Laughing] Oops!

JORDAN: But you would expect that others would be able then to get through wherever they are on their little rocks.

ANGELOU: Yes, it is according to their intelligence—not their intellect, but their intelligence, their deep intelligence. Intelligence affords people freedom. Courage and intelligence afford freedom. Ignorance makes people live in mean little narrow tunnels down some mean little narrow streets for about that long. That's a length of light about that long.

JORDAN: Ignorance.

ANGELOU: Ignorance. So when I see ignorance I don't indulge it at all. I have no patience. I respond to it and I think, "Get away. Get away." It's like poison and it's unfortunate; it's contagious.

JORDAN: You're made uncomfortable often, aren't you?

ANGELOU: Terribly. So I respond to it.

JORDAN: To sum up what we have heard this morning, there are two powerful forces at work in us: the force of good, the force of evil. It is our hope that through the human mind we would be able to bring these two forces into some kind of balance so that the one will not overtake the other. The forces in us are a given. There is nothing we can do that would relieve us of having the one or the other in us. It's a given. And since it is there, the accommodation of the two must be a given. We must try to balance these two forces so that we will understand not only evil but good also—and be better human beings as a result.

NOTES

[1] From 'Facing Evil, with Bill Moyers', a co-production of Public Affairs Television, Inc. and KERA/Dallas, March 28, 1988. Transcript by Journal Graphics, Inc., New York, 1988, p. 3.

[2] Richard Wright, 'Between the World and Me', *Partisan Review* 2 (1935), pp. 18–19. Reprinted in Ellen Wright and Michel Fabre (eds.), *Richard Wright Reader* (New York: Harper & Row, 1978), pp. 246–247.

[3] Maya Angelou, *And Still I Rise* (New York: Random House, 1978).

[4] Daisy Gaston Bates, a leader in the 1957 desegregation of Little Rock schools, is the author of *Little Rock: A Memoir* (New York: David McKay, 1962).

[5] Maya Angelou, 'Willie', found in an earlier version in *Poems* (New York: Bantam, 1986), pp. 141–42.

[6] Bob Dylan, 'Gotta Serve Somebody' on *Slow Train Coming* (New York: Columbia Records, 1979). "You're gonna have to serve somebody, Well it may be the Devil or it may be the Lord, But you're gonna have to serve somebody."

[7] Edna St. Vincent Millay, 'Conscientious Objector' in her *Collected Poems* (New York: Harper & Brothers, 1956).

[8] *The Complete Poems of Paul Laurence Dunbar* (New York: Dodd, Mead & Co., 1943), p. 71.

[9] Maya Angelou, 'When I Think About Myself', in her *Poems, Op. cit.*, p. 26.

[10] Maya Angelou, 'Song for the Old Ones', *Poems, Op. cit.*, pp. 100–101.

[11] Maya Angelou, 'Still I Rise', *Poems, Op. cit.*, pp. 154–155.

4

THE EVIL ONE

Jeffrey Burton Russell

Jeffrey Burton Russell is profes-
sor of history at the University of California, Santa Barbara.
He has been chair of religious studies at the University of
California, Riverside; director of the Medieval Institute and
professor of history at Notre Dame University; and dean of
graduate studies at California State University at Sacramento.
He has been a Fulbright Fellow to Belgium, a Harvard Junior
Fellow, a Guggenheim Fellow, and a Medieval Academy
Fellow.

Among his articles are an essay on evil in the *Encyclopedia of
Spirituality* and essays on the Devil and witchcraft in *The
Dictionary of Biblical Tradition*. Russell's books include *A History of
Medieval Christianity: Prophecy and Order; Witchcraft in the Middle
Ages; The Devil: Perceptions of Evil from Antiquity to Primitive
Christianity; A History of Witchcraft: Sorcerers, Heretics, Pagans;
Satan: The Early Christian Tradition; Mephistopheles: The Devil in the
Modern World;* and *The Evil One.*

I will not talk with you today about either the history or the
theology of the Devil, though I will be glad to at any other time at
the drop of a hat. History and theology are enormously important, but this conference is about identifying Evil, facing it, and
converting its energies to the good.

The energy of Evil is tremendous. I am sometimes asked
whether I really do believe in the Devil. Most of you remember
the famous film interview with Jung when that great man was
asked, "Do you believe in God?" Jung replied, "No, I don't
believe. I know." So, I do not believe in the Devil. I know.

Stop. Do not panic. Don't run for the exits. Once when I
was giving a public lecture a girl in the audience sitting next

to a friend of mine said, "If he really believes in the Devil, I'm not going to sit here and listen to such nonsense." A priest friend of ours had a discussion group which had greatly enjoyed reading Dr. Peck's *The Road Less Traveled*. When he proposed *People of the Lie* to them later, he said, "they would have no more of him." I hope that *you* will be more patient and consider how an idea that appears to be obsolete may not only be true but even practical.

But what do I mean when I say that I know the Devil exists? If I were speaking theologically, I might reply that being a Christian entails belief in the Scriptures and in the tradition of the Christian community. I am a Christian, so I believe in the Devil. And it is true that the term 'the Devil' was invented and developed in a religious context. But here I want to examine whether the idea has any validity beyond religion. What do I mean, then, when I say here that I know that the Devil exists? I mean that I know that a powerful, centered, destructive, focused force of hatred exists within us—in our minds. I know this from experience. This notion certainly resembles the traditional idea of a hateful personality that everywhere seeks to destroy and annihilate—what Goethe called *der Geist der stets verneint* ('the spirit which always denies'). But call this focus of destructiveness what you will: call it the Devil, call it original sin, call it the lie, call it the shadow, or call it—this is perhaps a term where more of us can find common ground—Radical Evil. Radical Evil exists in every one of us. I will refer to this Radical Evil in my own terms as the Devil. By "Radical Evil" I mean a fundamental warping of the will that underlies individual actions. I reject the argument that there are evil actions but no evil people. I believe that there are people who have allowed their wills and personalities and lives to be swallowed up by Radical Evil.

I want to discuss Radical Evil within individuals first and later turn to societal and transpersonal evil. The central point I want to make about Radical Evil is this: unless we recognize it, name it, and deal with it as a real phenomenon, we can never convert its tremendous energies to good. The fathers and the mystics understood this. Jung understood this. Lately Dr. Peck has argued this to a wide audience as I have to a smaller one. It is not, granted, a popular idea today. But we dismiss it to our own harm and to the harm of our neighbors and of our planet.

I am not allowed to hedge. Although honesty may be a fault as well as a virtue, I do not feel that I can speak here with integrity without telling you of two intrusions of the Devil into my own life. One is recent: I shall call it 'The Snake in the Manuscript'. The other, 'The Snarling State', occurred twelve years ago and was the center of the most destructive moment of my life. There have been other intrusions, but I choose these two as examples. First the destructive episode, then a happier one. First 'The Snarling State'.

Thirteen years ago, I was living, quite reasonably happily, in Riverside, California, with my wife and four children, a nice big house, and a tenured position as full professor of history at the University of California, Riverside, where I was one of the best liked and most influential members of the faculty. I mention these things not to boast but only to provide contrast to what followed. In 1975 I was offered a phenomenally attractive position at a university in Indiana, where I would occupy an endowed chair and also be director of a well-established research institute. Objectively, if there is such a thing, it looked good to me and to my colleagues. It did not *feel* good to me or to my family. To begin with (please forgive the chauvinism) we are all Californians; I am a fourth-generation Californian on both sides; my great grand-parents on one side came to northern California just after the Gold Rush; those on the other side were among the first settlers of Anaheim, now the home of Disneyland; unfortunately they did not hold onto their real estate. The point is that with all its faults we loved California deeply. I also felt an intense loyalty to the University of California, where three generations of my family have studied. I was brought up half a block from the Berkeley campus and had studied and taught at the University of California for over 20 years. We had a wide and close circle of friends whom my wife and I loved; and our children were settled happily (on the whole) with their own schools and friends. 'Objectively' the new job was a good one; *really* it was a very bad one.

But there were two powerful temptations to take it, both of them destructive. The first was pride, ambition, the temptation of power and prestige. Understandable, given human folly, but nonetheless destructive. The other temptation was much worse: it was anger. For various reasons I was angry at my wife, angry at a close friend and colleague and angry at the University. Additionally I felt—foolishly—that the University did not appreciate me enough. So I struggled to decide whether to go.

As the time came for a decision I had a vivid dream. I dreamed that I was sitting in my study with a jigsaw map of the United States before me on the table. I placed my left hand on California and my right hand on Indiana. For a while, in the dream, I seemed to concentrate. Then, with uncontrolled violence I swept my hands to and fro over the puzzle map, knocking the pieces on the floor. I knelt down to retrieve them. By the door from the study into the garden that I had worked many years to build and grow, lay California. I felt a pang of separation, but I reached over to my right and picked up Indiana instead. Gripping Indiana in my right hand and thrusting it aloft, I rose to my feet, growling the word 'Indiana' as an affirmation.

The next day I asked a close friend who was an amateur psychologist what he thought. "I think it means I have to go, don't you?" I asked him. "Oh, absolutely," he said. And so I made the decision. And I felt terrible. I needed professional advice, so I called the man who had been our marriage counselor and made an appointment with him. I told him the situation and the dream, and Jim agreed that I should go. But that night he called me and asked me to come back for another appointment the next day; he said he wasn't satisfied. The next day we went through the dream again, and Jim told me that on deeper reflection he was sure that it meant the opposite of what it seemed. He didn't like the way I had left California forlorn by the door, and he liked even less the hostile, phallic, gesture I had made rising with Indiana held aloft like a bloody sword.

That night I had another dream: a quick and terrifying one. I dreamt that the puzzle piece of Indiana was sitting by the basin in the bathroom and when I picked it up it had an eye that glared at me. In a harsh, guttural snarl, it called my name. I dropped the snarling state like a poisonous viper and woke up shouting.

Such is the folly of human nature that it will not surprise you to know that in spite of all this, I decided, after more to-ing and fro-ing, to take the Indiana job. It will amuse fans of Jungian synchronicity to know that the day we left Riverside the hills behind our house went up in a giant brush fire, and our last look at our house was of flames moving down the hill behind it. Or to know that our car broke down crossing the desert and that we had to be towed across the California state line into Nevada, sitting in our towed car, facing backwards, towards California. The sad part is that the new job was a disaster in itself, that our marriage nearly ended, that our children were miserable, and that we lost a large amount of money. The most lastingly painful thing is that it turned out that, because our children were growing up, we never all lived as a family together again. After several years of agonized searching we finally found jobs back at the University of California. But our family was permanently separated.

The role of the Devil here is clear. I made a decision, against my rational judgment, and even against my deep emotional feelings, that was a destructive, evil decision. I did so because I had allowed a focus of hatred and anger and pride to grow within me and to take charge of my decisions. (I hope it is clear, by the way, that of course I do not regard California as 'good' and Indiana as 'evil', but that they had become symbols of good and evil in my psyche at that time.) Call it what you will, I call it the Devil that spoke to me in the Snarling State.

One does learn something. More recently I became very upset at my present job and had sunk into a bitter, angry depression. But I had learned to practice a meditative or prayer technique in which I lie back and let a picture come into my mind that illustrates my feelings. The picture that gradually surfaced was that of a medieval manuscript of a kind that you have all seen or seen pictures of, with an elaborate illuminated initial letter. The letter was an I. As I allowed the picture to take shape, I felt that my anger and hostility and malignity centered in that initial I. Part of this meditative technique is then to try out different names for the figure. You know you have hit the right one when your body suddenly relaxes. I tried all kinds of names for that 'I', trying to get to the root of the matter: I tried Anger, Fear, Sex, Marriage, Money, Promotion, Disease, Depression—none seemed quite to hit the spot. Then I noticed that the 'I' had begun to move. The top part of the I began to extend itself out to the right above the text; gradually it began to move its head back and forth. And then I saw what it was. I named it Satan, and my body relaxed, my teeth unclenched, my stomach unwound. It was The Snake in the Manuscript. At first I shouted angrily at it, "God damn you, you bastard, get out of my mind." But my anger only increased the intensity of its malignancy. Then I took a different tack. "God love you", I said. "God cleanse you. God fill you full of light and love and make you happy and whole." As I repeated such prayers, and the serpent cringed and shrank and backed away until, turning into a cockroach, it scuttled off the imaginary manuscript and plopped under the imaginary table into the darkness—from which I know it will try one day again to emerge.

Now whether the Satan in the state or the Satan in the manuscript were 'real' in some 'objective' fashion, whatever those terms mean, they were certainly real in my mind. So then of course what one must do is to apply to oneself what one had applied to Satan. With the manuscript, for example, I readily understood that the Serpent represented the anger, fear, and hatred I had allowed to build up within myself. Remember that the illuminated letter was an 'I'—in other words a 'me'. So I asked God to pour the light and love into me. When I thought of myself, the picture that came to mind was a little leather sack, all closed and pulled tight by the drawstring. The light and love could not flow in through the closed opening. So I had to lie there and let God pull that sack gradually open with His hands and pour in the saving grace. I knew it needed to keep on being poured until my tightness and constriction were broken. The sack turned out to be much tougher, heavier leather than I had thought, much more resistant than I had thought, but under the weight and pressure of gallons upon gallons of grace (which appeared as water in the picture), the skin stretched and stretched, and finally burst. Then the water of grace just rolled in over it like surf, and the malignancy was gone. Immediately the depression and anger diminished by 90 percent—and floods of energy returned. That time at least, I allowed myself to be saved from the Devil.

Some observations about the nature of the Devil emerge from these stories.

A close friend of ours, a British psychologist, who has written books on depression, says that she is struck by the fact that a large number of her patients cling to their neuroses tenaciously. It is as if, she says, they have so identified with their neurosis that if they shed it they would cease to be themselves, cease to have an identity. I think this is precisely what Satan does. When you offer him truth and light and beauty and love, he cringes, shrinks and runs. Malice, hatred, evil dominate him to the extent that they have become his identity, and he clings to them because he fears that without them he will cease to exist. We are all tempted, I suspect, to cling to our resentments, our angers, our lusts, our prides, because we fear that freed from them we will be transformed to something else—it might be better, but it won't be us, and we fear losing our identity. Most of us struggle against this destructive lethargy and keep our heads above water. But some do not. Dr. Peck has shown that there are people who, like Satan, allow the forces of hatred and malice to become a black hole that drains away all light and life. These people not only do evil things; by allowing themselves to be identified and taken over by the focus of evil, they become evil people. I have (thank God) not myself known many of them. But I have known at least one; from experience I know that Dr. Peck is right.

Of course this focus of evil within works with our own proclivities: to ambition, or avarice, or sexual irresponsibility, or backbiting, or power, or lying, or anger, or physical violence, or whatever. What I suggest that is different from what most psychologists believe is that underneath these individual destructive proclivities is a focus of malice and destructiveness that unites and energizes the variety of destructive, hateful forces within us. This focus of destruction creates its own hidden agenda, its own policy, which is destruction for its own sake. Take avarice as an example. I may begin with real financial need; it may then transfer into sheer greed; and it may reach the point where it gets out of control and begins destroying other people and oneself. At some point along the way, the focus of evil within us seizes that greed, energizes it, and utilizes it for its own purpose of destruction far beyond the scope of the original avarice. This focus of evil, having an agenda of its own, a purpose and a will, may we not call it a person?

The focus of evil may completely dominate some people. What is one to say of Adolf Hitler? With most of us it does not dominate, but it is always there, threatening to do so. It has become fashionable to deny the existence of this Radical Evil within, but it is there nonetheless. By denying it in ourselves, we fail to face our own problems squarely and so lose the opportunity to resolve them. Worse, by denying the real evil within us, we project it upon others. When I deny my own hostility to Person A, I project it onto him or perhaps onto Person B, assuming their hostility to me and therefore justifying a destructive response on my own part that I falsely believe to be entirely defensive. This process is so well known that I need not dwell on it here. But we do need to keep in mind that the Devil disguises his intentions well. Repression of malice and failure to face it in ourselves produces the self-righteousness that provides us with ready justification for our cruelty and insensitivity. It enables us to claim vices as virtues, justifying our violence, our prejudice, our intolerance, on the grounds that the evil is not found within ourselves but in others.

It is my experience that the Devil never gives up. When you have won a victory over him he will lie low for a while and then return in full force when you give him the opportunity. Sometimes he will ride back on an old vice; sometimes he will attack you from a new direction. But the destructive force of malice is always lurking within you waiting for its next opportunity. It is also my experience that the Devil is always defeatable. He can never win over if you don't allow him to. But he is defeatable only if we open our hearts to life and to love. If we only perfunctorily and grudgingly ask him to be gone, if we secretly cling to our hatred, our anger, our vice, then we are really cooperating with the destructive force, and its power over us will increase unless we finally change and truly will to stop it. When we do really decide that we want light and love and not darkness, the Devil immediately loses his power over us.

The activity of the Devil within individuals readily transposes to his activities within societies. Governments, businesses, universities, churches—every human institution—is open to the Devil within, and to the process of denial, repression, and negative projection that immensely enhance his powers. The personal proclivities to self-righteousness, prejudice, and righteous violence express themselves socially in slavery, genocide, apartheid, violent revolution (such as the Cultural Revolution in China), war, and exploitation. All such things can be justified when the victims are demonized, and the demonization of others is possible when we fail to recognize the demon within ourselves. Ronald Reagan characterized the Soviet Union as the Evil

Empire. Certainly the Soviet Union is the source of much evil, but the United States is not? What about our own greed, irresponsibility, drugs, crime, violence, ethnic discrimination, and exploitation of other countries?

Of course we should also not be surprised that our own nation or society has faults. I believe that the illusion that there *can* be a society without evil, that we can build such a society, is the root of the most destructive behavior of humanity. The belief that we can build a perfect world—if we can just destroy those evil people who block our noble efforts—is what lay behind Hitler and Stalin and Pol Pot. Do you remember a photograph in *Newsweek* when the dark days of Cambodia were beginning? A young revolutionary was turning a family out of their house. On the young man's face was a look of pure demonic hatred. One group of people led by the government of Pol Pot, collectively denied all the evil within themselves and projected it upon those who were labeled 'capitalists' and, having identified these so-called capitalists as completely evil, justified treating them with inconceivable brutality. Inconceivable, that is, unless one recognizes and understands the appalling power of Radical Evil, the force of destruction within.

But what is happening when a society gives itself so completely over to evil? Are we simply adding up a large number of individual angers and evils, a lot of individual devils? Or is something more sinister and frightening actually happening? Social psychologists have long been investigating mob behavior, but it is fair to say that we still know a great deal more about its effects than about its mechanisms. Lewis Thomas and other biologists have pointed to the intense social behavior of other animals. Swarms of bees, for example, seem to act not so much like individual bees in a group as a large organism in which the bees have become functioning parts—we might almost say cells—of the whole. The swarm is in effect an organism. It seems to be able to act, even perhaps to decide, as a whole, communicating its collective will by mechanisms that we are just beginning to understand. Comparable behavior has been observed in human groups—in mobs particularly, but other groups as well—when individual wills seem to be submerged in the will of the whole. The behavior of the Nazi crowds at Nuremberg or of the Chinese Red Guards are notorious examples. The phenomenon does not have to be evil, of course, and is not always so. Altruism and constructiveness can communicate themselves in groups as well. Unfortunately it appears that groups are most likely to coalesce when confronted by something perceived as an external threat; the results, of course, are destructive.

Now if this group psychology is really at work, if there is some kind of collective unconscious that rules groups, then it is reasonable to suggest that a focus of evil similar to that in the individual unconscious may exist in the collective unconscious as well. It seems improbable that adding up individual sins, even in large numbers, can produce something as appalling as the Nazi Holocaust. It seems more likely that a collective focus of evil is at work with its own agenda and purpose, a composite of evil raised to a new dimension of intensity and malignity. Again, having will and purpose, such a focus may be considered a person.

Let us go one step further. If, as Jung suggested, there is such a thing as a collective human unconscious—if humanity, in other words, is less a collection of individuals than something like an organic unity—then there may be a focus of evil, a malign force with its own will and agenda, operating within humanity as a whole.

This is moving away from the more sure to the less sure, from the less speculative to the more speculative. Let me continue to do this for a moment longer. I have just been suggesting the existence of a transpersonal Devil, a focus of evil transcending that of the human individual. What about a transgeneric focus of evil? Whenever we imagine or conceive of intelligent, socially-organized extraterrestrials, we usually conceive of them as having will as well as intelligence, that is of having the ability to choose good or evil. If this is so, they would likely have a focus of evil within them as well. Is it possible that in some sense life throughout the universe may form some kind of whole, and, if that is true, that there may be a focus of evil throughout the entire cosmos? If so, that brings us very close to the Judeo-Christian idea of the Devil. I think, by the way, that the more one examines the human concepts of extraterrestrials and angels, one sees that the extraterrestrial occupies very much the same part of the human mind in the materialist twentieth century as the angel did in the Christian seventeenth century. For angels, like extraterrestrials, are persons: nonhuman beings having something analogous to human understanding and human will.

Clearly such speculations are not susceptible to anything like scientific validation, at least unless we establish firm contacts with extraterrestrial intelligences. They do, however, find religious corroboration in the Jewish-Christian-Muslim conception of the Devil. When we experience the Devil within ourselves personally, or when we observe its appalling social manifestations, we immediately realize that it is essentially a force determined on destruction. The traditional religious idea of the Devil is precisely of a force intent upon destroying and annihilating the cosmos to the greatest extent it is allowed to do.

If we reflect upon the threat of the nuclear annihilation of the planet, it is clear that whatever the Devil may ultimately be, we are running the risk of identifying with him. Humanity seems to have set no bounds on its own destructiveness. No species has had anything remotely like the destructive effect upon the planet that we have had. Even our primitive ancestors wielded enormous destructive power. It is now believed that within a thousand years of crossing the Bering landbridge from Asia into North America during the ice age, Clovis humans, nomadic hunters before the beginnings of agriculture, exterminated many of the dominant species of mammals in the Americas, including all the vast herds of mammoths. The effects of agriculture have been the denudation of the Earth's forests and erosion of her fertile mantle of soil. We all know what the advancing technology of war has brought. We are now in a position to annihilate all vertebrate life on this planet. Further, we are poised to develop bases on the Moon and Mars early in the next century, and we are already moving ahead with weapons in space. Who can doubt that during a space war we in our fury would dash atomic weapons against Mars if the allegedly Evil Empire had bases there? Who could doubt we would annihilate Jupiter and Neptune if it were militarily advantageous and feasible? If we could extend our power to other star systems, would we spare their planets when we are ready to destroy our own? If we felt we needed to destroy the whole galaxy, would we not do so if we could? What restraint would check us from annihilating the entire universe if we had the power to do so? Indeed, if the theory of the anthropic principle in physics is correct, we may really *be* able to annihilate the entire universe by annihilating the only creatures—ourselves—capable of observing it.

And this leads me full circle back from speculation to observation. Whether the Devil exists outside of or beyond humanity we do not and perhaps cannot know. That a will to destruction, a focus of annihilating malice, exists like a sucking void within humanity, unlimited except by the practical boundaries of our physical power to destroy, *that* is clear. Whatever else the Devil may be, wherever else he may be, he is certainly within ourselves.

In conclusion, a few suggestions. First, virtually everything I have said here is in the nature of suggestion, not an effort at proof, which would have been vain. What I am doing is calling for an open-minded consideration of the question of Radical Evil—or the Devil if you like. First of all, it may be true, and to know the truth is always a good in itself; secondly, to recognize the name *Evil* may allow us at last to combat it effectively. Unless we do so, we run terrible risks: the destruction of our mother and sister the Earth; and even failing that ultimate of all evils, endless wars—there are more than 40 being waged in the world even today—tortures, genocides, and all the agonies caused by both individual and social negative projection.

It only remains for me to go on and offend by suggesting what I do *not* think will get us out of our mess.

First of all, I believe that the dominant ideal of contemporary America, optimistic, liberal progressivism, is not solving, and cannot solve, the problem. Human nature is not intrinsically good; we cannot remove evil by well-meaning social projects. We cannot do so because evil is radical; it is embedded in human nature. As Yochelson and Samenow observed after their long and intense involvement with the New York State penal system as psychiatrists, some people have no desire for the good at all; their lives have been turned over to the void. And the rest of us, who are not hardened criminals, is the worm not within our rose as well? Is the Evil Empire always somewhere else? Liberal progressivism will not save us.

Much less will traditional American conservative capitalism save us. The policies of the current administration are showing the fallacies of that idea as if they had not been evident before. An ideology based upon personal selfishness—remember that Ivan Boesky exhorted the graduating class of the Berkeley School of Business last year not to be ashamed of greed—can never do anything but drag us down. Liberal progressivism at least has the virtue of aiming at alleviating real human miseries, and it sometimes wins victories. The civil rights movement, though we all know how much inequity still exists, nonetheless made substantial gains against racial exploitation. I shall continue to vote for, and support, liberal policies and liberal candidates. It is better to treat the symptoms of a problem and alleviate some of the pain they cause than not to treat it at all. But for all the admiration I have for workers for liberal causes, they are not penetrating to the heart of darkness.

Nor, for all the strength I see in traditional religious views of evil, do I advocate a return to old-fashioned religion. Let me first name the strength, since the dominant worldview of our society so often ignores or denigrates it. The Jewish, Christian, and Muslim traditions have for 2,500 years thought seriously about the problem of evil. No other religions or ideologies have confronted the problem so directly and courageously as these three, which formulate it in such a poignant way: how can radical evil exist in a world created by a good God? How can it, yet it does? This creative tension within the theology of the great Western religions for two and a half millenia have produced thousands, even millions, of serious, truth-seeking people, many of them brilliant intellectuals, many others deeply spiritual, still others astute psychologists, who have wrestled with the problem. This creates a reservoir of wisdom that is ridiculous to dismiss, as leading voices of our dominant world view have done. Anyone who doubts, for example, that the study of evil can be linked with astute and sophisticated psychology, should read the church father Evagrius of Pontus or the medieval anonymous author of *The Cloud of Unknowing*. The concept of the Devil and of Radical Evil is one of the fruits of these two and a half millenia of wise reflection, and we have much to learn from it.

However, it must be granted that in times and places where this wisdom is itself the contemporary worldview, evil has not noticeably decreased. To take only the most lurid examples, we need only remember the Albigensian Crusade or the Ayatollah's Iran. Partly this is because religious leaders—in the sense of the political leaders of religious communities—seldom have deep insight into their own best traditions. Perhaps the very effort to construct 'a Christian society', for example, violates and distorts the essential purpose of Christianity, which is to serve as a source of radical prophecy against the values of this world. We cannot, and should not even if we could, attempt to construct a religious society along traditional lines.

If these things will not work, what will? I suggest coping with the problem of evil on a variety of fronts.

First, to avoid doing evil, we should avoid being allured by abstractions. Democracy, socialism, national security, women's liberation, free enterprise, Christianity, right-to-life, communism, free enterprise, Zionism: the list of causes is endless. The question here is not whether one or another of these causes may be good or bad. The point is that to allow any cause (however good its intent or appearance) to encourage us to hurt individuals or to fail to help individuals, is the greatest cause of evil in the world.

Next, I suggest continued liberal, political action to treat the symptoms of evil wherever we can. We must do what we can to control and to end war, racism, greed, exploitation, crime, ignorance, violence, and the other blemishes on society that are so painful to its victims. Nothing that I have said about liberalism's not addressing underlying causes is intended to undermine our efforts to relieve the pain. Only to delve deeper.

Next, I suggest open-minded research into the nature of evil, using the insights of psychology, biology, sociology, history, literature, and theology—all the resources of the human mind and spirit. This research should not be narrowly limited to fit the narrow mindset of modern academia, modern media, and the entire modern, materialistic establishment. We must get out of the habit of dismissing huge reservoirs of wisdom as irrelevant; we must begin to practice what we preach about pluralism and open minds and cease being blindered and dogmatic.

Next, I suggest greater attention to both individual and social self-awareness, particularly awareness of our own motivations and of the evil that exists in each one of us and in every society. To this end, I suggest that psychological awareness be taught in our schools (I do not mean the superficial 'how to adjust to society' classes that are now given) and that the media too take a creative, responsible role in advancing such education.

Along with that, I suggest an increasing awareness of our own ability to make choices voluntarily. The argument as to whether genetics or environment determine our behavior has raged for decades. Neither has the full answer, nor do both together. Each of us has within us a 'still, small point' of freedom of will where we can stand and decide for good or for evil. We are not entirely determined by our genes and our milieu. It is debatable whether the severely insane or the severely mentally handicapped may be said to have this freedom, but most humans certainly do.

Finally, I suggest that each of us search for and find that point of freedom—often it is buried under decades of hatred and anger and selfishness—and summon up the power of light and love within us against the power of darkness. As Dante said, love takes us ever outwards, opening wider and wider, freer and freer, lighter and lighter, in a sparkling spiral into an ever more beautiful world; hatred takes us in the opposite spiral, ever narrower, ever tighter, ever darker, into a world of ugliness and pain. And at this small still point of our freedom we will find help.

If the Devil does exist, what is he? If the concept has any meaning at all, he is the traditional Evil One—a mighty person with intelligence and will whose energies are bent on the destruction of the cosmos and the miseries of its creatures. What the Devil represents in the ultimate scheme of the world is impossible to know. But here on earth he represents the will that holds the nuclear weapons poised in threat. We are called to fight and strive against that evil with every syllable of our sanity.

We are also called to know *how* to fight that evil. It is not effectively fought with guns and bombs. Evil cannot be defeated with evil, negation with negation, terrorism with terrorism, missile with missile. The process of negation must be reversed. Only affirmation can overcome negation; evil can be integrated only by good; hatred can be overcome only by love. The only response to evil that has ever worked is to live a life of love. That means what it has always meant: visiting the sick, giving to the poor, helping those who need help. Above all, it means fostering children, loving them not harming them, so that future generations may be less twisted than we.

Everyone knows that the life of love is no easy thing. It is easier to go the Devil's way, with hatred and violence. But the Devil's way is not only morally wrong; it is stupid. It will never work; it has never worked. Violence always provokes violence; hatred everywhere provokes hatred. Daily we are reminded of this, and reminded too that we have not yet learned. The Devil stands like a blind man in the sun, seeing only darkness where he stands among the green and brilliant fields of God's creation. We have thought the Devil's way long enough. It is time for a new way of thinking.

This new way of thinking, I suggest, is to pursue the life of love not by denying and repressing the Devil within ourselves but by recognizing it, facing it, and transforming it into positive energy. It is the task of the twenty-first century to show us how to do this. We have no other choice: we will learn to do this or we will kill our children and our grandchildren and the planet that nourishes them.

RESPONSE TO JEFFREY BURTON RUSSELL

Philip Hallie

The clarity and the reasonableness of Jeffrey Russell's remarks showed a lot of guts. I review books for journals and institutes on Evil. The books I've read are all concerted attacks on the Devil or anything like a demon. They demythologize Evil. The whole tendency of current historical thought—about slavery, about what happened in the third empire of Hitler, about psychological analysis, about philosophic work on good and evil—all of these things conspire to flatten out evil and make it a kind of sickness. That means, if somebody's done some destructive work—sick, sick, sick—the person is thought of as a patient in a hospital. How can you blame somebody who is sick? How can you become angry at somebody who is sick?

Yet that word, that quasi-scientific word, that vague, vast metaphor 'sick' is what people find themselves fashionably and technically using instead of the word 'evil'. In fact, they always speak shamefacedly when they speak about Evil.

I could give you about two dozen instances offhand, but I'll just mention one. An English philosopher named Mary Midgley wrote a book called *Wickedness*.[1] When I saw that title *Wickedness*, I said, "Oh, isn't that terrible?" She just didn't like the word *evil* at all. Everybody is scared of it. It's full of demons, and the Devil, and these terrible things. The great path of treating evil as a kind of sickness that we can cure by putting somebody on a couch, or giving them an injection later on, or something like that.

What this book does is say that wickedness is made up of perfectly healthy, perfectly splendid drives, desires, and motives that are just peachy. Self-preservation, pride in oneself, all these things make up a Hitler or Stalin. When they do turn up in a Hitler or a Stalin, however, they get mixed up in a funny way. So let's unmix them and we've got the problem people all solved. It's a beautiful book, absolutely out of this world, but it's perfectly typical of all the work I've seen on history, psychology, philosophy, and that whole business of evil.

Therefore, in my opinion, Jeffrey Russell had to have guts, in the face of all of this, to say that there is a person with an agenda. That person is the Devil, and the agenda is death and destruction. To say this takes a lot of courage.

There are three things I'd like to highlight or explore. Although he touched on at least one of them very heavily, they are about evil, and about the usefulness, the power, and the truth of the phrase 'there is a Devil'.

The first thing is perverseness: doing things because they are wrong. That's very different from pragmatic evil—doing things because you want a low price to pay for your cotton crop, or doing things so that you can get certain supplies that you need for your war effort, and get them as cheaply as you can. These are pragmatic kinds of ways of destroying human beings, pragmatic justifications. But as Raul Hilberg will point out, so many of the things that happen in history as well as in our most intimate personal lives are just simply perverse. They are not done for some good, clean, healthy (as Mary Midgley would say) ulterior motive, but they are done for the sheer rottenness of doing them.

Edgar Allan Poe talks about this in 'The Imp of the Perverse'.[2] He's not a full-grown devil, the imp of the perverse, but I think he's got the makings of one. Poe says, when you stand on a cliff, right near the edge, and you're thinking, 'Well, Hell, wow, wouldn't it be something, just killing myself, just tipping over, just, just bending just a little bit more and then dying and smashing and then oh, oh, wonderful', and then maybe you don't and then maybe you do do it.

Or you talk just a little bit longer, keeping Jeffrey Russell from talking, but a little longer than you should, just for the hell of it, as we say. Just for the hell of it. I'm trying not to do that.

Sheer perverseness: the destruction of the native Americans, the slavery of our Black people in this country, Jim Crowism—these activities went way beyond pragmatic factions or motives or good healthy Mary Midgleyan 'Hello, aren't we peachy basically' sort of attitudes. These were diabolic, done for the hell of it. We need, Poe says in the middle of 'The Black Cat', we need "to vex ourselves."[3] We've got to do something to go against the goddamned grain. This was the theme of Robert Frost's poem 'West-Running Brook' as well, going against the grain.[4] The French use that word *à rebours*, 'against the grain'. They love it, and they know what they're talking about.

That's one element. A tough one for us to fight even with Russell's help. I find it in myself, ever since I killed people in the last world war and watched them burn. When we used white phosphorous instead of regular high-explosive shells, we watched them burn. And we watched them gleefully. It's the adverb 'gleefully' that carries all the meaning of things like perverseness.

Second, and Russell touched on this very heavily and very well, I think—the Devil lies. The Devil, if you take this interpretation of the Bible, turns up, as you know, in the third chapter of the Bible. The first thing he is described as is being the most subtle (that's one translation) of the wild creatures. Forked tongue, subtle. The first thing he does is lie to Eve.

Lies are a part of this temptation of which I am speaking that's characteristic of the Devil. Because of the lies, we always do evil in the name of good when we're not being perverse and doing it for the evil's sake itself. We do it in the name of good, to use Maya Angelou's expression. That lying is much more subtle than saying, 'Well, it's dark outside' when it's light. You can check that out in a second, but the lies that are characteristic of evil, of destruction, cannot be checked up on.

They lie in people's hearts, those lies lie. That Blacks are inferior and deserve to be slaves. That native Americans are inferior and deserve to have been 'Lo, the vanishing Indian'. Westerners used to use one word when they talked about a native American: 'Lo'. That was short for 'Lo, the vanishing American'. These were lies that no possible confirmation or disconfirmation had anything to do with. Lies are lies because no evidence can touch them. They lie in the heart. They lie there, and how they lie.

Finally, and this to me is one of the most interesting handles on the Devil. I'm talking about modes of temptation. The Devil is a force. I have a friend who tells me that we have in this core of our brain system (if you want to call it that) or cerebral system, a serpentine element, a cold-blooded serpentlike mechanism. What this does is to bite back, cold-bloodedly back—what Melville called "the reactionary bite of that serpent".[5] Step on him.

That's the one. That's the handle on the Devil that I have found most often in my work for decades now on evil. Reacting. Hitler built the SS troops as guards for defense. We're going to defend our species to death. We're defending ourselves in this country. Russia's defending itself. Everybody is defending her or himself. We're going to defend ourselves personally, publicly to death because of the reactive bite of the serpent.

I'm not talking about perverseness and I'm not talking about the naming of things as good. I'm talking about a simple reflex action that's deep in our brain system.

I want to conclude with one very strange remark that echoes Jeffrey Russell's beautiful talk, the ending of it as well as, I hope, the spirit of the whole. Aldous Huxley, when he was in his sixties, was asked, "Well, what's the upshot of your life so far, Mr. Huxley?" He'd written *Brave New World* and all these works that had been there to liberate humankind, give it a certain dignity or at least remind a person that he or she could find a dignity.

He said, "You know, I'm very sad to say that all the work I've done, defending, explaining, invoking, praying for human freedom and dignity comes down to one stupid little sentence, one stupid little sentence. And the sentence is: 'Try to be a little kinder.'[6]

Look, as Simone Weil used to put it, more with a loving look. Look more with a loving look. Look at words. Look at your own perverseness. Look at your own rationalizations, but above all, look at their victims with a loving look.

I beg you to come back after all these brilliant, insightful, deeply humane talks that you're having and I'm sure going to have, to the simplicities, to that loving look. It's not shallow; it's as deep as you are. It's as wide as your life can be. So I'll just repeat it. It's enough. Try to be a little kinder.

DIALOGUE

Question: What about the banality of Evil? When Elie Wiesel talks about the camps, he certainly talks about the cruelty of the Nazis, but if you read his work carefully you see he says that the indifference and the apathy of the onlookers was far worse.

JEFFREY BURTON RUSSELL: Yes, I think that's a very good point. Of course, it's not really the most horrible part of the Holocaust, but it certainly is a horrible aspect the way people went about so methodically that office workers sat there typing forms and checking columns as if this were normal office work selling insurance. It gets mixed up with petty virtue, for example. We always think that hard work is a good thing, but as my older daughter has pointed out many times, work is not a virtue in itself. People worked hard building Auschwitz. They worked very hard, and did a very efficient job. Hard work in itself is not a good thing; it depends on what the aim is. I think you are entirely right that we disguise what may be something hideous that we're doing by just the banality of day-to-day living. We don't think of what we're doing, of what it's leading up to.

PHILIP HALLIE: Perhaps you were thinking of Hannah Arendt's book, *Eichmann in Jeruselum: A Report on the Banality of Evil.*[7] The big danger in emphasizing that too much, and I think Arendt falls into this danger, is to say that evil itself can be banal. Part of evil can be banal. Let us say the mind of Adolf Eichmann sitting in the dark in Jerusalem talking bureaucratic clichés by the bucketful is certainly banal. This is what Arendt explores in her brilliant book. But she excludes the suffering that Eichmann's mind generated. The deeds of Eichmann are the suffering. So you can talk about the banality of evil, and you must because it is crucial, but don't leave out the fact that the thing that makes it evil is what it's doing. It's what it's doing to the victims and that's not banal. Never—death is always cruel no matter how short.

PAUL WOODRUFF: There is an old theory that evil is the absence of good. We haven't really talked about that. Some of what you've said fits this and some doesn't. The image of evil as darkness, which is an absence of light, and the talk of evil as the absence of love or kindness, seems to go along with that. Is evil the absence of good? Or is there more to it?

RUSSELL: A very good question. I think that there is more to it. I've never been satisfied with that. There are a number of Christian theological answers to the question, or efforts at answers. One of the more typical ones is that evil is merely the absence of good. It derives less from the Bible than it derives from Platonism and neo-Platonism—where the universe is described in stages and where you have good equals God equals perfection equals truth at the top and then you descend stage by stage till you get to that which is the farthest away from God, the least true and so forth as the privation of all those good things—that's where evil lies. I think there's some value in that argument, but it doesn't go far enough because it seems to leave you with the feeling that evil is somehow only a kind of emptiness. Well, it is, in a way. Perhaps one of the best analogies for total evil I've heard is the metaphor for evil as 'absolute zero' cold—that is to say, what is cold but the absence of warmth? What is warmth removed from molecules? If you have absolute zero, you have absolutely no movement of molecules, no life. And so cold—absolute zero—is the absolute deprivation of any kind of warmth.

I think all of that has certain value but it does not quite come to the full answer because it leaves out the idea that there is a real absolute power operating here. Another analogy would be a vacuum, a real vacuum. The real vacuum is what? It's nothing. But it also has an enormous effect on things. If you put a real vacuum in the center of this room, we'd all be sucked into it and destroyed. So the real vacuum, the real deprivation, can act as a really destructive force. All these metaphors perhaps do leave us with a too empty sense of evil, but I think that it is a real force operating in the world.

Wayne Holtzman: I would like to ask about the 'racial unconsciousness' of all of us. We have grown up in a tradition of thousands of years of Judeo-Christian or Islamic teaching and beliefs in which evil is epitomized by icons, images, devils, demons; and the other side by angels. We all carry certain icons around by which to short circuit our thinking, conceptualize various things in our own life experiences, and provide meaning to life. In the last 15 years, many of the things we thought had been pushed out of our society—like witchcraft, mysticism, and mythologies—have grown rapidly. The sociologists tell us that these are far more endemic in our society than we ever believed. Witches still live. And some of the movements today, whether they are charismatic Christians or fundamentalists or within the Catholic Church—you name it—have to do with these unconscious symbols or beliefs in which all of us in one way or another emotionally may be exorcizing the devil while intellectually denying that we're involved in the process at all. I'd like to hear what Jeffrey Burton Russell might have to say about that, since he's an expert on witchcraft.

Russell: I'd like to begin by saying that some of my best friends are witches, but that wouldn't quite be true. In my research on witchcraft, however, we did have some witches over for dinner one evening. That's kind of a trivial point because I think that most of these modern witch groups are extremely benign. These people were interested in nature worship, planting redwood trees, and singing songs about Tolkien. I don't think modern witchcraft is anything like a sinister force at all.

There are some groups that are very sinister. There are some satanic groups, fortunately not very many of them, but some of them are extremely dangerous. And of course we have satanism perpetrated in a lot of lyrics of what's called 'heavy metal music'. Not all heavy metal groups are into them but some, like 'Twisted Sister', really do have lyrics that are very satanic indeed. So, yes, there's been a growth of the irrational in the last 20 years and some of it is very sinister. You're quite right.

NOTES

[1] Mary Midgley, *Wickedness: A Philosophical Essay* (London: Routledge & Kegan Paul, 1984).

[2] Edgar Allan Poe, *Complete Tales and Poems of Edgar Allen Poe* (New York: Modern Library, 1938), pp. 280–84.

[3] "It was this unfathomable longing of the soul to vex itself—to offer violence to its own nature—to do wrong for wrong's sake only—that urged me to continue . . . " (*ibid.*, p. 225).

[4] From 'West-Running Brook', *Complete Poems of Robert Frost* (New York: Holt, Rinehart and Winston, 1964):

> Speaking of contraries, see how the brook
> In that white wave runs counter to itself.
> It is from that in water we were from
> Long, long before we were from any creature.
>
> It is in this backward motion toward the source,
> Against the stream, that most we see ourselves in,
> The tribute of the current to the source . . .

[5] Herman Melville, *Billy Budd, Sailor* (Chicago: University of Chicago Press, 1962), p. 78.

[6] C. Fadiman, (ed.), *The Little, Brown Book of Anecdotes* (Boston: Little, Brown, 1985). pp. 295–296.

[7] Hannah Arendt, *Eichmann in Jerusalem: A Report on the Banality of Evil* (New York: Viking, 1963).

CREATIVITY AND EVIL

Rollo May

Rollo May is an author and psychoanalyst who lives in Tiburon, California. A Columbia University Ph.D., he has been president of the William Alanson White Psychoanalytic Association, faculty member at the William Alanson White Institute and the California School of Professional Psychology, and a visiting professor at Yale, Harvard, and Princeton Universities, and the University of California, Santa Cruz. Among his many honors, May received the 1971 American Psychological Association Award for Distinguished Contribution to the Science and Profession of Clinical Psychology. In 1987, he received the Psychological Professional Gold Medal Award. His books include *Art of Counseling*, *Man's Search for Himself*, *Psychology and the Human Dilemma*, *Love and Will* (which received the 1970 Ralph Waldo Emerson Award), *Power and Innocence* (which received the New York Society of Clinical Psychologists' Special Dr. Martin Luther King, Jr., Award), *The Courage to Create*, *The Meaning of Anxiety*, *Freedom and Destiny*, *The Discovery of Being*, and *My Quest for Beauty*.

I was moved by Laurens van der Post's words because it seems to me they are saying in somewhat different words exactly what I will say this evening. The Shadow is not in itself evil. But there is a capacity in human beings to use the Shadow to run amok. This is what's so terribly fascinating—people run amok when they have lived in meaninglessness for as long a period as they can stand it. And then they let themselves go in killing and in other aspects of gross evil.

I want to talk about the very difficult problem of how we use evil. It is wrong to think that if we wiped evil out, everything would be fine. Even if such were possible—which it obviously is not—the meaninglessness would be infinitely greater. But what we need to do is to see that human beings have the capacity through what Laurens van der Post calls consciousness and awareness to *move into* a way of life that will help us use evil for constructive purposes.

There is a point in a child's development (somewhere between the ages of one and two) before which he looks at you directly, and without self-consciousness. After that he is very different; he looks at you with suspicion or with guilt or love. From then on, he can lie. As Sartre says, "Lying is a behavior of transcendence." This birth of self-consciousness does not come with the birth of the baby itself. It comes about nine months or a year and a half after that. With that consciousness comes the capacity for evil. Not only can he or she experience life as vitality but he or she can experience the depth of meaninglessness.

When, as Laurens van der Post so beautifully said, meaninglessness is the situation in our country (and has been for several decades, as it is characteristic of the twentieth century), when meaninglessness goes beyond the point of absorption, whole nations may run amok. The most educated nation in Europe—the nation that has given us the greatest of many kinds of art—this nation, Germany, went amok. And we have not understood it yet.

Now it's about these problems that I come to Texas to talk with you tonight and to listen during our other times together, because these problems are to my mind the most difficult problems facing humankind. We may really run amok; it is not at all impossible. This is why I think the problem of evil must be taken very seriously and this is what I hope we do in these three days.

Stanley Kunitz, who was the poet of the Library of Congress for a number of years, a great poet, was at our house for dinner. There happened to be also in the group a very young man who wanted to be a poet; and he had brought in his pocket some of his poems which he wanted Kunitz to read. Now Kunitz does not like to be put on the spot like that, but he is a kindhearted person and he listened as the boy read them. Then he said, "There is not enough rage in them."

Now, what did he mean in saying there is not enough rage to

make a good poem? What is necessary, we know, in creativity is the concentration of all of one's passion, one's love, one's anger, one's rage, one's hatred—the concentration of all of these, with one's sensitivity, into a poem. This is why Dylan Thomas writes about the death of his father,

> Do not go gently into that good night.
> Rage, rage against the dying of the light.

What does this mean? These persons are not at all saying, 'Be nice'. What they are saying is that for any great creation there must be a rage. I also would interpret Laurens van der Post as saying that this rage comes out of our final inner decision to break through the meaninglessness—the meaninglessness of death in Dylan Thomas's father's case, and the meaninglessness of a poem that is insipid, in this young man's poetry.

We know that creativity also begins with consciousness. (This, incidentally, is the meaning of the fall of Adam.) It is the parable of the birth of self-consciousness in the growing child. Before that time there is no anxiety in Eden, there is no guilt. After that moment there is anxiety and guilt. They are afraid. And after that time, there is guilt. They realize they are naked. They walk together to the gate of paradise. They look out on the vast world, and as Milton puts it so beautifully, to see where they would spend the night:

> The world was all before them, where to choose
> Their place of rest, and Providence their guide:
> They hand in hand with wandering steps and slow,
> Through Eden took their solitary way.
> (*Paradise Lost XII.* 646–49)

Now I want to talk about the confronting of evil, not the wiping out of evil. I think wiping it out is quite impossible and is itself the most evil thing imaginable. This is the great danger in the short-sighted view of many religions and also of our own Christianity—that we think we can put the evil in somebody else, like the Devil, and if we can keep free from this Devil we will survive. Nothing could be more dangerous than that very idea. For evil cannot be put out of human life, as Jung noted that one could not erase the Shadow. And if one tries to put it out, then the rage is put out with it and the capacities to create are thrown aside with the so-called evil.

In Goethe's *Faust*, which he finished when he was 80 years of age, the question is put by Faust to Mephistopheles, "Who are you?"

And Mephistopheles answers, "I am that which always does evil which turns into good" (Part I, Lines 1335–37).

I agree, though I think that Goethe oversimplified the problem somewhat. He lived in the age when everybody was optimistic, the Enlightenment and the Industrial Age, which invented trains and all kinds of mechanical things. I don't think it's that easy. Nevertheless, it is interesting again that he puts Evil as that which originally is caused by the Good.

In the Book of Job, for example, God and the Devil talk together. They are certainly on speaking terms. Satan was a worshipper of God to start with, he was not an agnostic. Lucifer was thrown out of Heaven. These devils are needed by God. Out of the capacity to deal with evil, there comes the ultimate good.

This is the reason there has been so much argument in our day. Can we get over evil? Erich Fromm writes that if we change society, we then would no longer have evil people, when it's obvious that it's this very society that helped make these people evil.

We must put aside all the easy answers to the problem to start with, and ask the deeper questions: How is evil formed in the paradox of human existence? In the paradox of human consciousness—how is evil formed that out of it may come creativity, may come art, and may come a very powerful and profound kind of love? This is why Freud and many others down through history have said not only that we cannot do away with evil, but also that evil is part of human existence and will continue to be.

Christian theology has tried to oversimplify this, at least in some quarters. I am sure that what Laurens van der Post was saying was tremendously refreshing to my soul because he does not oversimplify. Christian theology has tried to put evil into the form of devils, and if you could then execute all of these devils, you would be that much freer from evil. But the Devil is always coming back into the picture. When William Blake drew his pictures of God, he had hooves on God. Just as I say, with the creativity of great poetry, the paradoxical struggle with Evil is that out of which the poem and the great work of creativity come.

Our contemporary age is an age of meaninglessness, of emptiness; we have the feeling that we don't know where we are going. One of the seniors at Stanford gave the testimony in his valedictory address a couple of years ago that the graduating class of Stanford had no real sense of relationship with life. It did not have meaning. It did not know where it was going. All these are examples.

I remember what my friend Paul Tillich used to say, that the best way to see the underlying meaning of any given age is not to read the philosophers, or even the poets or the theologians, but rather to look at the art. If you look at the art in modern museums, you will discover that what these artists are trying to do is to paint the conflict that their struggle with evil gives them. In any museum you may walk through, in the Renaissance art you have the feeling of great joy that is there. You walk through, say, the art of Rembrandt from the seventeenth century, and you see the great meaning in his portraits. Then you walk through the art of the last of the nineteenth century and you see Van Gogh and Gauguin and Cézanne struggling to keep whatever meaning they have.

But then you come to the twentieth-century artists and what you see is a great white canvas with several slashes of black on it, and this is hung up and called by a number—not a name. Or you may see a Motherwell, these great huge forms that seem to many people to have no meaning at all.

In the Metropolitan Museum, they now have a room for twentieth-century American art, and they have a big sign, "The Age of Anxiety". They are exactly 50 years late, but this is the way with museums, and we have been in this age of anxiety ever since the first jazz age. We are now in the second jazz age (I hope it is an age that will give birth to the new twenty-first century). But in the jazz age back in the 1920s, the beginning of this contemporaneous art told us several things. In the first place, the artists are trying to say 'how lonely I am'. They are also trying to say there is an anger in the world—beware of it.

When I had my office in New York in the Master Hotel, which is on the corner of 103rd Street and Riverside Drive, there was an exhibit of contemporary, twentieth-century art. Several of the artists put up an exhibit outside in a park just across the street; they couldn't get it into the museum. It was a wrecked car torn to pieces, with blood and intestines hanging all over the steering wheel. People called the police, who came and hauled the exhibit away. But I think it was a tremendous work of art that they produced. What these artists were trying to do was to cry out as loudly and vividly as they could, that this is what your technology is leading you to, and when the whole world is a mass of broken bodies, then you'll know what it means to have lived in this century.

This will not occur, I hope and pray, but what the artists are trying to tell us (as Paul Tillich so rightly said) is the meaning-lessness of life. They are trying to tell us the ugliness of life. De Kooning paints pictures of Marilyn Monroe with horse teeth—obviously a great deal of submerged hatred toward women as a whole—but that's not the main point. The main point is that the artists are trying through their expression of the unconscious to make signs, symbols, pictures of what the underlying soul of the twentieth century is.

Picasso painted a picture,*Guernica,* which many of you have seen. When this picture first came to this country, I went down to see it at the Museum of Modern Art in New York. I walked into the room and there was this large picture, all in white and grey and black, a picture showing bull's heads cut off, babies impaled upon swords, torn women lying in the agony of the bomb. The impression on me was so powerful that I could not stand any more than two or three minutes. I had to run out again and walk up and down the street until I could come back and look at it again. This is a painting with very little color—nothing but grey and white, and a little yellow. It's a picture in which Picasso is trying to say, 'This is what happens when Hitler drops his bombs over the helpless Spanish town of Guernica. This is what happens and this is my rageful heart trying to tell this to you.'

What we need to do here is to have a couple of sentences that will help you understand why it is that human beings are involved in these problems. First of all, we are beings along with the other beings, and anything that exists must assert itself, its own center. Up in New Hampshire, where we have a farm, when the top of a tree is cut off the tree sends up some other branch (where it gets it, I haven't the slightest idea), but it sends up another branch to be the center. It must keep its own centeredness, as all beings must preserve their centeredness.

In the second place, all beings must move out from their centeredness into other relationships, as animals do for food, as plants do in giving birth to other plants. Now this being is that which has within it the evil. And it is inescapable. It is not that we can say that if we do away with all these things, everything will be fine, but rather it is that evolution, the birthing of ourselves, the experience of our own being, requires that we take a stand. This stand will have some evil in it and the problem is the paradox of love and hate, the paradox of good and evil out of which we can create important and wonderful things. Whether or not we will survive to do it, I don't know and you don't know, but we can do our best to try to find what reality is available, what possible answers there may be to the problems that come with the evil and particularly with the evil of the twentieth century.

I was on a radio program where people call up and you talk over the phone. Several people had called me talking about the great amount of drugs used, especially in California where I live, and the fact that the suicide rate of young people in this country has gone up 300 percent the past 20 years. These things are certainly regrettable. Then a professor called up from one of the universities; he agreed with what we had said about the difficult problems of living at the end of the twentieth century.

I said, "Tell me about your students."

He said, "I have no trouble at all with my students because, you see, I teach music."

I remembered I had been in a hamburger joint when two young men walked in. One had a violin case and the other carried what I assumed was a clarinet or a flute. One was humming a tune. He said to the other, "That's from Mozart. Isn't it lovely?"

The other said, "Yes, but did you ever hear this?"

And he hummed another tune, also from Mozart. I thought as these young men sat down (they obviously were music students) that these men had something to love. They lived in our tumultuous world in which things are torn to pieces right and left, but nevertheless they had found something in this that they could love.

The particular aspect of evil that I want now to emphasize is the evil that we have exerted against young people and also against the development of our own culture. That is that we have turned our American culture over to illiteracy, a situation in which the majority of students can graduate from college never having taken one course in the sources of our modern civilization, namely Israel and Greece. Sixty-seven percent of them can also graduate from most colleges in this country without ever taking a bit of history. The idea that was believed, when I was in college, was that if you learn another language, you also learn the culture with it. This is certainly true. Now, in the majority of colleges, there are no languages required at all. What has happened is that more and more America has been learning less and less.

But I did not come here to trouble you about such things. One of the things I wanted to do tonight was to point out that, as shown in the book by Bloom, *The Closing of the American Mind*, and the one by Hirsch, *Cultural Literacy*, we have lost our love for the classics, for literature, or history.[1] Dante is read by only one of the students at the institute of psychotherapy where I teach. The Greek plays are not read any more. And these have been the source of joy for thousands of people.

When I was a student at Oberlin College, I had a little poem that wasn't terribly great poetry, but it helped me very much:

> Hold fast your dreams.
> Within your heart,
> Keep a place apart
> Where dreams may go, and sheltered so
> May thrive and grow.
> Where doubt and fear are not,
> Hold fast, hold fast your dreams.

When I was 20 years old I had some contact with the Greek language. I had wandered into the library one day, past the seminar room to one where there were seven or eight students studying Greek. I didn't know Homer from what the baseball players these days are knocking over the back fence. But I thought this must be interesting, so I signed up and took the course. It turned out to be the best course I ever took. What it did was to open up a past, a dynamic past that is also present, and opened up a future because I could read Aeschylus. I could read Plato as he wrote about Socrates when he was being tried for heresy by the Athenians and condemned to death. And I could read of Socrates's last talks with his followers.

Now these things have all but disappeared from our society. I believe this is a great tragedy. I had hoped that in this second jazz age, as I chose to call the last eight or ten years, we would recover some of these things that gave the students something to dream about, that in fact did give these music students something to love.

In this dreaming that we were doing out there, and in the music that we heard, there is both evil and good. But there is also the greatness that comes from the great works of art. Beethoven writes great music by putting things together that otherwise would be discordant. This is what gives his music such great power.

There is thus in these classics the exemplification of evil combined creatively with good. This present illiteracy is the destruction of the souls of modern young people. We load our TV programs mostly with trash and we have lost, as I have said, a great deal of our literacy.

What we need to do is to recover a familiarity, a love for those areas in which evil is absorbed into good, and vice versa. We need to recover a way of life, and I hope, a new world and a new love for the classics, for humanities, for literature. Darwin once said, "If I had my life to live over again, I would read some poetry every day because I have been so concerned with the evolutionary facts that my poetic sense has atrophied." There is another poem that I want to quote to you that made a lot of difference with me, George Eliot's 'The Choir Invisible'. I used to be saying to myself, as I walked across that campus:

> Oh, may I join the choir invisible,
> Of those immortal dead who live again
> In minds made better for their presence: Live
> In pulses stirred to generosity,
> In deeds of daring rectitude, in scorn
> For miserable aims that end with self,
> In thoughts sublime that pierce the night like stars.

I leave you with no answers. I leave you, rather, with my own imperfect statement of what I think is happening in our world. I want to do this through reference to another myth, to another great writer who is also a great comfort for us in our day, Christopher Marlowe. In his version of Faust, he has Faust say, as he nears the end of his stay on earth, "The devil will come, and Faustus must be damned." Faust says to himself:

> Oh, I'll leap up to my God!
> Who pulls me down?
> See, see, where Christ's blood streams in the firmament!
> One drop would save my soul—half a drop! Ah, my Christ!
> Ah, rend not my heart for naming of my Christ;
> Yet will I call on him—Oh, spare me, Lucifer!
> Where is it now? 'Tis gone, and see where God
> Stretcheth out his arms and bends his ireful brows,
> Mountains and hills, come, come and fall on me
> And hide me from the heavy wrath of God!
> No, no
> Then I will run headlong into the earth.
> Earth, gape! O no, it will not harbor me.
>
> (Act V, Scene ii)

And always he has to say, 'No', until the final bell rings and he is thrown into Hell. Different from Goethe who lived in the Enlightenment, Christopher Marlowe lived in the Renaissance a couple of centuries earlier and he knew the seriousness of Faust. We have forgotten this in our day, with the help of Goethe and people of our century who want to say, 'if only we could learn how to make more money for more people, we could then forget all the poor people who are increasing faster than the multimillionaires', people who want to forget that in our second jazz age and go on without a care.

This, Marlowe says in *Dr. Faustus*, is not possible. It does matter whether one is cast into Hell or not, no matter what one's view of Hell may be. It is, as Paul Tillich used to say, "what one sees every time one looks at oneself in the mirror". But this Hell, which we deal with certainly in the death cycle analysis, is there, and as Marlowe says, it is a pitiful thing and is a destruction of our love, and a destruction of our hearts and ourselves.

I have put before you a glimpse of the end of the twentieth-century as I see it. I think the understanding of evil is exceedingly important in our moment of history. It's important enough for me to get out of bed and come here to speak. It's important enough for all of us to find that understanding we can arrive at, what we can learn to love. There still can be discord, as there often is in Beethoven; but these great discords are turned into great beauty.

One of the ways we can do this is to recover our culture, our love, our understanding of other people. We can find again the greatness that was partially there in a previous America. Perhaps the most important reason for doing this is that we then can pass on to the younger generation a world that is worth living in.

NOTES

[1] Allen Bloom. (New York: Simon & Schuster, 1987). E.D. Hirsch, Jr. (Boston: Houghton Mifflin, 1987).

[2] George Eliot. The first seven lines of "Oh May I Join the Choir Invisible," *Poems*, Vol. II. (Boston: Dana Estes & Co., n.d.).

6

SMALL SINS AND LARGE EVILS

Karl E. Weick

Karl E. Weick held the Centennial chair in business administration in the Management Department of the University of Texas at Austin at the time of the symposium. Previously he was the Nicholas H. Noyes professor of organizational behavior and professor of psychology at Cornell University in Ithaca, New York. A Ph.D. in psychology of Ohio State University, he has been professor of psychology and director of the Laboratory for Research in Social Relations at the University of Minnesota, Minneapolis. Weick has also been visiting professor at Stanford University and the State University of Utrecht in the Netherlands. He received the 1986 Distinguished Career Award from the Academy of Management and was cowinner of the American College of Hospital Administration 1972 Book of the Year Award. His books include *Productivity in Organization: A Metatheory of Work and Its Assessment, The Social Psychology of Organizing,* and *Managerial Behavior, Performance, and Effectiveness.*

The decision of the Institute for the Humanities at Salado to focus on the topic of Evil is a significant act. The significance derives from the fact that "the evil of our time is the loss of awareness of evil, for to be conscious of evil is a dimension of the understanding of what one does and what the meanings of those actions are."[1] The symposium on Evil is about awareness and what happens when awareness grows weak.

This article was printed in the booklet on "Understanding Evil" (Harry A. Wilmer, ed., 1987) which was given to all speakers and registrants prior to the Symposium on Understanding Evil.

Awareness can weaken in unexpected ways. For example, the simple fact that only one-fourth of today's population was alive at the end of World War II takes on added significance when rephrased as "three-fourths of today's population has no first-hand knowledge of the dramatic evils of the Holocaust, Hiroshima, or mass lynchings."

First-hand knowledge is important because we need information and a capacity for rational judgment to deal with evil. Camus in *The Plague* wrote "the evil that is in the world always comes of ignorance, and good intentions may do as much harm as malevolence if they lack understanding . . . the most incorrigible vice being that of an ignorance that fancies it knows everything and therefore claims for itself the right to kill."[2] To resist evil we need to ask what it is and how it works since we cannot detect or resist something we don't understand. The difficulty comes when we try to understand evil and simultaneously reject it. To understand is to run the risk that that evil becomes stripped of its raw wickedness and seems more distant and acceptable. To reject evil is to run the risk that we ignore possible ways in which evil insinuates itself into everyday life. To understand without accepting requires a difficult balancing act of emotion and thought as well as sensitive associates who listen constructively and seriously to one another. Those are the resources provided by the symposium.

Evil comes in so many forms that it is fruitless to argue over whether a specific item ought to be included on a list of evils. Doob[3] hints at the futility of mere lists of evils when he shows how diverse human groups are in what they designate as evil:

American Indian: 'vice, crime, pollution, and even misfortune'.

Babylonian: 'an unconscious violation of the ceremonial regulations'.

Buddhist: ' "folly" as a result of ignorance'.

Celtic: 'gods being offended by neglect.'

Chinese (Confucius): 'theft robbery, . . . malignity, perverseness, mendacity, vindictiveness, . . . vascillating weakness, . . . being unfilial'.

Christian: 'The explicit or implicit claim to live independently of God, to put something else, be it the world or self, in His place'.

Greek: 'all conduct which by omission or by commission, in overt act or inner meaning, is offensive to the supra-human Powers'.

Hebrew: 'neglect of certain external acts'.

Iranian: 'a refusal, on the part of the free choice of the human will, to conform to the divine will'.

Muslim: 'pride and opposition to God . . . infidelity or the ascribing of partners to God, murder, theft, adultery, unnatural crimes, neglect of the Ramadan fast and of the Friday prayers, magic, gambling, drunkenness, perjury, usury, disobedience to parents'.

Roman: 'enmity with superhuman forces'.

Teutonic: 'blasphemy, perjury, adultery'.

While those examples are striking in their diversity, they do share some common features. Thoughtful people who have tried to define evil suggest what some of those common features may be. Here are seven attempts to define what evil is:

1. Evil is a "line of conduct which destroys resources necessary for existence: the pollution and destruction of the environment, as emphasis on short-range goals at the expense of larger purposes, the damaging of trust and of legitimizing values that results from bigotry and jingoism."[4]

2. The term evil "is most appropriately applied to situations when force, violence, and other forms of coercion exceed institutional or moral

limits."[5] Thus, evil can occur when people not empowered by a legitimately accepted order to exercise coercion do so (for instance, armed robbery), when people legally empowered to exercise coercion exceed the legitimate limits of that exercise (such as police brutality), and when the institutionalization of the exercise of coercion offends some higher standards of humanity or morality that we feel ought to be observed (for example, a police state).

3. Evil is "the use of power to destroy the spiritual growth of others for the purpose of defending and preserving the integrity of our own sick selves. In short, it is scapegoating."[6]

4. Evil means "not that an act or pattern of life is necessarily a sin or a crime according to some law, but rather that it leads to damage or pain suffered by people, to social destructiveness of a degree so serious as to call for use of an ancient heavily freighted term."[7]

5. Evil "refers to an individual who knows the better but follows the worse course of action."[8]

6. Evil "is the dramatic absence of good."[9]

7. "Evil is not simply a matter of pain or death but of what people do to each other's minds, to each other's understanding of themselves and of their opposite numbers. In fact, staring at bloody events can render us too callous to understand the unselving of a human being that is at the heart of victimization."[10]

The evil portrayed in these definitions is vivid, dramatic, stark, crude, heavy-handed, conspicuous and revolting. But evil is also sometimes a subtle event that starts small. Evil is like an amoeba: hazy, shifting, changing shape, not hard-edged, subtle, parasitic.

The subtle side of Evil is visible in a definition not listed above. Doob[11] suggests that there are two criteria by which people can judge whether evil is present. The first criterion is psychological: evil is "a condition in which one or more persons experience pain, unhappiness, frustration, or other negative, aversive feelings." The second criterion is social-moral: evil is "a condition in which aversive feelings or the actions of one or more persons are considered undesirable by one or more judges." Evil occurs when *both* of these criteria are satisfied.

When we first read this definition we rejected it as not strong enough. Evil sounded more like an irritant than an outrage, more like normal, natural trouble than a threat to humanity. And yet, evil seldom starts full-blown. More often it is built up from small sins, occasional oversights, unwarranted deference and sluggish mentation. Evil is such a dramatic event that it is easy to fall into the trap of thinking that it takes an equally dramatic cause to produce it. If we spot no big causes, then we expect no large evils.

The evil-as-amoeba metaphor captures the fact that evil starts small. And that's why, when Doob grounds evil in the event of aversive feelings felt by one person that are judged by another person to be undesirable, he captures a truth about evil. A dramatic absence of good often starts undramatically.

Evil often starts small when people try to establish a sense of identity, a sense of who they are, a sense of where they leave off and others begin. Identity is a decision about difference. The kind of act required to build identity is implied in the word 'decision'. The word 'decision' is contrasted with the word 'incision'. Both mean to cut (cision): an incision means 'to cut into', a decision means 'to cut away'. A decision about identity is made when I cut away definitions of who I am not until I am left with a residual which suggests who I am (for example, I am not you or a woman or a Texan or a moonie or a . . .).

The innocent exercise of building an identity can have a darker side because it also involves labeling, classification, stereotyping, and typification of the selves we discard. The danger is that "typification becomes prejudice and ultimately the inability to see or feel."[12] The differences and stereotypes that produce identity need not lead to aggression and projection, but they have the potential to do so.

Stereotypes and separation of myself from others make it easier for me to treat those others as objects. And when I see the other as an object, I am more likely to use that other, dismiss that other, and exaggerate how different we are. The innocent act of building an identity, which leads to the small sin of stereotyping, can be kept by empathy from growing into the large evil of dehumanization. Kant knew this when he wrote the second of his three maxims of common human understanding: think for oneself; think from the standpoint of everyone else; think consistently.[13]

To think 'from the standpoint of everyone else' is hard for a person with a distinct identity because identity encourages a preoccupation with self. Once a self is marked off with boundaries of what it is and is not, then it is more tempting to pay attention to it. Self-absorption means that little attention is left over to discover and correct the sterotypyes attributed to other people in the interest of identity. With self-centeredness comes detachment and misperception. Faced with war crimes, lynchings, the homeless or death squads, self-centered people say, in essence, "I can't take the responsibility of the world on my shoulders too strongly myself . . . It upsets me. I'm having my own problems and can't take this stuff too seriously since it causes me worries and problems."[14]

If I have an identity in which I have become absorbed, then it also becomes harder for me to admit that I am an imperfect person capable of failure. As I become more self-absorbed I see myself as more coherent and less flawed which means that when I do fail, I need to disown the failure. And it is here where those 'different' other people, the ones I discarded when I cut away selves I was not, come in handy. I project my failures onto other people whom I have lumped together, labeled, and avoided. I preserve my self-image by sacrificing theirs. This sequence sets the stage for evil especially when it goes on without awareness. "The acknowledged shadow is terrible enough, it is the unacknowledged one which is the real killer."[15]

The unacknowledged shadow has the potential to become "the real killer" because it is the failings of the others—failings which I put there—that become the evil I crusade against. If I crusade against the Devil in others, but I put that Devil there in the first place by projecting my own dark side, then the devils in them will stick around just as long as I remain blind to the devils in me.

And now we see why crusades seldom make the world better. Crusades have such poor results precisely because crusaders find it harder to deal with their own dark side, but easier to deal with darkness in others. The 'discovery' of darkness in others can encourage impulsive, reckless, evil acts because "he who does evil is typically convinced that evil is about to be done to him."[16] The Kent State tragedy, internment of Japanese in America in World War II, and justification for the Nazi actions against the Jews all share the quality of preemptive evil made to forestall 'their' evil intentions.

Identity, difference, self-absorption and shadow projection serve as small sins that encourage large evils in another way. Words like choice, self-responsibility, fatalism, pawn and resistance crop up repeatedly in discussion of evil. For example, "most evil is done by people who never made up their mind to be either bad or good."[17]

There is agreement that morality consists of drawing a line somewhere. But there is also agreement that we now live in an age where people are either unwilling to draw lines at all or are willing to draw lines but they do so arbitrarily with neither reflection nor caring.

The issue of choice and line drawing is mentioned most often in the context of Adolf Eichmann's statement that he was just doing his job while exterminating human beings.[18] The tragedy of Eichmann is "that he did not inherently lack the faculties of understanding, judgment, reason and will, but merely gave up the active and individual use of these faculties—that he deferred in all important aspects to faculties of others."[19] Deference and conformity in group settings often encourage evil.

In the prologue to their important book Sanctions for Evil, Sanford and Comstock retell a story from the 1930s that illustrates the close ties between evil and groups: "We are reminded of the cabaret joke current in the early 1930s in Germany: 'Show me one Nazi.' 'What do you mean? Here is room full of Nazis.' 'Yes, but show me one Nazi.'[20]

"Obedience and support should always be considered and never automatic."[21] The necessity for awareness and deliberation in groups is clear if one thinks carefully about the appeal which led Eichmann and others to do what they did. "In order to persuade a good moral man to do evil, then it is not necessary first to persuade him to become evil. It is only necessary to teach him that he is doing good."[22]

The list of conditions which encourage evil, unfortunately, is long. But the biggest danger of all, and the danger toward which this symposium is dedicated, is indifference. Indifference, understanding and awareness have a strange relationship to one another. If we understand evil and how it works, then it may be easier for us to dismiss it or become indifferent to it. "How evil contributes to good is NOT something we are permitted to know, because if we did know, we wouldn't take the battle seriously."[23]

Thus the difficult assignment for people at this symposium is to see evil both as mysterious, to forestall indifference, and as intelligible, to forestall resignation. We need to listen carefully to one another, in order to demystify those causes of evil, including our own self-absorption, that we can do something about.

Although we gather in Salado to understand the polarity of good vs. evil, that may not be the most productive way to pose the issue. If we are to build responsible individual positions on this issue, we have to personalize it. And a more personal way to pose the issue of this symposium was suggested by Martin Buber in 1966:

> There is not as we generally think in the soul of man good and evil opposed. There is again and again in different manners a polarity, and the poles are not good and evil, but rather yes and no, rather acceptance and refusal. And we can strengthen, or we can help him strengthen, the one positive pole. And perhaps we can even strengthen the force of direction in him because this polarity is very often directionless. It is a chaotic state. We could bring a cosmic note into it. We can help put order, put a shape into this. Because I think the good, what we may call the good, is always only a direction, not a substance.[24]

The point is not to battle over examples (substance) but over directions; not to battle over abstractions, but over concrete yeses, noes, acceptances and refusals; not to battle over self as much as over others; and not to battle over the large issues that announce themselves as evil; but over the small slights that foreshadow it.

NOTES

[1] C. Drekmeier. 'Knowledge as Virtue, Knowledge as Power', in N. Sanford and C. Comstock (eds.), *Sanctions for Evil* (Boston, Beacon, 1971), p. 198.

[2] Albert Camus, (New York: Modern Library, 1948), p. 240

[3] L.W. Doob, *Panorama of Evil* (Westport, CT.: Greenwood, 1978).

[4] Drekmeier, *op. cit.*, p. 242.

[5] N.J. Smelser, 'Some Determinants of Destructive Behavior', in N. Sanford & C. Comstock (eds.), *Sanctions for Evil* (Boston: Beacon, 1971), pp. 15–24.

[6] M. Scott Peck, *People of the Lie* (New York: Simon & Schuster, 1983).

[7] N. Sanford and C. Comstock, 'Sanctions for Evil' in N. Sanford and C. Comstock (eds.), *Sanctions for Evil* (Boston: Beacon, 1971), pp. 1–11

[8] Doob, *op. cit.*, p. 8.

[9] S. Dossa, 'Hannah Arendt on Eichmann: The Public, the Private, and Evil', *Review of Politics*, 46, (1984), pp. 163–182.

[10] P.P. Hallie, 'Justification and Rebellion', in N. Sanford and C. Comstock (eds.), *Sanctions for Evil* (Boston: Beacon, 1971), pp. 247–263.

[11] Doob, *op. cit.*, p. 8.

[12] Drekmeier, *op. cit.*, p. 242.

[13] B. Clarke, 'Beyond "The Banality of Evil",' *British Journal of Political Science* 10, (1980), pp. 417–439.

[14] E.M. Opton, Jr., 'It Never Happened and Besides They Deserved It', in N. Sanford and C. Comstock (eds.), *Sanctions for Evil* (Boston: Beacon, 1971), pp. 49–70.

[15] M. Midgley, *Wickedness: A Philosophical Essay* (London: Routledge & Kegan Paul, 1984).

[16] Smelser, *op. cit.*, p. 17.

[17] Dossa, *op. cit.*, p. 166.

[18] H. Arendt, *Eichmann in Jerusalem: A Report on the Banality of Evil* (New York: Penguin, 1963).

[19] Clarke, *op. cit.*, p. 428.

[20] Sanford and Comstock, *op. cit.*, p. 3.

[21] Clarke, *op. cit.*, p. 437.

[22] Doob, *op. cit.*, p. 99.

[23] M. Garner, *The Whys of a Philosophical Scrivener* (New York: Quill, 1983).

[24] M. Buber, *The Knowledge of Man* (New York: Harper, 1966), p. 181.

7

WHY EVIL ATTRACTS US

Gregory Curtis

Gregory Curtis, editor of *Texas Monthly*, has worked with the magazine since it was founded in 1972. After graduating from Rice University in Houston, he worked as a freelance writer for a variety of publications and was the founding partner of a small printing and publishing company. From 1972 until 1977, he was a senior editor at *Texas Monthly*, where he wrote scores of feature stories on subjects ranging from artists and politicians to murderers. He was named executive editor in 1978 and editor in 1981. Under his editorship, *Texas Monthly* has won numerous honors, including many nominations for the National Magazine Award.

A few years ago, I walked alone through the concentration camp at Dachau. I had arrived there by commuter train from Munich—to my mind, one of the most appealing cities in the world. The art and music is the equal of anywhere and the food would make even a Parisian take notice. Dachau is a small village only eight miles away, and the camp is a good long walk from the train station. I asked someone there for directions. As I walked on and on, I almost thought that the man had misled me, perhaps out of shame for himself or for his village or for his country. Later I thought perhaps if he had misled me, it had been for more benevolent reasons, as anyone of good feeling would try to protect another from horror.

At the site of the camp, really very little remains except for the huge white wall that encircles it. The grounds are mostly empty now, covered by thick white gravel. Near the entrance, there is a museum where you can learn the history of the camp.

The whole horror is overwhelming. Most affecting for me were the accounts of merciless experiments involving children. At some distance from the museum, at a far corner of the camp, buildings remained where there were ovens. Their bricks are crumbling but their iron doors seem impervious to use or to time. Near that building is another containing so-called interrogation rooms. These are small cement cubicles with no adornment and with thick wooden doors. There is nothing there to tell you what went on in these rooms and really nothing needs to tell you.

All this was very sad and terrible to see. It made me feel empty and helpless at a time when I would rather have felt a justified anger or righteous strength. At the same time, as horrible as that was, it's impossible to say that evil is not sometimes attractive. I don't mean that it is good, but that it is appealing—even seductive. How can evil that is so appalling and enervating at Dachau be in other circumstances energizing and spirited? Why, in short, when evil is so terrible, does it ever appeal to us?

For one thing, I think, the good can be very difficult to get along with. There is a painting by Velázquez in the National Gallery in London. It shows Christ visiting a humble house. In the foreground is the kitchen. Through a window, you can see into the main room of the house where Christ is seated talking to a group of adoring listeners. In the kitchen is a woman with a tremendously sour expression on her face. She is grinding garlic. Someone, after all, has to prepare the meal for Christ and for his listeners. This task has fallen to her. Christ may have been revealing the true path to heaven in the other room. She's stuck in the kitchen with the garlic.[1]

That's how exasperating the good can be. It assumes that someone will cook for it. It can make us its servants unfairly and against our will. Had the serpent come to the woman in the kitchen, who could blame her for listening?

There are other reasons why evil is attractive. We must search for the good while evil seeks us out. In Eden, Eve did not go looking for the serpent; rather, it came to her. Evil accepts us. It does not require us to improve. No matter how great our faults, evil will embrace us. Evil validates our weaknesses and our secret appetites. It tells us we're all right. Evil does not ask us to feel guilty. You are what you are, evil says. In fact, if you want to, you can get worse. This is a tremendously appealing and seductive attitude. No stern lectures—instead, an accepting indulgence.

On the other hand, If we don't want indulgence but instead want to have more or know more, evil can do that, too. Remember, after all, what it was that the serpent promised Eve. "In the day ye eat thereof," he said (that is, eat of the forbidden fruit), "then your eyes shall be opened, and ye shall be as gods, knowing good and evil" (Genesis 3:5).

Surely the grandest portrayal of evil in our literature is the character of Satan in Milton's *Paradise Lost*. It is a truism of Milton scholarship that, despite the poet's stated goal of justifying the ways of God to man, instead he created a God that seems as strict and stubborn as an old-fashioned schoolteacher, while Satan has a complex psychology that's appealing. His pride led him to rebel and his rebellion caused his fall, but the reader (despite Milton's genius) finds himself rooting for the rebels and sympathizing with their leader.

Milton's Satan may be pure evil, but like anything that is pure, he has his own integrity. Early in the poem, Satan has just been cast into Hell, and for a moment, he considers his predicament (Book I, lines 106–116).

"All is not lost", he says. He has been cast from Heaven, he faces an eternity in Hell, and yet he says, "All is not lost." The reason is that he is still in possession of his own will. Later, he explains this further:

> To bow and sue for grace
> With suppliant knee, and deify his power
> . . . that were low indeed,
> That were an ignominy and shame beneath
> This downfall.

In other words, Satan's simple pride leads him inevitably to a kind of moral code. He won't relent. "That were low indeed", Satan says. There are things that even Satan won't do. There are depths to which even he won't sink. Having made a decision, he will live with its consequences.

Thus, evil can be attractive because, after all, it has values. Satan has made it impossible for him to live in heaven, but he has not made it impossible for him to live with himself.

But there is a connection in Milton between the prideful, tormented, and attractive Satan and the horror of Dachau. At the end of Book One, Satan rallies his fallen army to hear him speak. Milton describes the assembled horde this way:

> And now
> Advanc't in view they stand, a horrid Front
> Of dreadful length and dazzling Arms, in guise
> Of Warriors old with ordered Spear and Shield,
> Awaiting what command their mighty Chief
> Had to impose. (Book I, lines 562–67)

It sounds exactly like a Fascist rally. Evil is no longer personified by one individual but has immense organization dedicated to awful purposes. The individual soldier at a Fascist rally is probably no better or worse than anyone else. Perhaps one even hopes, at least at first, that soldier felt the same individual helplessness that I felt at Dachau. But then the rally, and all that goes with it, serves to convince our average soldier that what might have seemed evil is right after all—that it is in accordance with some natural law. Thus, he who otherwise may be kind to children and pets and donate to charity commits evil acts without a flicker of conscience.

In Milton, Satan knows he is evil. In Shakespeare, Iago knows he is evil. What we have to fear in the twentieth century is evil that does not know itself—that is, in fact, convinced it is good. What contaminates one's spirit at Dachau is the knowledge that this immense engine for evil could not have been constructed and operated in the name of evil. Such energy could only come at the service of some ideal. How could this have happened, one asks? And the answer is, they believed.

NOTES

[1] 'Christ in the House of Martha and Mary' (ca. 1618), by Velázquez (1599–1660).

PART II

IN THE VALLEY OF THE SHADOW

THE HOLOCAUST

Raul Hilberg

Raul Hilberg is the John G. McCullough professor of political science at the University of Vermont, Burlington. He was born in Vienna and served with the U. S. Army from 1944 to 1946. He has been a member of the President's Commission on the Holocaust and is a member of the United States Holocaust Memorial Council in Washington, D.C. He holds a Ph.D. in public law and government from Columbia University and an L.H.D. (hon.) from Hebrew Union College. Hilberg is author of *The Destruction of the European Jews* and *Special Trains to Auschwitz,* and editor of *Documents of Destruction* and *Warsaw Diary of Adam Czerniakow.*

In 1976, I went to a small town in Württemberg, Ludwigsburg, which has the headquarters for investigation of so-called National Socialist Crimes, an office maintained by the provinces of the Federal Republic of Germany. About 30 prosecutors were housed in that particular building. I went there to study court records, various affidavits, and other materials.

One afternoon they said, "We're having a party today. Would you join us?"

"Why, yes."

"We have one bottle of wine for each person," they said.

After a while, I chanced to talk to the deputy chief of that office.

"I've been troubled by one question," I said. "I'm afraid I went into print with something that isn't entirely accurate, and that is the role of Adolf Hitler himself in the annihilation of the Jewish people in Europe. I know you're only concerned here with live individuals, and you do not investigate the dead. But still, what do you think?"

"Ach!" he said. "We've often fantasized about drawing up an indictment against Adolf Hitler himself, and to put into that indictment the major charge—the final solution of the Jewish question in Europe, the physical annihilation of Jewry. Then it dawned upon us—what would we do? We didn't have the evidence." And he laughed.

Elie Wiesel and other survivors sometimes ask, 'Where was God?' The German prosecutors, the political scientists, the historians ask a more modest question, 'Where was Adolf Hitler?' The question has enormous importance for Germany today—and beyond even Germany—for our appreciation of what a totalitarian system is. When I touch upon the simple question of the role of Hitler in the initiation of the final solution, I speak of something that Christopher Browning addressed in a book called *Fateful Months*[1]—how was the decision of 1941 made? We've long known that the process of destruction was a step-by-step undertaking. No one in 1933 had a clear idea of what would happen in 1936. No one in 1936 anticipated 1939. No one even in 1939 foretold 1942. There was no blueprint. There was no central office for destruction. There was no planning in any fundamental, central way of this process.

Yet a point was reached—after the Jews had been concentrated in ghettos within Polish cities, after they'd been deprived of livelihoods, after their food rations were cut—when the open question was asked, 'What now?' We know what happened, but there is a strange darkness amidst all the thousands and tens of thousands of materials at our disposal pertaining to the central figure, the main character: Adolf Hitler. Despite the plethora of books about Hitler, we still have not found out everything about this man. We have, however, some basic knowledge about his youth, including his encounters with Jews.

The physician who treated Hitler's mother for cancer was a Jew. The mother died. One might think that this episode itself would have led him to rave against Jewish doctors. Oddly enough, however, when Hitler marched into Austria in 1938, he gave very specific orders that this particular doctor who was still alive was not to be touched. He was to be given every opportunity to leave with whatever he had.[2]

Hitler lived in Austria until 1913. He left the country for a number of complex reasons, one of them being that he wasn't really quite successful. What had he been doing? He had been painting pictures, as you know. He sold some of these pictures to Jewish art dealers.[3] Never did he complain about being taken advantage of by these dealers, even after he could have done so with impunity in the years after the First World War.

Hitler's success as an artist was very moderate and his future was dim because he had not been accepted by the Academy of Fine Art. His departure from Vienna, however, was prompted by yet another reason. Hitler had not responded to a draft call. Evading conscription, he went to Munich. When Austrian authorities caught up with him in Germany, he returned to Salzburg and was turned down for military service as "unfit, too weak". Immediately after the outbreak of the First World War, he joined the German army and was sent to the Western Front. He served long and hard but was not promoted to non-commissioned rank because he was deemed to lack leadership qualities. In 1918 he was recommended for an Iron Cross First Class, but did not receive it. The request was initiated again, this time by First Lieutenant Gutmann of the reserves, a Jew. Now he obtained his medal.[4] During the Second World War Hitler would not wear civilian clothes in public. If you have seen a photograph of him taken at that time, you will have noticed that unlike many other Nazis bedecked in splendor, Hitler wore only a simple uniform and his Iron Cross.

Three significant encounters with Jews—three that we know of. In 1919, Hitler wrote the first tract, the first letter, against the Jews. Before then, he might have said something or other orally, but, well, who didn't in Vienna? The Vienna of Mayor Lueger was not a philosemitic city. As of 1919, Hitler was still in the German army. The army was trying to democratize itself by order, of course, of the government. There were discussions, and in Hitler's unit one soldier raised a question about the Jews. The commanding officer assigned Hitler to answer the question, and this is the first anti-Semitic tract we have that Adolf Hitler wrote. He was already 30 years old.

In the lengthy letter, dated September 16, 1919, Hitler said that the Jews were exploiting nations, undermining their strength, and infecting them with a racial tuberculosis. Yet he rejected an anti-Semitism based on emotions that would lead only to temporary violent outbursts: pogroms. What he wanted was an anti-Semitism of reason *(Vernunft)* that would be implemented with legal steps against the Jews and that would result in their total elimination.[5]

If you were to assign characteristics to Adolf Hitler, almost any one of them would fit something or other that he said or did. If you were to select rationality or reason, you could affix it to his letter of 1919. A sense of proportion that actually heightened his status as the all-encompassing leader dictated his wearing of the unadorned uniform, and that same sense impelled him to order the Vienna Gestapo to acquire three of his signed watercolors and to have them destroyed.[6] He did not want one of his pictures hanging over the sofa of some Viennese citizen.

Hitler is always depicted, if anything, as the most decisive man in history, yet we have enough evidence of indecision. One piece I discovered in a rather crucial diary that was kept by a German major, Engel, who was the adjutant posted by the army to Hitler's headquarters. Engel was in Hitler's company four or five years, sitting in on every conference—although in the background, of course, never saying a word, and keeping a diary. On or about February 2, 1941 (he inserted the dates later), Hitler met with some of his party stalwarts in—this is unbelievable—a freewheeling discussion without agenda.

These party fellows frankly had nothing to do any more. They had very little power, but they were still the old entourage. Everybody was talking this way and that, sometimes without even paying attention to Hitler. One of them, Ley, the chief of the German Labor Front, raised the question, 'What about the Jews?'

As if caught by surprise, Hitler said something about Madagascar.

That was like pushing a button because Madagascar was an old idea. An island in the Indian Ocean, it was a colony of France. The so-called Madagascar Plan was cooked up in the German Foreign Office but had antecedents prior to the time it was drafted in 1940. It was to have been the final solution of the Jewish question. That was the notion. All the Jews of Europe were going to be sent to this island. After all, they couldn't migrate as individuals anymore. Hence they would have to be sent there by the millions in ships.

The only problem was that Madagascar, as I say, was in the Indian Ocean. Obviously, after France was conquered in 1940, there was some sense that the plan could be made to work. Yes, yes, yes. We're going to have a peace treaty with the French to cede Madagascar to Germany. We will place Madagascar under a German police governor, and all the Jews of Europe will go there. The problem was that prior to concluding a peace treaty with France, they would have had to finish the war with England. Of course, so far as the Germans were concerned, the British had no reason to fight on. The Germans didn't want anything from England, so that in the West the war was to be ended very quickly, but that did not happen.

By February 1941, the planning for the invasion of the Soviet Union was far advanced. When Hitler said, "Madagascar", one of the other party stalwarts said something like, "But, *mein Führer*, how are we going to get to Madagascar?"

And Hitler said that he would mobilize the entire German merchant fleet to send all the Jews to Madagascar even now, but that the British fleet, British submarines, would sink the German ships. So that wouldn't work.

"What then?" he was asked. He just answered cryptically, that he had other thoughts now, "less friendly".[7]

Speer was once asked, "How did you know when Hitler made a decision?" This is a very important question because as the Nazi regime developed over the years the whole structure of decision making was changed. At first there were laws. Then there were decrees implementing laws. Then a law was made saying there shall be no laws. Then there were orders and directives written down but still published in ministerial gazettes. Then there was government by announcement: orders appeared in the newspapers. Then there were only the hidden orders—the instructions that were not published, that were given within the bureaucracy, that were oral. And finally there were no orders at all. Everybody knew what he had to do.

There, you see, is where Stanley Milgram failed altogether.[8] He thought these people were button pushers, but they weren't. They were innovators, initiators. They knew from the very structure of the whole undertaking what they had to do—without a plan, without even jurisdictions, without a legislature, without a budget. One of the SS men was asked in a postwar trial, "What is jurisdiction? What is the meaning of 'jurisdiction'?"

He answered, "Jurisdiction belongs to him who gets something done."

The bureaucracy moved on a track of self-assertion. But in such a situation, what is a Hitler? And what is an order by Hitler? If he says, 'Ah, I think we ought to do something', is that an order?

So Speer was asked a question, "How did you know?"

He said, it depended on Hitler's tone of voice, that when he was very angry, his outbursts were not necessarily considered his final word, but when he spoke quietly, and in a low tone, then his listeners knew that a decision had been made.[9]

A few years ago the German historians, becoming more acutely sensitive to the Holocaust and its implications, decided that all the people who had ever done research in this field, all the footnote writers of the world, were going to be invited to a conference in Stuttgart where they were going to deal with the central question, 'How was this decision made?'

There were two schools of thought.[10] I sat there listening, everybody wondering what I would say. One of the arguments astonished me. It was voiced by Martin Broszat, the head of the Institute for Contemporary History in Munich, and by Hans Mommsen. They said that there was no Hitler decision. There was no Hitler any more. He was a figurehead. There was automation—decision making itself had been automated. That which was latent in the whole bureaucracy now came to the fore without signals or orders. The next step was merely a matter of logical consequence. I always had some difficulties with this theory because I wondered, as did Christopher Browning, how it was that death camps were built all at the same time? Were the decision makers engaging in telepathy?

In this controversy, I had placed considerable weight on the opinion of Helmut Krausnick, a very important researcher in Germany. I had first met him in 1968 when I visited his institute in Munich. He said to me, "I wanted to write to you, but I didn't."

"Why didn't you?" I asked.

"Because I thought you would not answer my letter."

"Why did you think that?" I said.

"Because I've made political mistakes in my youth."

Oh, yes. He was in the Foreign Office in Paris during the occupation in France.

In 1982 I met him again at a conference in Paris. There, this man who incidentally is the author of the most lucid essay on the destruction of the Jews ever written[11] attacked the 'automation' theorists and said: "But gentlemen, this could not be. You do not understand. However much one wanted to do it, one could not do so until one had authorization from Adolf Hitler."

And I said to myself, "Yes, he's right."

One must listen to men like him, not because he was a bureaucrat in Nazi Germany. Rather it is as Judge Bork said about the Supreme Court interpreting the Constitution of the United States: one must always think about what the framers—as he said, the ratifiers—had in mind. In construing the Constitution, one pays special attention to the court decisions made early in the history of the United States, because those judges were very close to those ratifiers, those writers who put the words on paper.

I had listened to Krausnick because he understood the language of the times, because he understood the atmosphere, because he could role-play. But in Stuttgart, Mommsen counterattacked, throwing the book away. In a conference, this is unheard of in Germany. This was a gathering in which people were seated in a room by rank. He threw the book away and said,

> I decline to approach the younger generation to say: Look at the time from 1941 to 1945, Hitler was responsible for the Holocaust; he did it and without him it would not have happened.[12]

So here it is, this enormous implication—who did it? I've always believed that ultimately a vast bureaucracy was involved. One cannot destroy a people—it's not possible—without employing all the institutions that a society has. The uprooting process alone required the specializations, the expertise of bureaucrats in all walks of life. Name any agency, any institution, of the Third Reich and I will tell you what it did to contribute to this process of destruction.

What was this organization like? It had been identified, even during the war, by one of the most astute political scientists

—Franz Neumann, a student of the Nazi government. He said that Germany was not even a state, it was a Behemoth (that's the title of his book). It was ruled by four hierarchies, which he identified as the Civil Service, the Military, Industry, and the Nazi Party.[13] It was a very shrewd observation. I remember even as an undergraduate becoming interested in this and wondering what the German system was like. I would examine books dealing with *Verfassungsrecht*, the German constitution, written as early as the turn of the century, and find an opening phrase with words such as 'The two pillars of the German state are its civil service and its army'. Were such a book to have been written 40 years later, an author would have had to add industry and, yes, the Nazi Party. Taking just the first two hierarachies, and looking at their personnel composition, one quickly discovers there was no purge to speak of. That whole organization in 1935 was roughly 95 percent of what it had been in 1932. A few social democrats were fired. Communists were hardly in the army anyway and there was no real turnover. There wasn't even any room for the party people, except for a few at the top. It was the same organization.

When I sometimes talk about my subject I speak of the Germans, and the executive director of the Jewish Antidefamation League was somewhat troubled. Once he walked up to me after a talk and said, "You seem always to say 'German' rather than 'Nazi.' "

I said, "What do you want me to call it? The Nazi Railways?"

Of course, the Nazi Party had its little domains, and what were they? The SS, the propaganda apparatus, and above all—occupied territories. In other words, there wasn't really room for the party in the establishment. A new establishment had to be created side by side with the old one. New jurisdictions had to be carved out by virtue of new tasks. One of these tasks was the destruction of the Jews. That is not to say that the anti-Jewish work was the exclusive job of pure Nazis—party members, initiators of Nazi party doctrines or of ideology. For that matter, what ideology? Where is the Karl Marx of the Nazis? There is no such person. The Jews were destroyed by the establishment and by the newcomers. For example, Speer, whom I just mentioned, was a young man, the architect of Berlin. He rose in power. He had an enormous role in charge of German war industry, and he was deeply involved with a variety of matters affecting Jews, ranging from apartment allocations in Berlin to supplying of material to the death camp of Auschwitz. There was also a symbolism in the elevation of Speer particularly. Why? Because Adolf Hitler and Speer shared a special interest. I discovered this connection very early.

Shortly after the capture of Munich on April 30, 1945, I found myself in that city at night. We were quartered in, of all places, the headquarters of the Nazi party. There I saw a bunch of crates, and having been a shipping clerk, I could not resist the temptation of opening some of them. There were about 60 and what did I find? Hitler's personal library. By the way, I never have found it since. I don't even know where it is now. I broke open a case or two and looked at some books and I found two topics: Frederick the Great and architecture. That was it, plus his old rent receipts from the 1920s. He didn't throw out the receipts. How were these books inscribed to Hitler? To Adolf Hitler, *den Erbauer des deutschen Reiches*, to the Architect of the Third Reich. For Adolf Hitler, everything was architecture. The war itself was an esthetic phenomenon, the destruction of the Jews an edifice, the whole *Götterdämmerunq* a controlled Wagnerian process.

What a strange phenomenon is the initiation of this undertaking by the bureaucracy. Their materials were proposals, suggestions, all kinds of measures—they all thought of measures, measures, measures. For the most part, these were not original thoughts. No, they were copied from canon law, from any place. Sometimes, however, initiatives were blocked. The proposal to mark the Jew with a yellow star did not become a decree until September 1941 in Germany, a very late date, because Hitler had evidently vetoed it.

Vetoes and limits were a way of modulating the process. There was a law made in 1935 of considerable significance—a criminal law drafted during the Nurnberg party rally. Jews were forbidden to marry Germans or to have extramarital relations with Germans; to do so was to be a crime.[14] The real significance, incidentally, of this decree is that it forced the German bureaucracy to face the arduous and difficult task of defining the term *Jew*, because how can one have a criminal law without defining the terms in it? In the enforcement of the law, however, something very strange happened. Adolf Hitler forbade, absolutely forbade, the application of the law to women. Only men were to be tried. Shall we call it chivalry? Or perhaps the feeling that a woman doesn't know any better?

Once, long after the killings had begun, a young Gauleiter, Greiser (in whose jurisdiction was located a death camp where already 150,000 Jews had been killed by gas), wrote a letter to the *Führer* chancellery proposing to deal with 35,000 tubercular poles in his *Gau* as he had done with Jews. The matter was handed to Hitler and Hitler vetoed it. Greiser became angry, not at Hitler, because that was impossible, but with the people who gave his letter to Hitler for a decision. Why did they bother the *Führer* about 35,000 tubercular Poles?[15]

For Hitler, the process had to have direction, balance, and tempo. He put on the red lights and the green lights so that it would flow smoothly. But who were these initiators, these innovators, these bureaucrats? They remind me of the opening of Hegel's *Philosophy of History* when he speaks of the world's historical men who know what is right for the times. These bureaucrats knew what was right for the times. They seemed to be there at the right moment with the right measure, just in the right sequence. We heard at the beginning of this conference from Dr. Rollo May about the importance of education. They were very well educated.

Let me give you just three groups: the lawyers, the soldiers, and the physicians. The lawyers were everywhere. They had to be because the process of destruction had to begin with ultracomplex, I'm inclined to say *surgical*, maneuverings to make certain that while the Jews were destroyed, the German population was protected. What, for example, does one do with a half-Jew? How does one deal with a mixed marriage? What is to be done with a contract between a Jew and a non-Jew? A Jewish corporation and a non-Jewish corporation? How is one to define the term *Jewish corporation?* Who do you suppose solved these problems? The lawyers, always. But not only that, the entire process of destruction was, in some sense, conceived of as a legal proceeding.

Thus, for example, we have the strange figure of Dr. Kröger, who was in charge of one of the *Einsatzkommandos*, one of the killing units during the invasion of the Soviet Union. These were units of the SS and police attached to the armed forces for the purpose of killing Jews on the spot by shooting them. Kröger had been educated in Germany; he was a Baltic German from Riga. He had his law degree and had done advanced work in international law. After the war had begun and the Russians had moved into Latvia as well as Lithuania and Estonia, eighty thousand ethnic Germans left those three Baltic Republics, called by their *Führer*, and came to Germany. The Germans never discriminated against other Germans, wherever they came from. Hitler himself, after all, was Austrian.

Kröger arrived and, given his academic achievements, he was immediately offered the rank of Lieutenant Colonel in the SS. When Kröger found himself only a year after his immigration in command of a killing unit, shooting Jews, he—the lawyer—made a speech. To whom? Why, to the Jews of course, to explain to them why they were being shot. It was, he said, a reprisal for murders committed by the retreating Red Army.[16]

Or take the rather insignificant case of another official, also a lawyer, Dr. Glehn. A decree had been issued in central Poland, whereby any Jew who left a ghetto without a pass was to be shot without any legal proceedings. The question arose about Jews in forced labor who were being sent from a particular ghetto to a site where they were performing the labor. What about the possibility, which occurred, of Jews escaping on their way from the ghetto to the place where they were supposed to work? The decree didn't cover this contingency. Nobody had thought of it. But the Germans had a principle. They have an almost untranslatable word called *sinngemäss*. It is a concept that means 'If I can do this, I can do that by analogy.' So he said, 'Why not extend the meaning of the ghetto to include these escapees so we can shoot them?' It was the lawyer who was thinking in these terms. Was he alone? Of course not. It was such a common principle.[17]

Here is another example—the very first measure in 1933, in April. Consider the lead time. The German government changed when Hitler came into power on January 30, 1933. By April 7, they had a crucial law on the books. Imagine how little time elapsed before they could institute a law calling for the "restoration of a professional civil service", which meant that communists were to be removed, and which also meant that Jews were to be dismissed. But what about scholarship holders, what about people with stipends at universities?

Ah, said the chancellor of Freiburg University, they're covered as well. They're like civil servants. That chancellor, by the way, was the distinguished Martin Heidegger, the philosopher. He too was familiar with the analogy principle.[18]

The military were not charged with or even trusted with the destruction of the Jews. That was somebody else's work. However, they governed several countries and regions: Belgium, France, Serbia, Greece, and large areas in the USSR. They were backup for concentration camp security. They were giving logistic support to killing units operating in occupied Russia. They were heavily involved. It was a war in that sense against Jewry.

And the doctors? Robert Lifton refers to something called the *medicalization* of the Holocaust, the notion that to the Germans it was a cleansing process.[19] Thus, the ghetto was conceived of as a quarantine to prevent epidemics. Euthanasia, the first killing operation—it must never be forgotten—was directed against the institutionalized Germans, those with so-called mental illnesses, of whom there were perhaps 300,000—80,000 were gassed. The retarded children, by the way, were not gassed; they were starved. I speak of German children now. But the same process, the same personnel, the same techniques were used to gas the Jews. Thus, for example, the first commander of the Treblinka Death Camp was a psychiatrist, and Euthanasia veterans manned also the Belzec and Sobibor death camps. Everything was in competent, experienced hands. Did all these men know what they were doing? Of course. They thought about it. Himmler, a man born in 1900 who commanded the SS and police, had seen no action in World War I. It was too late; He was only 18 when the war ended. He saw none, of course, in 1939 either, because by then he was high ranking. In August 1941 he came to a shooting operation to see what it was like. These were the first dead bodies he had ever seen. He was shaken and said he wouldn't even like it if German men did such things gladly. Again and again he made speeches about conduct and honesty in killing operations. Finally in 1943 he delivered a long address to his SS generals. It is the famous one in Poznan, in which he said: "Most of you know what it means when 100 corpses lie together, when 500 lie there, or when 1000 lie there. To have endured this and—apart from exceptions caused in human weakness—to have remained decent, that has made us hard. That is a page of glory never written and never to be written."[20]

RESPONSE AND DIALOGUE

Douglas Kinnard

Douglas Kinnard, a retired general in the U. S. Army, is a combat veteran of World War II, Korea, and Vietnam. He served as special assistant to the Supreme Allied Commander in Europe. Kinnard is professor emeritus of political science at the University of Vermont, Burlington. He has written *Of War Managers*, and is currently writing a book on decision making concerning some sixteen decisions made in the Vietnam War, *General in Camelot*.

Raul Hilberg and I were colleagues for a dozen years at the University of Vermont and I think now the story can be told without hurting affirmative action. Raul brought me to Vermont as the chairman of the Political Science Department because I was a veteran. Professor Hilberg is one of the very top scholars in the field on this subject anywhere. He spent his life in it.

My only direct connection with the events described was as a lieutenant in World War II when I participated in liberating a concentration camp. This was not a monument; this was a camp in action. I was with the 71st Division, the furthest east division in the European theater, and we liberated a Hungarian Jewish labor camp. There were 3,000 people lying on boards in a hut built for three hundred people, people dead lying next to them and they were starving vomiting, hadn't had food or water for five days. That was over 42 years ago, but it is still etched in my mind.

Given the subject of the conference, Professor Hilberg's theme was directed toward one central question: how was it possible for a modern state to carry out an act of evil involving the systematic murder of a whole people? After talking about the seminal role of Hitler within this area, he made the point that a few top leaders could not carry out genocide on this scale, that the process was remarkable decentralized, and that those who carried out the final solution were specialists in all parts of German life. The bureaucracies he mentioned were not just cogs in the wheel—they turned the wheel themselves. Their evil was no less great because they were merely carrying out orders.

Second and even more chilling were the professionals—lawyers, soldiers, doctors. It was a little more difficult to conceive that they did not know the evil of their deeds.

A third group, which he did not discuss, but has on previous occasions, was the individuals who for various reasons of rewards and personal psyche were part of the process. But the bottom line, which he brought out clearly, pertains to all groups—none considered themselves to be evil. But they were.

There are two other areas into which Professor Hilberg's research has carried him that are worth mentioning: how was it possible for the world to stand by and let this evil happen without halting or retarding the destruction? A second and more central question, and a little more difficult to come to grips with, is how it was possible for a whole people—the Jewish people—to allow itself to be destroyed. There are several factors involved, obviously.

I would like to ask a question in a broader scheme than the Holocaust. Pol Pot (who came to power in April 17, 1975, in connection with the fall of both South Vietnam and Kampuchea) was, as you know, the type of communist whom Lenin defined in his tract *Left Wing Communism: An Infantile Disorder*—very left. By 1978 after three years, he was responsible for the genocide of two million Khmer—one quarter of the population. I am asking if you would react to a statement in the best-selling book on Vietnam by Stanley Karnow: "The full dimensions of Cambodia's martyrdom will probably never be known or understood. Nevertheless, the evidence accumulated until now already makes the Nazi Holocaust seem tame by comparison."[21] The question is, what reaction do you have to that statement?

HILBERG: If I had been the editor I would have asked him to consider that sentence again. The death of every man diminishes me. I well recall members of the U.S. Holocaust Memorial Council, of which I still am a member, traveling at their own expense to Thailand (to the border of Cambodia) to stand there demonstrating the unity of mankind—the totality of its fate. Were it not for people like Elie Wiesel or the late Bayard Rustin or Father Theodore M. Hesburgh, members of the Council, remembering the Holocaust—then who would pay attention to what happened in Cambodia? But this autogenocide in Cambodia was fundamentally different from what happened in Nazi Germany because the Germans were concerned with protecting Germany and that is to say, with protecting Germans—that's why they spent so much time trying to define the term *Mischling* of the first degree, a half-Jew who didn't belong to the Jewish religion. That's why so much time was spent worrying about German creditors of Jews who had been deported, why so much time was spent over and over and over again in a kind of careful surgical procedure tying every knot to assure least damage to Germany while Jewry was destroyed. What happened in Cambodia seems to be a gigantic enlargement of a purge, a whole class wiped out—perhaps similar in some basic way to the cultural revolution in China except much more vicious. There is another coincidence between the two fates, the Jewish fate and those of the Khmer. Auschwitz was liberated by the Red Army. Most Jews who were alive at the end were saved by communists. The communists didn't intend to—it wasn't in their minds—but they did. When I read in the newspapers that it was of all people the North Vietnamese who were putting an end to the disaster in Cambodia, I could not help seeing in this event a historical irony almost beyond belief.

JORGE LARA BRAUD: Like everyone else in this room, Professor Hilberg, I found it hard to listen to what you are saying. It stirs up taboo emotions that one would prefer to keep unmoved. I was tantalized at the very beginning of your address by the question, "Where was God in all of this?" Knowing that besides being highly educated, the people whom you have described—the most educated of the western societies known to us until then—were among the most *religious*. They were a deeply Christian society in which the understanding of God himself was harnessed in order to justify the vindication of the German people against the threat of the Jews. This did not come as an accident; it had a long, long history, which we call the teaching of contempt. For the Christian West, this has such ancient roots that because of their ancientness we tend to dismiss them. And that is the very early disengagement of Christian identity from its Jewish roots, and the idea that God had reneged on the chosenness of his people. And wherever that has happened, the pogroms are not too far away. It seems to me that you may prefer because of the nature of your work not to address the answer to the question, 'Where was God?' In this symposium I think this has been one of the absent concerns. It is a very large one. After the Holocaust we can no longer think of God in the ways in which we used to. This is a God who himself is wounded, infinitely wounded by this tragedy. If there is one major lesson from the incalculable evil unleashed against the Jews in Germany, it is that God, the God of the United States, could conceivably be harnessed into the destruction of otner people from whom we have become disengaged. If we became disengaged from those who gave us the roots of our own Christian faith, how much easier it would be to become disengaged from other people and to call on God to bless that disengagment.

MAYA ANGELOU: Thank you, thank you so much, Dr. Hilberg. There was a statement when you were speaking about Krausnick and the generous compliment you gave to Krausnick as having written the most lucid chapter on this horror, a human horror; and I was thinking about the statement of the sadly late Primo Levi and his encounter with the German scientist, an inadvertent encounter with the scientist with whom he had worked, in fact, during the years of horror. I was thinking about how they started a dialogue and how he, Mr. Levi, invited that German scientist to Italy to visit him. Now, I'm a lover of Primo Levi. He had a spirit in which the victim and victimizer come together. Is it possible, then, that in that joining one eradicates evil, suppresses evil itself? What I seem to see in that is hope and probably the only way in which evil can be suppressed. Am I right?

HILBERG: I think the relationship between Jews and Germans is extraordinarily complicated. A person who has suffered may, I suppose, forgive the tormentor. And that is in some existential way even easy. But how does one forgive the killing of millions of people? On whose authority do I forgive? I have not been elected to do that. There is no Jew anywhere who feels that he or she could. A few years ago Elie Wiesel finally consented to set foot on German soil and he gave a lecture from which virtually everybody was barred. The Germans desperately wanted a statement, something that would sound like conciliation. He would not oblige them. For it is not a matter just of what had happened to him, but what had happened to others. It is simply not possible to extend a formal sense of forgiveness. Given this situation there is an admonition for silence. There is nothing more important than to know when not to speak and what not to speak about. I speak to Krausnick, yes, and I've spoken to others. They have identified themselves to me in a way that sounds like a confession. There's no reason that they have to say to me, 'I have made political mistakes in my youth.' They do it, especially in my case, because they do not wish a situation to exist where they would know who I am, but I would not know who they are; that's not cricket. Therefore they tell me, in an anguished way, but not for forgiveness. It's possibly a small step which will take generations to develop into larger steps.

KINNARD: Professor Hilberg has elucidated for us in a most brilliant way the nature of an evil of staggering proportions—the destruction as an end in itself of six million Jews (two out of every three European Jews, in an area in which two-thirds of the world's Jews lived in 1939). Someone raised a question to me yesterday as to the relevance of the Holocaust to the evils of our own time—that is to say, questioned its relevance. I think there is a profound relationship. While each major event is unique in its totality, and this is one, there are common elements or threads of evil here that pertain to all people at all times. But a caveat. One must, I think, be cautious that the magnitude of the event not cause us to turn away from perhaps more subtle, but nonetheless devasting, evils of our own time and country, which have been so intelligently elucidated by previous speakers.

NOTES

[1] Christopher Browning, *Fateful Months* (New York: Holmes & Meier, 1985).

[2] The doctor, Eduard Bloch, wrote of his experience in 'My patient Hitler', *Colliers*, March 15 and 22, 1941.

[3] Bradley F. Smith, *Adolf Hitler: His Family, Childhood and Youth* (Stanford: Hoover Institution, 1967), pp. 137–38, 149. J. Sydney Jones, *Hitler in Vienna 1907–1913* (New York: Stein & Day, 1983), pp. 147–48, 163–64, 178, 201, 229.

[4] Ernst Deuerlein (ed.), *Der Aufstieg der NSDAP in Augenzeugenberichten* (Munich, 1974), pp. 74–80.

[5] Text of the letter, *ibid.*, pp. 91–94.

[6] See the correspondence from August 28 to October 27, 1942, in the National Archives, Record Group 238, T 175, Microfilm Roll 69, Frames 585510–585523.

[7] Diary of Gerhard Engel, entry of February 2, 1941, in Hildegard von Kotze, ed., *Heeresadjutant bei Hitler* (Stuttgart, 1974), pp. 94–95.

[8] Stanley Milgram, *Obedience to Authority* (New York: Harper & Row, 1974).

[9] Affidavit by Albert Speer, June 15, 1977, in Arthur Suzman and Denis Diamond, *Six Million Did Die* (Johannesburg, 1977), pp. 109–112.

[10] See Browning, *Fateful Months*, pp. 8–9.

[11] 'The Persecution of the Jews', in Krausnick *et al.*, *Anatomy of the SS State* (London: Collins, 1968), pp. 1–124.

[12] Eberhard Jäckel and Jürgen Rohwer (eds.), *Der Mord an den Juden im Zweiten Weltkrieg* (Stuttgart, 1985), p. 196.

[13] Franz Neumann, *Behemoth*, 2d ed. (New York: Oxford University Press, 1944).

[14] Law for the Protection of German Blood and Honor, September 15, 1935, *Reichsgesetzblatt* I, 1146.

[15] Arthur Greiser to Heinrich Himmler, November 21, 1942, Nuremberg trials document NO-249.

[16] Indictment of Dr. Erhard Kröger by the prosecutor with the *Landgericht* in Stuttgart, January 30, 1968, 18 Js 139/66, p. 18.

[17] See the report by Dr. Karl Glehn, *Kreishauptmann* of Tomaszów, April 8, 1942, High People's Tribunal, Trial of Josef Bühler, folder 285, Glowna Komisja Badania Zbrodni Hitlerowskich w Polsce.

[18] Announcement by Martin Heidegger in *Freiburger Studentenzeitung*, November 3, 1933, reprinted in Guido Schneeberger (ed.), *Nachlese zu Heidegger* (Bern, 1962), p. 137.

[19] Robert Jay Lifton, *The Nazi Doctors* (New York: Basic Books, 1986), p. 14.

[20] Speech by Himmler at Gruppenführer meeting at Poznan, October 4, 1943, Nuremberg document PS-1919.

[21] Stanley Karnow, *Vietnam: A History* (New York: Viking Press, 1983), p. 44.

2

CRUELTY: THE EMPIRICAL EVIL

Philip Paul Hallie

Philip Paul Hallie, author and poet, is Griffin Professor of Philosophy and Humanities at Wesleyan University in Middletown, Connecticut. He received a Ph.D. from Harvard University. He is a veteran of World War II with three Battle Stars. He has been a Harvard traveling fellow, a Fulbright scholar, a Guggenheim fellow, and an American Council of Learned Societies fellow. He has served as American representative at the International Philosophy Congress (Mysore, India) and at the International Congress on Morality (Oslo, Norway). He has taught at Trinity College, Oxford University, and at Vanderbilt University. His book *Lest Innocent Blood Be Shed* tells the story of a small village in southern France that devoted itself to rescuing refugees from the Nazis—at the risk of the villagers' lives. It has been printed in French, Norwegian, Dutch, German, Italian, and Japanese, as well as English. He also contributed to the book *Sanctions for Evil* edited by Nevitt Sanford and Craig Comstock. Hallie's other books include *Maine de Biran: Reformer of Empiricism; Scepticism, Man and God; The Scar of Montaigne;* and *The Paradox of Cruelty.*

Before I begin to talk about cruelty itself, I want to tip you off that since I'm a teacher of philosophy, a student of philosophy, I've got a method that I'd like very, very briefly to describe to you. That method is something my wife hates me to describe this way, but I'm going to do it anyway. I'm a skeptic.

A skeptic is somebody who is skeptical or dubious or doubtful about high abstractions. For instance, evil as the *privatio boni*, or the privation of good, and that whole medieval business and all the medieval fright that comes with the word *evil* give me the jumps as a skeptic. I'm a little dubious about it. But there is a positive side to skepticism, aside from dubiety about the otherwise very useful abstractions.

Skeptics used to be doctors, and I'm in a tradition of people who think you've got to look for therapy in your philosophizing, and you've got to look for the facts. In fact, you've got to believe that only in the facts is there anything like therapy—no ideas but in facts; no ideas but in things.

For this reason, the two things that I most cherish are, one: the clear facts that are more or less observable to people with their eyeballs unaided by vast ideologies, and two: the passions of people. Lucidity and passion. That's my motto. Lucidity and passion. Clarity of fact and allowing yourself with the best discipline you can muster to be moved by your passions instead of by abstractions. Having said that, let me just say, therefore, that I have found it most natural for myself as a descendent of the doctors who were the original skeptics in Greek antiquity to be concerned with cruelty instead of evil.

Cruelty is something that's got authorities. There are some people who really know when it's happening, and they're the authorities. Evil—theologians argue about it, philosophers argue about it, and a lot of people say it doesn't exist. There's a lot of fiddling about evil. We happen to have a very congenial group here and there seems to be a great deal of agreement about it, but I dare say in other groups we'd really be in a mess.

Cruelty has authority and that authority is its *victims*. The victim of cruelty has an empirical authority like the authority of a doctor who's observing a patient, or better yet, like the authority of the patient about his or her own feelings.

I want to talk a bit about my experiences as a skeptic understanding cruelty. The crushing and grinding of human beings is something that we love and hate. The literature of humankind is full of it. The literature of humankind is almost nothing else but an excuse to be involved in torture and revolution, escape from or continuing torture. Crime, punishment, the original Greek tragedies—from then on, literature has been full of pain; it has been a real jolly circus. We love cruelty as much as we hate it in our literature.

Our religions offer us similar scenes illustrating our love/ hate relationship with the crushing and grinding of human beings. Our religions—with their Crusades, their crucifixions, and their bloodshed of various sorts (depending on which religion you happen to be concerned with)—find their own excuses for having this kind of relationship to cruelty that kids have when they're looking at a scene that they want to see but don't want to see, so they put their hands over their eyes and then they spread their fingers, in order to see and yet not see the horror.

I don't know if you have ever talked with a state policeman, but a state policeman will hasten to tell you that his biggest problem in highway accidents is rubber-neckers. Rubber-neckers are amongst his biggest problems because they usually stick around like glue. They just stand there and they get in the way. You can't get the ambulances through. With a fatal wreck the incidence of people loving cruelty goes up.

I needn't even mention the films, but I'm going to anyway. In wartime, we have one kind of film. In peacetime, if there is such a thing, we have films that deplore war. They hate war—hate it—in peacetime because that pays. In wartime they really love it because *that* pays. This relationship to destruction is paradoxical. Destruction is always slow despite the dopamines, despite the various dopes that get kicked into our bloodstream while we are dying. It's still always painful to die, at least for a little while.

Our relationship with suffering has been one of love *and* hatred. We pay good money to enjoy it in films. We pay lip service to compassion through literature, religion, and various other activities of our so-called civilizations, but we love and we hate torture. The queer thing about this love/hate dance of death with violence is that when it comes (at least in the last few decades) to people who theorize about it, they don't just open their hands like this and look through their fingers. They put their hands over their eyes completely. Psychologists, philosophers, historians, economists—so many of them, although not all of them (certainly not Jeffrey Russell)—commit two fallacies about this violence. They're really in the opposite of the condition of humankind that I've just been trying to describe, this love/hate relationship.

The first fallacy is what you might call the 'vanishing victimizer'. Nobody is really to blame for slavery. Nobody really did any harm. After all, slavery was an activity that was there as labor was needed in a labor intensive economic situation. Slavery was there to make a profit. There are economic and political structures that account completely for slavery and take everybody off the hook as far as blame for it is concerned.

I've heard a lecture that I'll never forget by a philosopher whose name I'm not going to mention because he's so well-known it might be damning if this ever gets out. It was done at the American Philosophical Association. The lecturer said that you can't find an evil person in the Nazi empire because everywhere you look the buck gets passed, and this gentleman proceeded to pass the buck. That's one of the modes of closing your hands, if you're a theorist, to evil.

The other fallacy is that of the 'isolated victimizer'. This fallacy says, 'Let's look into the *mind* of this person that you say is a victimizer and let's see what we find in that mind. Let's look *deep* into his motives, her motives, and see what we find.' The fallacy of the isolated victimizer is another way of blinding us just as surely as the first way, to the nature, existence, presence of this crushing and grinding that I speak of in terms of cruelty.

I mentioned early this morning that Hannah Arendt wrote this very fine book called *Eichmann in Jerusalem: A Report on the Banality of Evil.*[1] She found Eichmann banal, trite, commonplace, ordinary, everyday boring—a drag. The reason this was so was that early on she says, 'Look, I'm going to distinguish the sufferings of all these gypsies, Jews, and God knows what all from the deeds of Eichmann', as if you could separate them, as if you could isolate the victimizer from the victim, as if there was a break that some philosopher could ordain; Eichmann was doing nothing really, just sort of talking bureaucratic jargon—which he was.

The fact is, of course, as it is for both the vanishing victimizer and the isolated one, if you just use your eyeballs you see the deeds—the whole deeds and nothing but the deeds. When people look at the facts the earliest skeptical doctors cherished so, they started making some progress in the way of understanding therapy. If you look at the facts you'll see people hurting people, you'll see lynchings, you'll see burnings of Blacks. You'll see all these things; but you won't see them if you are blinded by one or both of these two dreadful fallacies. When we are blind to the facts the love/hate relationship becomes such that we hate or fear cruelty so much that we can't look at it at all. Can't look at it at all, can't stand it at all. Then we raise this blindness to a virtue. If you don't want to *look* at cruelty, just don't make any claims about it.

I mentioned to you that as a skeptic I believe that lucidity of fact and candor of personal passion are the two poles of my whole understanding of what philosophy is all about when it's alive. I have to tell you a little about my life. I was raised in the slums of Chicago, and spent a good part of my life in a building quite aptly named the 'cockroach building', on Roosevelt Road near Kedzie. My father was always getting fired, so he could never make a living. And so we lived in the cockroach building. In order to walk down the street in our neighborhood, you almost always had to run a gauntlet of some sort. In those days, my mother would send me for a loaf of Silvercup bread.

Maybe nobody here is old enough to remember Silvercup bread. The Lone Ranger advertised it: 'Dum dadadum, dadadum, dum dum', and when you pick up this bread, it squinches in your hand and becomes a little tiny ball. It's got a red and white wrapper. Just about every other evening my mother would say, 'Go out and get some Silvercup bread'. So I'd go down and sombody'd jump me. Then, if I were lucky he wouldn't give me a very hard time—he would just give me a sock or two.

One day when I must have been eight or nine, somebody jumped me—a great big blond kid. He started pounding the back of my head down on these big rough stone pavements we had in Chicago. I felt the blood sort of gather, coming down my neck.

He said, "You son-of-a-bitching Jews, you killed Jesus. You bastards, you killed Jesus."

I hadn't heard too much about Jesus. I'd heard rumors about him, but my immediate response was, "I didn't do it." That didn't stop him. He must have seen my eyes glaze or something, however, and so after a while he let go and took off. I went to get the Silvercup bread, because I was a fairly tough kid.

When I came back to our house, my mother's kid brother was sitting in the kitchen. He's a fighter—used to work out with Joe Louis sometimes, very seldom.

He said, "Pinky, whose blood is that on you? Is that somebody else's blood?"

I said, "No, Uncle Louie." (Everybody had an Uncle Louie in Chicago.) "No, it's my blood, Uncle Louie."

He said, "Oh."

He was quiet. He was with my mother, his big sister. She was a mystic and loved everybody, so he wasn't going to bring up anything. The next morning my uncle came by. Instead of taking me to school, he took me to his house and he started to teach me fighting, not boxing. I learned that a little later from him. Street fighting, which is murder—just murder. It's very different from boxing.

I got pretty good at this. It was a lot of fun. People kept a nice large area around me as I would go for my Silvercup bread or whatever. I felt a great deal of joy and power in it all. The boxing was even better. I had some faults—small hands, an easily bloodied nose—but I was fast and mean. So I did a little boxing and that was fun, too.

Later on, I went into war (considerably later) and had fun, as I suggested to you before, shooting shells with white phosphorous warheads into Mannheim on the Rhine River and watching people burn.

This was fun. This was my life. This was my joy, and when I studied philosophy and picked up the tools of philosophy, the first major thing I turned to was a work on cruelty, which was my great interest. Let me tell you a secret. You do not only imitate your enemies as we've been saying earlier today; you imitate your loves as well. And I loved violence as much as I loved my Uncle Louie. It turned out, in ways that I won't go into here lest I get too autobiographical, that the violence to Black people was one of the important facts in our Chicago life.

It just so happened that early on I discovered perhaps the greatest nonfiction book of the nineteenth century in America, *The Life and Times of Frederick Douglass.*[2] Somehow that was the beginning of understanding the facts of life for me. The facts of life had to be cruel because life was joyously cruel for me (we were victoriously cruel: we Allies won World War II and as a kid I kept bringing the Silvercup bread home). The involvement with this, in my opinion, one of the greatest works of the nineteenth century in America, taught me a few things about this crushing and grinding. The first thing *The Life and Times of Frederick Douglass* taught me is that cruelty is not to be understood in terms of its origins—etymological, word origins. In Latin, it comes from *crudus*, which means bloody or bleeding or something physical.

What I learned from Frederick Douglass was that cruelty—this crushing and grinding, this destruction of the soul—need not involve bloodshed at all, not at all. Let me read you an advertisement in the New Orleans *Bee:* "Negroes for sale. A Negro woman, twenty-four years of age, and her two children, one eight and the other three years old. Said Negroes will be sold separately or together as desired. The woman is a good seamstress. She will be sold low for cash or exchanged for groceries. For terms apply to Matthew Bliss and Company, 1 Front Levy." It fit the laws. It fit the customs. It fit a way of life. Quiet, peaceful, genteel.

The second thing Frederick Douglass's life and times and my other work in slavery taught me was just about as important. I mentioned this toward the beginning of my remarks: that if you want to find out what cruelty is or when it's happening, don't ask the victimizer. Don't ask the one who's doing it. Don't get zeroed in on the victimizer. Ask the victim.

Maya Angelou says there is the unknowing majority, 'it', and the knowing minority, 'you'. *Victims know when they're being cruelly treated and victimizers are usually the unknowing majority.* The sword does not feel the wound. The flesh on which that sword strikes does. The empirical, skeptical authority for cruelty is the victim and the victim alone. There are moments when the victim—by various devices of custom, law, habit, or uses of language—is blinded or numbed to the actual humiliation and crushing that is happening, but those moments are rare, much more rare than people think. The victim is the authority on it. When Frederick Douglass talked about his life as a slave struggling for freedom (and not only struggling from a slavery technically but also afterward in all sorts of ways), he was speaking as the authority.

Finally, I learned from Frederick Douglass that there is a power relationship between the victim and the victimizer, between the unknowing majority and the knowing minority. This relationship makes cruelty happen the way a spark jumps from a higher to a lower voltage in an appropriate conductive atmosphere. When you have a majority with overwhelming economic, political, or legal power and a minority with much less power, cruelty can happen, and it does. What Frederick Douglass taught me throughout the whole of his book, but especially in the last three-quarters of his expanded version of *Life and Times,* was that only when the victim equalizes the power in some sense does the spark stop leaping the gap—because there is no gap to leap. This equalization is like my being able to walk down the streets because I would kick people in the groin if they came too close, or like my firing at people in the last world war.

In Frederick Douglass's case, it was an entirely different mode of power. It was a whole range, a symphonic range, the powers that I'm not going to go into now. It began with fighting Covey the slavebreaker.[3] The range of his idea of power was so great that after Frederick's emancipation, he went back to his old master and saw him just before the master died. His power was immense at that moment. He was loving. These are the three things that I learned about this crushing and grinding.

I did my book on cruelty[4] and then I noticed, as I mentioned to you before, this law of mimicry. You mimic what interests you. You imitate what you love, the way I imitated my Uncle Louie, the way I wanted to imitate Frederick Douglass. I noticed that I hadn't really studied the kind of cruelty that I had somewhat experienced when I was in Europe and the last world war: namely, the experience of the concentration camps, the *facts,* because I am a skeptic. I started looking into the medical experiments. I spent a lot of time studying just exactly how white-coated doctors would cut gypsy, Jewish, or Jehovah's Witness children's eyeballs out or parts of their rib cages or members of their bodies—often without anesthesia. I learned how they would put children and adults in hot water and cold water, and low air pressure and high air pressure experiments, and so on.

I studied those experiments, and a curious thing started happening because of this law of mimicry. I found that I wanted to kill the victimizers. I was going to imitate them; or I felt as if I was the victim and I was imitating *them.* But worst of all, I found that when I wasn't feeling like killing the victimizers, or wasn't feeling identified or thinking of my children as lying on these dissecting tables, I was indifferent—and that was the worst. I was as indifferent as the monsters who were doing and ordering it done. Ask my poor wife, Doris. I became one of the indifferent monsters myself, when I wasn't becoming a fantasizing murderer or victim.

One day, I was sitting in my office reading about these horrors and I couldn't bear it anymore. I really didn't want to live. I didn't want to kill anybody as I went out. I just wanted to go. The world was simply unbearable. And so I thought I'd take a look at some of the things I'd been trained in the Army to investigate, mainly the story of the French Resistance. As I opened a page and started reading, my cheeks began itching. I reached up, and my cheeks were covered with tears. I was reading about the little village of Le Chambon, the way it saved lives without killing or hurting or hating anybody. I realized that this might be my salvation, that by becoming interested in it—assimilating it, imitating it, mimicking it—I might be saved.

This village of love gradually taught me about this force, which I found so clearly exemplified in my own life and so much more vastly exemplified in the life of Frederick Douglass than I even knew then. (It took me years to understand just exactly the range of power in Frederick Douglass.) I learned that his kind of reaction to cruelty by love, by hospitality, by kindness—this has its own power. It has its own power. And then the range of power Frederick Douglass had—that opened up to me. It was not clear to me before—the power of love. Their gray little church that they had in this tiny little mountain village was perched on a plateau on a high mountain in south-eastern France. This tiny little church was like a battery charged with love, charged with such a power of love that the Germans were disarmed in the literal sense. Their arms weren't relevant. It was like a disarmingly innocent child. The village wanted to save the Germans as much as it wanted to save the kids. They wanted to save the Germans from doing more evil.

I wrote *Lest Innocent Blood Be Shed*[5] and became converted, a different person for awhile. Then I said to myself, 'Wait a minute, something in your heart resents the village.' They didn't stop Hitler. They did nothing to stop Hitler. A thousand Le Chambons would not have stopped Hitler. It took decent murderers like me to to it. Murderers who had compunctions, but murdered nonetheless. The cruelty that I perpetrated willingly was the only way to stop the cruel march that I and others like me were facing.

How could I begin to deal with cruelty in my mind? I had, on the one hand, the idea that you could, first of all, stop its march and then harness its power by force, by equalizing power, and, on the other hand, by love. How could I take these two such different forces and turn them against the cruelty I was growing to hate, especially after my work in Le Chambon, with such an intensity that it was unclouded by any skeptical doubts?

The result was a vision, and this is where I now stand. I feel—in line with everything that has been said so far in our conference—that we are in the condition of cruelty. We are in the food web. We eat whatever we can eat and whatever can eat us eats us. We are in the food web. We are killers, if only of plants, and we are killed. Yet in the food web, there is room. There are spaces in the food web.

We had a hurricane in Middletown, Connecticut a couple of years ago. We watched it uproot our favorite chestnut tree. Then, all of a sudden, the sky was blue overhead. Even little birds were just living it up, up there—singing, doing all sorts of acrobatics, and having a wonderful time—right there in the middle of the hurricane. Around this blue was a vast raging hurricane. But in the blue, peace: beauty and space—room.

George Santayana, in one of his sonnets, says, "As in the midst of battle, there is room for thoughts of love".[6] In the midst of that blind, agonizing, destructive force, there were those little birds. My mother, when she talked about the kids who were killed in the Holocaust, called them 'little *Faygeleh*'—little birds, whirling inside the blue.

I feel now that we can push back and expand the blue, the eye, but it's the hurricane we're in. Don't forget it. We can push back the eye. Some people don't push it back very far. For instance, according to the writer Albert Camus, Heinrich Himmler used to come in the back door of his house after work, and he would come in quietly. He'd come in very quietly and not make a lot of noise. Why? Because he didn't want to wake up his canary. He was the murderer of millions, but he loved his canary. Then there was Frederick Douglass, and there was the village of Le Chambon. There was the blue. All of us had it, this moment, this space of blue. We have to make room for love, even the most vicious, destructive of us—perhaps especially the most vicious and destructive. Some people make a larger space for blue, for peace, for love. The making of that space takes power as well as love. It takes force of will. It takes assertion and commitment. The people of Le Chambon made a large space in the middle of the hurricane, and so did Frederick Douglass.

I mentioned at lunch today that I don't like ethics anymore. I've really had it with ethics. Why have I had it, after three or four decades of working in it? Why am I retiring? I can get good Social Security, that's one of the reasons. But another reason I am retiring is that I feel ethics is irrelevant. Let's put it this way: it's a means. A means of joy. Joy, the joy Maya Angelou is always expressing in every line she writes. The joy of living itself. There are even the joys we have in pain, because we still have that tiny thread of the joy of living. If you do not have joy, then your ethics is a blinding, puritanical, dried up, self-destructive and life-destructive force. If you do have that joy, your life is as wide as you can make it.

I am convinced that we can express a larger need for joy, and a larger capacity for joy than we have ever done. Each of us, every next moment, can do so. The way we can do this is to get interested in people who have it. To get interested, not in the evil ones, not in the ones with that tiny eye of the hurricane that looks so tiny, like Himmler's, because it's made so tiny by the vastness of the storm around it. Not that way, but by being interested in—if you can, by falling in love with—people who love the lives of others as much as they love their own lives. That's an unbelievable mystery for me. I'm from Chicago—how can I believe it—that there are people who love the lives of others as much as they love their own lives? But if you love such lovers or at least are interested in them enough, you begin to mimic them. You begin to love life the way they do and you begin to love the larger life, the life of those who are beyond you and connected with you. You begin to love them with passion and lucidity. By choosing such people to care for, we choose life, the breath of life. And in that choice, we will find joy, the very breath of joy, the joy of living together.

DIALOGUE WITH PHILIP HALLIE

Barbara Jordan

BARBARA JORDAN: We have heard an interesting and provocative talk by Philip Hallie. He told us some things that I think we need to talk about for a long time. I'm going to make a couple of comments, Philip, and I'd like for you to respond to them. You talked about the power differential between the victim and the victimizer as being endemic, really, to the condition of cruelty. I believe that thesis, Philip; but if that is correct, you may be telling us that it is impossible for us to become reconciled as victim and victimizer because it is very difficult for us to alter power allocations. I don't see that alteration occurring. Are you telling me, in effect, that reconciliation is really not possible?

PHILIP HALLIE: That's an absolutely central question. It's the one I've been wrestling with ever since Frederick Douglass became important to me because in some way or another, toward the end of *The Life and Times*,[7] he was still dealing with Auld, his former master, who was still a member of the White majority, who still had all the verbal equipment for seeing Frederick Douglass as an inferior, socially, politically, and so on. Douglass's description of their meeting is the most delicate nonfiction prose of nineteenth-century America. He describes how, when he walks into the room, Auld says to him, "Hello, Marshall Douglass." (He was then U.S. marshall to Haiti.)

Frederick Douglass said, "Frederick to you."

And that changed everything, because what happened was that Auld took his hand, trembling, and they talked for a few moments. Even though all the ancient differences of power—political, economic, aesthetic, verbal, were still pretty much intact in Auld's mind, there was a personal relationship between the two individuals, not only because of those words, "Frederick to you," but also because Frederick Douglass *was* there sitting by the bedside of this dying man. (He died the next day.)

Douglass was in such a relationship to Auld that even the word *equality* was irrelevant. They weren't talking about it, because that was almost a condescending term compared to what was happening between those two men. What was happening I cannot believe was anything but what I call *efficacious love*. It was in that last scene between those two people—one dying and the other in the full vigor of his manhood, yet to do some of his greatest things. In that personal relationship, your question got an answer at least in that case: Personal power of will has a generosity that surrenders nothing.

JORDAN: Then I think it is important for us to see here that we can understand evil, we can understand cruelty, but it is unlikely that we are going to be able to get beyond that point in a general sense because the power allocations are going to remain what they have been in the past and what they are now. There may be isolated instances of adjustment, as perhaps occurred in the case of Frederick Douglass, but on a massive scale we are not going to see it. That may be one reason why in this country we hear more talk about liberty and freedom than we do about equality. The president of the United States said that he was not aware of any tension between equality and liberty and freedom, and of course we can excuse that as due to an abysmal lack of knowledge. Be that as it may, it will remain a central problem.

Now on another point, Philip, that I would like to hear you respond to, you don't like the term *evil* and I can understand that because you said it's a little bit too abstract and you're very skeptical of abstractions. But the point is, evil is not really abstract because it is the result of conscious activity and not unconscious activity. It doesn't just happen. For evil to come about, somebody has to do something right or wrong.

HALLIE: Oh, yes. Usually somebody has to do something with some intent. My daughter is a lawyer and she is concerned with intent as a lawyer, a litigator. So am I, as somebody who finds in criminal law a very interesting set of guides to my work. And as a skeptic I find it difficult to understand *intent*. I think it can be said that when somebody is sadistic or perverse or just doing some harm for the sake of the harm itself and for the vexing of one's soul, as Poe put it, then it's very clear what intent is. It's damning. I think it's evil, and it's plainly evil, as you say. But there are so many very important degrees between that and having some ulterior motive that keeps you blind to what you are really doing. The victimizer is so blinded by her/his own interests or goals or ideology or whatever. They could even be religious abstractions. For instance, in the *autos-da-fé* the burnings at the stake were for the benefit of the victims who were being saved from hell fire by earthly fire. They were being helped into purgatory. These were acts of faith, *autos-da-fé*, because the people doing them were so concerned with the goal. They weren't sadists for the most part. They were really well-intentioned. God protect us from the well-intentioned! They were people who simply didn't see the victims. There are so many victimizers who don't see the victims. That's what Ellison's book is all about.[8] In such cases of blindness, not even deliberate blindness, there's something almost gallant about these bastards. They really are innocents, and it's because there are such cases of intention that I try to stick to the *victim's* point of view on cruelty, rather than the intent of the victimizer.

JORDAN: Now on another point, Philip, do you think you're being a little hard on Hannah Arendt and her thesis of the banality of evil, vis-à-vis Eichmann? There is a point where Jewish people and Black people are made to feel guilty for their circumstances. When that occurs, we get on the defensive. I am wondering whether this was a defensive mechanism. In writing *Origins of Totalitarianism*[9] and in other places, Arendt was really distraught about how the Jewish people seemed to acquiesce in their condition. Black people have that same problem. How do you see that?

HALLIE: That's an important part of Hannah Arendt's thinking. She wants to separate the victimizer from the victim, so as to take the victim off the hook. That's a summary of what you just said. I think it's a very important force in her thinking. I think she shouldn't have tried. If the victim is on the hook, then he or she should be on the hook. Something along these lines is what Hannah Arendt was thinking.

I worked with her when she came to Wesleyan as a fellow in our center for almost a year. We talked a lot about these things. She was finishing the writing of *Eichmann in Jerusalem*, just after her return from Jerusalem. When we talked, it seemed pretty clear to me that she was exploring his mind, not the world outside his mind. She was doing what you might call 'a work in psychology.' It was a very important work, I felt. I told her then, and I still believe it—an absolutely vital work. It is terribly important how commonplace, trite, ordinary, and uninteresting evil can be in the minds of the people who are the victimizers. That's terribly important to realize. It should warn us that when we isolate the victimizer and don't see what he or she is doing to the victim, then we are in great danger of being blind to the crushing and the grinding.

JORDAN: I'm wondering, Philip, is it possible for us to orchestrate good in people? We heard Rollo May say that there was about a year or year and a half when people are impressionable. They're not thinking anything in particular for that first year or so. Then when they begin to see good and evil, and right and wrong, that is the time they formulate these ideas and an essence of self. I'm just wondering if, because we know we have a window of opportunity to work with, could we in a massive way orchestrate good in people versus the predominance of evil? Is that possible, do you think?

HALLIE: I'm as scared of it as I am hopeful about it. If I had to assign people the job of teaching our young, I don't know how I or anybody else would interview them. I'm always so scared of nurture engineering. The teacher's job is so vital. One of the most horrific things about this world we live in is that we don't see how vital the mother's and the teacher's jobs are, and yet how effective and worthwhile they can be as individuals. There is no one rigid little pattern that the social sciences have come up with that they all agree on, and that we agree with, too (whoever the *we* might be), that we'd say is *the* pattern that we want to have our teachers follow. I've got my fears about it.

JORDAN: Right. If you and I could do it . . .

HALLIE: If you did it, I'd take it. I wouldn't even interview you. [Laughing]

JORDAN: I'm sure that you have read Allan Bloom's *The Closing of the American Mind*.[10] He makes an interesting statement about the way young people view evil. He is talking about books in this book, and he says that young people don't read the classics, that they don't enjoy the Greek writers any more. Then he comments that, instead of asking his students about the books they read, he would ask them about the people they respect and admire, and the people they view as evil people. So he asks his students, 'Whom do you view as evil?' The answer was immediately, 'Hitler.' He said a few mentioned Stalin, but not many had heard of Stalin. In a real sense, however, the young people did not believe that there was any such thing as evil. They distrusted even its presence as a force. Do you find that credible?

HALLIE: Oh yes. But you know, when I teach ethics to kids in terms of facts or details or stories—preferably true stories, but even in novels—a curious thing happens. To my colleagues, it doesn't happen, but it always happens to me. We agree. But when my colleagues stay way up there on high levels and define words like *goodness* as producing more happiness than pain for the larger number, they have all sorts of fights with their kids. But when I tell them a story of, say, a lynching in Detroit (not with the power, of course, of Richard Wright's poem,[11] but something approaching the detail), I have never had anybody tell me that there is no evil. Never. No student.

JORDAN: Do they understand the force, the power?

HALLIE: Yes. They see the destruction, because the details of the actual description lay out the destruction. I've had a couple of descriptions that match in detail what Richard Wright's description does. It's a curious thing. It makes me overjoyed as a skeptic because I don't have to argue with them up there in the stratosphere. Many years ago, a freshman in a sociology course would say, 'Well, it all depends on your point of view. It could be this. It could be that. It could be evil, could be good.' When I first got the job of teaching such kids, such smart alecks, I would pick them up and put them up against the wall and say, "I'm going to kick ya. Now is that good or bad? Is that indifferent? If it's indifferent, I might not kick ya." So I got a rise out of them that way: 'It's bad, bad, bad.' But now I am older and they can beat me up, so what I do more or less is to stay close to fact. I mention a particular lynching or a particular passage, especially the Covey slave-breaking passage in *The Life and Times of Frederick Douglass*.[12] Or I'll mention something that happened more frequently than most people know, except Raul Hilberg, that a guard or a soldier will take an infant out of a mother's arms and throw the baby up against the wall and kill it. There are dozens of witnesses to this. It just happened again and again in front of the mothers: They just dash the baby up against the wall. Now any young person who ever says, 'Well, that depends on your point of view'—I've not met such a person.

JORDAN: You know, *lynching* is a very loaded, heavily value-laden word. That's why I found it so curious when I heard the president of the United States talking about a political lynching just because some person could not be confirmed as a justice on the Supreme Court. It just kind of defies me. I just had to get that in. But back to cruelty and evil . . .

HALLIE: As if we left it.

JORDAN: We never did leave it. I wonder, do we understand how evil and cruel is the maiming and crushing of the *dignity* of people? Are we aware of what we are doing in a destructive way—that it can be so crushing to one's individual dignity? Ignorance of this is as great an evil as any mentioned at this conference. And that's why we must be ever vigilant in our actions, for fear we may perpetrate an act of cruelty or an evil notwithstanding our intent.

HALLIE: Exactly. That's the ultimate thing.

HARRY WILMER: There is a worldwide cruelty that I have had a little experience with, dealing with some of its victims, that should affect all our consciousness and that we might be able to do something about—that is, the torture of people that is so widespread in the world. Would you say something about that?

HALLIE: As you know, torture is a very special aspect of cruelty. It usually involves crushing somebody for purposes of extracting information. There are two ways, in general, that we torture or hurt other people. One way is for pragmatic reasons. There is something we want that's valuable, much more valuable to us than the life or the happiness of this person, so we destroy that happiness to get the something that we want. The other way is sheer perverseness—that is to say, *sadism*, you might call it, or the sheer joy of seeing another's pain. The experience of dissonance between your own pleasures and the pains of the other is sometimes called *sadism*. Now these two forces are so powerful that even when you can conquer the perverseness, you can hire people who are not sadists to be your torturers. This is very important, and was very important to Himmler. He wanted to hire people who were not sadists because sadists might stop having fun. They might get tired of it, and then they would no longer be functional. So he hired almost entirely nonsadistic people. What I am trying to say is that I have no answer to your question at all, because once you get rid of your sadists you have single-minded adherence to a cause that makes you eager to torture.

NOTES

[1] Hannah Arendt, *Eichmann in Jerusalem: A Report on the Banality of Evil* (New York: Viking Press, 1963).

[2] Frederick Douglass, *The Life and Times of Frederick Douglass* (Hartford: Park, 1881).

[3] Edward Covey was a slave breaker. "[Douglass's master] resolved to put me out, as he said, to be broken; and, for this purpose, he let me for one year to a man named Edward Covey. Mr. Covey was a poor man, a farm-renter. He rented the place upon which he lived, as also the hands with which he tilled it. Mr. Covey had acquired a very high reputation for breaking young slaves, and this reputation was of immense value to him." *Narrative of the Life of Frederick Douglass, an*

American Slave, Written by Himself (New York: New American Library, 1968), pp. 69–70. Originally published in Boston: 'Published at the Anti-Slavery Office', 1845.

[4] Philip Paul Hallie, *The Paradox of Cruelty* (Middletown, Conn.: Wesleyan University Press, 1969); paperback edition: *Cruelty* (Wesleyan University Press, 1982).

[5] Philip Paul Hallie, *Lest Innocent Blood Be Shed* (New York: Harper & Row, 1979).

[6] George Santayana, "As in the midst of battle . . . " First published in *The Harvard Monthly*, 21, no. 1 (October 1895): 6 as Sonnet IV. First published in book form in *Sonnets and Other Verses* (New York: Stone & Kimball, 1896) as Sonnet XXV. Reprinted in many sources including Irving Edman (ed.), *The Philosophy of George Santayana* (New York: Modern Library, 1936), p. 25.

[7] See above, p. 136, note 3., *Life and Times of Frederick Douglass*, p. 442.

[8] Ralph Ellison, *Invisible Man* (New York: Vintage, 1972).

[9] Hannah Arendt, *Origins of Totalitarianism* (2d edn. London: André Deutsch, 1986).

[10] Allan Bloom, *The Closing of the American Mind* (New York: Simon & Schuster, 1987).

[11] Above, p. 22, and p. 44 note 2.

[12] Above, p. note 3.

3

THE SOUNDS OF EVIL

Tony Schwartz

Tony Schwartz has explored the effect of sound on people for over 40 years. He has won over 360 awards, including Academy Awards; first place at the Cannes, Venice, and International Film Festivals; Art Directors Club Awards; International Broadcasting; Clios, Andies, and the Prix Italia. He became professor of auditory perception at Fordham University and together with Marshall McLuhan shared the Schweitzer Chair in Communication. He received a grant from the National Endowment for the Arts to study our changing communications environment. He has produced over 20,000 radio and television commercials for more than 650 clients. Schwartz has written *The Responsive Chord* and *Media: the Second God*.

For the last 45 years, I've been carrying around a portable tape recorder. The first one I carried around was big and weighed 20 or 30 pounds. Today you can take something little, like a Radio Shack recorder, to record people and it would be just as good quality as the one I carried when I first started. Over the years, I've recorded thousands and thousands of people from all walks of life. I've recorded presidents, I've recorded the Pope, I've recorded workers on farms, workers in their factories, children in school—in the wealthy schools and in the poor schools.

I started thinking the other day about the fact that I have many recordings about good and bad. Or you might say about good and evil—*evil* is a word that, in a way, means bad. I started thinking about evil, and I thought: we get our values and our thoughts about what is good and bad from our parents and our teachers and our religious leaders and radio and television.

I started thinking I had recordings of my father telling me what happened to him in Romania. Other than the American Indians, all Americans either directly, or indirectly through their relatives, came from other countries. Here's my father telling why he came from Romania when he was eight years old:

> The hoodlums, the hooligans would be coming running down the street with bats and clubs in their hands looking for old Jews with beards. And I remember very keenly how we had to hide our grandfather in the cellar to make sure that they won't see him and attack him. We weren't free to go to school. We weren't free to get the education that all the other Romanian children got. When I came to this country, I was able to go to a public school and got the same treatment, the same summer school playgrounds, and everything that everybody else did. And such things are everlasting in my mind.

Well, that was my father telling why he came here, because they would beat up his grandfather and he couldn't go to the regular schools in Romania, but here he got treated as an American, just like anybody else.

And my mother taught me many things. Here is one comment of hers that's very important: "I always had the feeling that if you don't hate right where you are, that'll cut down the amount of hate in the world." It's an important thing. If you're a good person, where you are, in your everyday activities . . . you help make the world a better place.

I put together a whole bunch of sounds and it's an interesting thing—the bad sounds, or evil sounds, are only sounds from people's mouths. There is no sound that's bad in itself. A gunshot is not bad in itself; it can be very good. It can be used by a police officer to shoot a mad dog that's running after children, or it could be used by someone to attack people. So, in itself, it's not good or bad.

When we take words, however, we find that each person, based on personal experience, had a reaction to whether something was good or bad. One thing most Americans thought was bad was Adolf Hitler in Nazi Germany. He wanted to conquer the world. I have a recording of him, with his people praising him and shouting 'Sieg Heil'.

One day I was recording a woman who came up from the South. She was telling about life in the South and what happened to her nephew. It was something that I thought was so evil and bad:

> My nephew was lynched by five White men who accused him of stealing a saddle. Later the saddle was returned, so then he didn't steal it. But yet my nephew was dead. No one was even punished for the crime. Just my nephew was dead from what they said, that he stole a saddle.

I had a Puerto Rican friend who told me that one day he went to look for an apartment. Here's what he tells about what he was told:

> When we first went to see about the apartment, we were sort of wondering if somebody would question the fact that we were of Puerto Rican descent. And he seemed to like us very much and he was very friendly. Then he turned to us and he said, "There's something else that you'll never have to worry about." I said, "What's that?" And he says, "No Puerto Ricans."

Can you imagine how he felt hearing that?

Then here's a woman who doesn't realize that her parents came from some other country also, but here's how she felt about anyone who just didn't sound like she sounded: "I wish they hadn't come here in the first place. They aren't welcome, they don't want to learn how to speak the language, and it's a shame that they don't stay in their own country." I wonder if people said that about her folks when they came here from another country—that they didn't want to learn to speak the language? They probably wanted to learn to speak the language very much, but it's hard to learn a new language.

Here's a man who wanted to test the law in the 1960s after the Supreme Court had passed a ruling that Blacks could ride equally in the front or the back of the bus. He wanted to test that law. He tells what happened when he rode in the front of the bus when Blacks previously were supposed to ride in the back of the bus:

I sat in the front of the bus. Then the cops come up, they arrest us, they told us to get in the back. We told them we felt that we had an obligation to sit in the front because the Supreme Court had made a ruling that Negros could sit front or back when they were traveling interstate travel. They said, "Well, that's what the Supreme Court may say, but we work for the state of North Carolina." Then they took us off and took us to the courthouse. At the courthouse, they gave us a trial. At the trial, they gave us 30 days on a chain gang. On the chain gang, they gave us a lot of work to do. We did it. We got off in 22 days—eight days for good time, God bless 'em—and then we came home.

Well, he was put on a chain gang. I have recorded the sound of men on a chain gang singing while they're working. They're chopping logs at the side of the road, and it's a hundred and two degrees in the shade. They're forced to work this way.

In one place, some Black people were holding a get-together where other people didn't want them to be and can you imagine what they were told? The people were throwing stones at them, and saying, "Go on back to Russia, you Niggers." It's unbelievable what some people will do.

Another group of young teenage boys and girls wanted to sing in the park but the police didn't want them there. The police started coming after them with clubs. The young people screamed when they were being attacked by the police. Don't in any way get the idea that all police are bad. On occasions we find activities of certain police very bad, but most of the time the police are very good people and are helpful to the community. They are necessary in our society and the majority of police are very good people.

Here is a woman during the civil rights movement in the South when the Blacks were protesting against the conditions under which they had to live. This woman was arrested and put in a detention camp. She was telling what happened to another older woman in this camp:

One day a lady who weighed approximately 300, who'd been pushed in the back and beat over the head, she was still sore. She was told to get up and move, and when she didn't fast enough the cops came and struck her to make her get up and called two more. One got one leg and one another and they tore her dress off and teared her dress up and she was naked and they actually beat her on her naked body. It was pitiful. We all began to cry.

I now have a recording that is one of the most amazing things I've ever gotten. A group of teenagers killed another teenager. I went to interview those kids in the police station and they were telling how they felt about it. [Here are several young boys' voices:]

—He couldn't run anyway because we were all around him. Someone punched him in the face. And then somebody hit him with a bat over the head and I kept punchin' on him.

—I kicked him, twice. He was laying on the ground lookin' up at us. I kicked him in the jaw or someplace and then I kicked him in the stomach. That was the least I could do, was kick him.

—I was aiming to hit him, but I didn't get a chance to hit him. There was so many guys on him, I got scared when I saw the knife go into the guy.

—. . . and turned around and stabbed him in the back. I was stunned. I couldn't do nuthin'. And then Mason, he went like that and he had a switchblade and he said, "You're gonna hit him with the bat or I'll stab you."

—I just went like that. I was standing with a bread knife, you know. I was drunk so I just, you know, stabbed him. All I heard was the guy screaming. Heh, heh, he screamed like a dog; he was screaming there. And I took that knife out of him and I told the guys to run.

—The guy that stabbed him in the back with the bread knife, he told me that when he took the knife out of his back he said, "Thank you."

—If I had gotten the knife, I would have stabbed him. That would have gave me more of a build-up. People would respect me for what I've done and things like that, and say, "There goes a cold killer."

You know, at one time in our society there were groups of people that thought they knew what Americans should be, and that if people had differing ideas from them, they didn't think they were good Americans. There was a senator who even felt that way, Senator McCarthy. During his time, he pressured all people to have loyalty oaths. Now, you'd be shocked if I told you they were giving loyalty oaths to the American Indians. But there was the chief of the Osage tribe who got a hundred-dollar-a-year check from the government. Therefore, they insisted that he take the loyalty oath and say that he was loyal to this government and did not represent any other government. Here is the chief of the Osage tribe taking a loyalty oath during the time of McCarthy:

> I, John Overly, do solemnly swear during such time as I am principal chief of the Osage tribe of Indians I will not advocate nor become a member of any political party or organization that advocates the overthrow of the government of the United States by force or violence. And I take this obligation clearly without any reservation.

Can you imagine an Indian chief having to say that he takes this oath without any reservation? It's almost funny.

In addition to the sounds of evil, or bad, that I've recorded, I've also recorded some sounds of good and I'd like to end with two sounds that I think are good. One is from a very important person—the Pope, Pope John Paul II—telling why we should be careful and why other countries should be careful in relation to nuclear weapons, because he feels they would bring an end to all humanity. He speaks up for humanity this way.

> We are troubled by the development of weaponry exceeding in quality and size the means of destruction ever known before. The continual production of ever more numerous, powerful, and sophisticated weapons shows that there is a desire to be ready for war. And being ready means being able to start it—it also means taking the risk that sometime, somewhere, somehow, someone can set in motion general destruction. It must be our solemn wish for the children of all the nations on earth to make such catastrophes impossible.

Now, remember I played you the sound of a woman telling about the three-hundred-pound lady being beaten on her naked body in the detention camp? Well, something made me want to ask this lady that I was recording, 'You're telling me about the inhuman things that you saw. What made you feel most human in your life?' It's amazing how simple things can make people feel human:

I was in Chicago for the first time of ever having been out of the South. I went up on the El and a White lady touched me on the shoulder and said, "Lady, your slip is showing." And that incident really made me feel more like a lady and more alive than I'd ever felt in my life. I felt that this lady says, "Here's another lady and because I'm a lady, I don't want to see another lady that is not properly dressed." And it just made me feel good to know a White person could think of me as being a lady.

So think of what you hear in your life and think of it against your background and also how you feel in your heart about the things you hear. Just because a lot of people are standing behind them doesn't make them right. Just because a few people feel the other way doesn't make it wrong. Go by your own heart and your own feelings and your own background.

An audiocassette and videocassette of 'Sounds of Evil' are available from AVW Audio Visual Incorporated. See page xiii.

4

THE SHADOW OF ACCIDENTAL NUCLEAR WAR: THE IRREPARABLE EVIL

Herbert L. Abrams

Herbert L. Abrams is professor of radiology at Stanford University School of Medicine and a member-in-residence of the Stanford Center for International Security and Arms Control. He is national co-chairman of Physicians for Social Responsibility and founding vice-president of International Physicians for the Prevention of Nuclear War, which won the 1985 Nobel Peace Award. An M.D. of the State University of New York, he has been Philip H. Cook professor and chairman of radiology at Harvard Medical School. He has been a research fellow of the National Cancer Institute, a special research fellow of the National Heart Institute, a special NIH fellow in the Department of Radiology at the University of Lund, Sweden; and Henry J. Kaiser senior fellow at the Center for Advanced Study in the Behavioral Sciences, Stanford. His books include *Coronary Autobiography: A Practical Approach*.

The following lecture was given on September 19, 1998, at 2 P.M. to undergraduates studying history at the University of Argentina in Buenos Aires.

"This course in Northern Hemisphere history", Professor Cordova said, "will deal selectively with the last decade from our modern perspective in 1998. Living and working at this university in Buenos Aires, we had the chance to watch the dangers of the nuclear age unfold.

"On September 24, 1990, Soviet leaders agreed to supply their Syrian allies with a few small nuclear weapons in order to 'maintain the military balance' with Israel.

"Two weeks later, on October 10th, a fundamentalist Islamic coup occurred in Egypt, and a Shiite faction of the Muslim brotherhood led by a Mullah named Mustafa Ibrahim took control of Cairo. Mustafa summarily rejected the Camp David accords and pledged to return Egypt to spiritual purity through strict adherence to Islamic law. On October 17th Mustafa's men seized the American embassy in Cairo. Shiite revolutionaries meanwhile took command of three American-made AWACs planes housed in an Egyptian airfield near Cairo. Civilian unrest intensified in Saudi Arabia, and a wave of defections swept through the ranks of the military.

"With the Mustafa in control of Egypt, the Isrealis began troop movements south into the Sinai Peninsula in order to secure their buffer zone. Syria then began to shift troops into Lebanon. Israel, realizing its limitations in manpower for a two-front war, decided to launch a pre-emptive air strike on Syrian airfields. The vast majority of Syrian fighter planes and surface-to-air missiles were destroyed in the October 25th raid. Nine to ten Soviet advisors were killed.

"The United States immediately disavowed any U.S. complicity and reprimanded Israel. The U.S.S.R. voiced its condemnation and accused the United States of inspiring Israeli behavior. Moscow placed five airborne divisions on alert in Eastern Europe. The Syrians proceeded to regroup and by the following day, Syrian tanks had rolled into northern Israel and the two nations were engaged in heavy artillery fire. Meanwhile, a band of Shiite revolutionaries invaded and took control of the Saudi airfield at Jidda and closed it to all air transport.

"The United States felt it had no choice but to intervene. On October 28th, the rapid deployment force of the 82nd Airborne Division began air drops into Israel. Soviet troops began to enter Syria through Iran. When the 82nd Airborne rallied to Israel's support, President al-Assad of Syria reasoned that once the United States entered the conflict decisively, the Soviets would back down, to avoid the risk of a strategic exchange. On October 30, 1990, the Syrian army initiated a tactical nuclear strike on Jerusalem. The devastation of the Holy City was total.

"The following day, a squadron of B-52s executed a limited retaliatory strike on Syria, dropping a handful of air-launched cruise missiles. The United States President held an emergency meeting with the Joint Chiefs of Staff and a decision was made that a Soviet attack was imminent. The bombers were scrambled, the submarines flushed, and a launch-on-warning command issued. The Soviet general staff detected American war preparations and concluded that war with the United States had become unavoidable. The decision was made to pre-empt.

"At sunrise on October 31, 1990, NORAD's early warning system picked up a massive ICBM barrage on its radar screens. The Strategic Air Command received orders to launch the MX missiles and the Minutemen.

"As the day wore on, the respective strategic arsenals were exhausted. Finally, as darkness came, fighting ceased and the agitated survivors began to look for food and shelter. Massive fires swept the subcontinents. Temperatures plummeted. Soot and dust encased civilization. The Northern Hemisphere was reduced to rubble and grew still.

"And so," Professor Cordova said, "as things happened in the last decade, many of the elements that thinking people had considered potential triggers of inadvertent nuclear war were lived out precisely: regional conflict, internal unrest, escalation of a conventional war, irrational leadership, proliferation, a local war between client states of the super powers, limited pre-emptive nuclear strikes, war preparations by the super powers, and then the decision to pre-empt because of misinformation and miscalculation.

"How lucky we were in Argentina never to have nuclear weapons," he said.

The nuclear age really began on August 6, 1945, when the bomb bay doors on the B-29 called Enola Gay opened wide. At 8:15 A.M., the bomb exploded over Hiroshima. Instantly, the blue sky was blanked out by the blinding light of the huge fireball. Over 250 feet in diameter, it was 100 times as bright as the sun, with a heat of 1,000 degrees centigrade, the same as the sun's interior. The fireball sucked up millions of tons of dust and pulverized debris, which began to form the great grey mushroom cloud. The city darkened and a dirty rain began to fall. More than half the population of 250,000 were instantly dead or incapacitated.

The event excited the imagination and the horror of the world. In its wake, paintings on the apocalypse and the Holocaust appeared. Others depicted the armored trains, the imprisonment and dispersion of man, and the shadows in the sky. Big Brother was watching. Mechanical man was upon us. Isolation in the metropolis of tomorrow finally gave way to chaos.

Since 1945, over 1,500 nuclear weapons have been exploded in tests, the bulk of them by the U.S.A. and the U.S.S.R. The strategic arsenal includes missiles in silos, submarines, and bombers, and is spread across the United States, the U.S.S.R., in England, France, and China. Among the great nations, the power and the number of the weapons have increased year after year. There is no sign of a leveling off. There are now roughly 60,000 nuclear weapons. These huge stockpiles are a major factor in the intense concern about accidental nuclear war: we know that no rational leaders would intentionally initiate a nuclear war because of their knowledge of its annihilatory effects. It is far more likely that it will come through misunderstanding, miscalculation, misinterpretation, or accident.[1]

An *accidental nuclear war*, as shown in Figure A, has genuine meaning primarily in the context of crisis. The term may serve as a contrast to the intent of all rational leadership to avoid the event. In this construct, the accidental nuclear war is undesigned, unforeseen, occurs by chance, is unintended, unexpected, unpremeditated. Inadvertence can be incorporated in this broadened definition: the nuclear exchange that occurs because of oversight, misperception, misjudgment, misunderstanding.

The triggers include technical-mechanical accidents involving nuclear weapons, weapons carriers, command and control centers, and warning systems. Human instability and devolution of command to lower levels may play an important role in accidents or unauthorized launch.

What is meant by 'inadvertence' is a series of pathways to conflict that produce crises, arise during crises, or intensify crises. They include client states under attack, regional conflicts, escalation of conventional war, a catalytic war precipitated by a third

ACCIDENTAL OR INADVERTENT NUCLEAR WAR

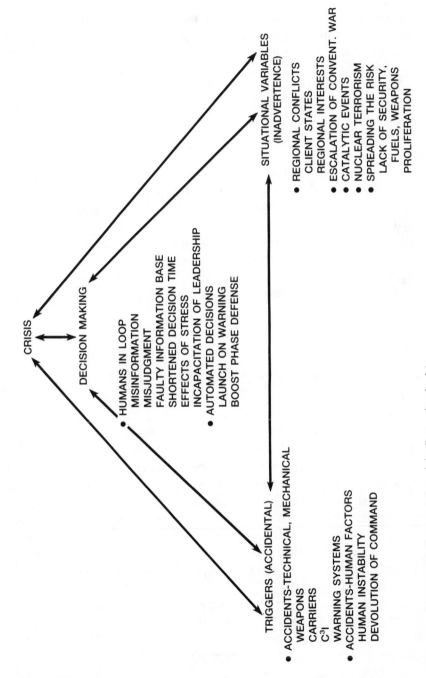

FIGURE A: Diagrammatic Representation of the Factors Involved in Accidental or Inadvertent Nuclear War.

power, and nuclear terrorism. The risk spreads through lack of security of nuclear fuel and weapons and through proliferation. All of the foregoing avenues to a major confrontation are inadvertent because a nuclear exchange was never originally intended by the great powers, although at some point there must be a decision to launch the weapons. Both parties believe that they are following programs that will minimize risk, but war erupts because an adversary is thought to have attacked, or to be about to.

In crisis, logic and clarity give way to emotions and irrationality when tensions are high and national pride is at stake. Accidents and inadvertence interact with each other synergistically to affect the decision making process. Many other factors alter the final quality of the decisions, including misinformation, misjudgment, stress, and incapacitated leadership. Perhaps the greatest threats are the shortening of decision time and the potential removal of humans from the decision loop (Figure A).

Nuclear Weapons Accidents

Among the potential triggers, nuclear weapons accidents require consideration. *Broken Arrows* and *Bent Spears* are the military code words used to indicate major accidents and less severe accidents involving nuclear weapons. A *Broken Arrow* has been officially defined as any unexpected event involving nuclear weapons resulting in accidental or unauthorized launching, fire, or use, which could create the risk of outbreak of war. Examples are nuclear detonation, seizure, theft, and loss of a nuclear weapon. A *Bent Spear*, which is less severe, covers any unexpected event involving nuclear weapons or components that results in damage to a nuclear weapon.

Because of the secrecy surrounding weapons accidents, their exact number is unknown. The Department of Defense officially lists 32 Broken Arrows between 1950 and 1980.[2] The most comprehensive study documents 125 nuclear accidents, major and minor combined, between 1945 and 1976—just about one every one-and-a-half months.[3]

If the United States stresses nondisclosure, other countries with nuclear armaments do the same to an even greater degree. At least 15 nuclear bombs have never been recovered from accidents.[4,5] In 1977, it was disclosed that nine U.S. nuclear bomber accidents had occurred over Canada or Canadian territorial waters. There have been at least nine occasions in which U.S. submarines have collided with foreign (apparently Soviet) vessels.

What are the actual hazards of nuclear weapons accidents? No accident has ever caused a nuclear detonation. Its likelihood is slim because the safeguards in weapons design have a great deal of redundancy.[6]

There are other dangers. Nuclear submarine accidents in peacetime may be reviewed carefully, and their causes determined. In time of crisis, however, the loss of a submarine may be interpreted as a deliberate act of provocation.

Accidental launches may be a far greater threat. The explosion of a nuclear weapon on an adversary's territory is the worst case. But accidental launching of nuclear capable missiles in time of crisis would constitute a grave threat. There have been at least five reported instances of U.S. nuclear-capable missiles flying over or crashing into or near the territory of other nations. These include a Mace Missile overflight of Cuba and a crash of a Matador Missile into the straits of Taiwan after an aberrant flight toward China.[7]

In spite of the present safeguards, the increasing number of weapons implies an increase in the number of accidents. As systems become increasingly complex, the possibility of malfunction rises. If developing nations acquire nuclear weapons, they will rely more on man-guided delivery systems and will lack the safety features of the industrialized countries.

Human Instability

On May 26, 1981, an American jet crashed into the flight deck of the nuclear aircraft carrier Nimitz off the southern coast of Georgia. The plane burst into flames in a tragedy in which 14 young men lost their lives and 44 others were injured. The pilot of the plane had six to eleven

times the recommended level of the antihistamine bromphe-
niramine in his system. A congressional committee concluded
that the effects of the medication at such a level—causing
sedation, dizziness, double vision, tremors—together with
stress factors, probably helped precipitate the pilot error that
caused the crash. Several government studies have found drug
abuse to be widespread throughout the armed forces.[8] This
situation assumes special importance in light of a 1982 report
by the House Appropriations Committee, which indicated that
many of the drug incidents and arrests have involved personnel responsible for controlling and maintaining our nuclear
weapons.

About 105,000–112,000 individuals are involved in handling
America's nuclear arms.[9] Most are responsible for strategic
nuclear weapons, but over fourteen thousand work with tactical
or theater nuclear weapons. The military is deeply concerned
with ensuring the stability of its weapons personnel.

The heart of this effort is the Personnel Reliability Program
(PRP) which screens candidates both for critical jobs such as
commanders of nuclear weapons delivery units and for less
autonomous control positions. The PRP selects individuals
thought to possess physical competence, mental alertness, technical proficiency, dependability, and flexibility. No psychiatric
interview or psychological testing is required.[10]

One measure of the program's effectiveness is the number of
persons appointed who must later be removed. From 1975 to
1984, 51,000 previously approved were decertified—an average
of more than five thousand a year. That represents 4 to 12 percent
at any one time. Drug and alcohol abuse or psychiatric problems
were the most common causes: over 30 percent were due to drug
abuse, 9 percent to alcohol abuse, and about 20 percent to
psychiatric problems.[11]

At any one time, therefore, thousands of potentially unstable
individuals have day-to-day responsibility for handling our
nuclear weapons. In a 1980 Defense Department survey of fifteen
thousand military personnel, 36 percent admitted illegal drug
use.[12] The drugs employed were not just alcohol and marijuana,
but also amphetamines, cocaine, hallucinogens, and many others. In the Navy, more than a quarter of respondents under 25
said that they had been *high while working* during the preceding

year, half of them on more than 40 days.[13] Alcohol abuse occurred widely.

The isolation aboard nuclear submarines and in nuclear missile silos, unnatural work shifts, and the stress of being responsible for nuclear weapons may intensify instability and affect job performance. The Soviet military appears to be confronted with many of the same problems.[14]

If it is true that nuclear weapons personnel of both superpowers are sometimes undependable, does it matter? In the United States, as in the Soviet Union, tactical nuclear weapons cannot be as tightly controlled as strategic arms during periods of international tension. Thus, tactical weapons are probably more vulnerable to misuse by unstable personnel. Most strategic U.S. nuclear weapons are fitted with 'Permissive Action Links' (PALs) that inhibit launch until the proper combination, supplied by the National Command Authority, is entered electronically. The 'two-man rule' is also operative as a safeguard, so that at least two people must turn the keys.

Controls over the firing of submarine-launched missiles are less stringent. The Navy maintains no Permissive Action Links. The captain and crew of a nuclear submarine are supposed to receive higher authorization. But if they should decide to act independently, there are no technical safeguards to prevent them from launching the weapons. In peacetime, the unauthorized firing of even a submarine-based missile is unlikely. The problem arises during crises, when measures to guard against inadvertent launches tend to undermine launch readiness. To ensure that their forces are able to respond rapidly to an attack, commanders on both sides might loosen safeguards.

DECISION MAKERS

Incapacity or instability in national leadership will surely affect the ultimate decisions. Acute and chronic organic illness has profound cognitive effects. It is important, therefore, to appreciate the demography of disease in our leadership.

There have been 16 U.S. presidents in the twentieth century. Eight of the twelve who are dead had heart disease, and three had cerebral hemorrhages. Of the seven Soviet leaders, four had heart disease and three had cerebral hemorrhages. Seven American presidents had violent attacks upon them, six had major surgery, and four died in office. One Soviet leader had a violent attack, two had surgery, and five died in office. Twenty percent of all U.S. presidents and 70 percent of Soviet leaders have died in office.

The most important underlying factor was coronary and cerebral arteriosclerosis, so frequently associated with increasing age. Impairment of ability to concentrate, lapses of memory, and periods of confusion are symptoms of cerebral arteriosclerosis.[15] Aging can also be associated with tendencies toward overconfidence, extreme choices, and difficulty in decoding problems.

Following Eisenhower's heart attack, he acknowledged that in the first week he could not have handled "the concentration, the weighing of the pros and cons, and the final determination" of a crisis.[16] The Twenty-Fifth Amendment of the Constitution is the only mechanism for removing a disabled president. Nowhere does the amendment state that medical or psychiatric counsel must be sought. As the assassination attempt on President Reagan showed, confusion over who is in charge may follow the acute disability of an incumbent president. No consideration of inadvertent nuclear war can avoid the conclusion that incapacity in national leadership is an important potential danger.

SYSTEMS FALLIBILITY

Faulty warnings in the nation's missile alert system occur when an odd movement or an infrared signature is detected by satellite guards, signaling the possibility that an SLBM or ICBM has been launched. In a year and a half, 3,700 minor alerts or routine missile display conferences were called to evaluate ambiguous sensory data in the warning systems.[17] False warnings can be caused by computer malfunction. A NORAD spokesman indicated that failures in computer or communications systems happen on average two or three times a year.

We all know that computers are susceptible to break down. In a test of our worldwide military command and control system some years ago, the computer network worked only 38 percent of the time in hundreds of tests—failed 62 percent of the time.[18] During an 18-month time span NORAD reported 147 false warnings serious enough to invoke threat evaluations.

The most serious aspect of false alarms is the decreasing time span we are allowing ourselves for efficient checking of errors. The shorter the delivery time of new missiles, the more likely we or the Soviets are to move to launch-on-warning policies. In June 1980, the display system in the Strategic Air Command of the United States Air Force indicated that the United States was under attack by submarine-launched ballistic missiles. Shortly thereafter, there were indications of ICBM attacks. It was a false alert due to computer error. The failure was traced to an integrated circuit chip in a Data General computer.

Perrow has suggested that major accidents may be inevitable in complex technological systems. Tightly interacting parts and processes are difficult to stop at any precise point because the interactions are so rapid and so closely linked.[19] High-risk systems can be characterized by the rarity of serious accidents coupled with the unacceptable level of damage if one does occur. When the consequences of mishap are so high, the systems cannot afford to learn from their mistakes—they simply cannot make mistakes. In the nuclear age, American and Soviet nuclear forces comprise a single system, for they are tightly coupled together.[20]

NUCLEAR TERRORISM

Given that it's possible to obtain nuclear weapon material, would there be an individual or group willing to take such high risks? Recent terrorist acts reveal developing sophistication in the use of technology, intelligence, and communications systems. How likely are acts of nuclear violence? There were 288 threats or acts of violence against nuclear facilities in the United States between 1969 and 1975.[24] What will the next attempt at nuclear extortion bring? Potentially a terrorist group with a nuclear device could render its opponent ineffective and remain anonymous or unlocatable.

PROLIFERATION

Proliferation is clearly feasible technically. There are 33 non-nuclear states capable of making nuclear weapons within the next ten years—ten in the short term, ten in the intermediate term, twelve or 13 in the long term. Proliferation itself replicates the inherent hazards of any nuclear weapons system. With weapons placed in the hands of more people, an increase in Broken Arrows must be anticipated. Reluctance to share computer technology and safety systems means that each nuclear power will have to learn from its own mistakes.

DECISION MAKING IN CRISIS

The Bay of Pigs, the Korean invasion in 1950, the escalation of the Vietnam War, and Pearl Harbor all attest to elements of failure in the national decision making process. The stress of crises degrades decision making.[25] Distorted individual perceptions, time pressures, and group dynamics interact in this process.[26] They raise serious questions about the assumptions of human rationality and predictability in crisis behavior. The interaction of 'triggers' and 'situational factors' during crisis inevitably affects the capacity of leadership—whether ill or not. Decision making is prone to error when information is insufficient, inaccurate, or ambiguous, and when stress factors are operative. Most errors in the decision making process can be moderated and the damage limited; mistakes that promote a major nuclear exchange will produce damage beyond control.

NUCLEAR WAR: THE CONSEQUENCES

If it happens, this inadvertent nuclear exchange, what can we expect? Let me summarize the conclusions of a recent National Academy of Sciences Symposium in which I participated.[27] In the wake of a massive exchange, deaths from the acute effects of radiation,[28] blast, and burn will go far beyond those of any other period in human history—hundreds of millions.[29,30] The impact of fire would be far greater than anticipated. The medical resources required to handle the living injured will not be available.[31] Climatic changes will occur with the injection of soot, smoke, and dust into the atmosphere. The degradation of agriculture by temperature change and the destruction of the world's breadbasket in Europe and the United States will cause hundreds of millions, perhaps billions of deaths from starvation. Large amounts of nitric oxide will alter the ozone layer and expose the surviving population of the planet to excessive and harmful ultraviolet radiation. The synergistic effects of ionizing and ultraviolet radiation, trauma, burns, and malnutrition will create an acquired immunodeficiency condition like AIDS in survivors. This condition will augment the spread of exotic infections and may underlie an increased incidence of cancer.[32]

INFORMED CONSENT AND THE NUCLEAR THREAT

In the nuclear age, there are questions more profound and more serious than ever before concerning the conduct and obligations of government, not only towards their own citizens, but also towards all peoples who may be affected by their policies and actions. In this light, an analogy can be drawn between the medical-legal doctrine of informed consent and the conduct of the superpowers, for surely governments have the same responsibility to inform their populations as physicians have to individuals. In the conduct of governmental affairs, informed consent implies that far-reaching actions must be explained: the risks, the potential benefits, the alternatives. The questions to be answered are not alone those of the 'involved' nations, but of all potentially affected nations.

In recent years, the malpractice doctrine has been considerably broadened to include the physician's duty to obtain an informed refusal, to warn third parties, and to notify patients whenever past procedures or treatment are discovered to be potentially harmful or risky.

Applied to the present international situation, this doctrine would mean fully informing the uninvolved world about ecologic effects and the hazardous radioactive fallout that would envelop Europe and other continents if U.S. and U.S.S.R. policies and stockpiles combine to cause global injury. It can hardly be said of the Soviet and American governments that they have systematically attempted to inform their own people fully, let alone those of other nations, of the potential consequences of their actions. Such actions have always been couched in terms of national security, rather than in terms of the extraordinary international insecurity they have produced. Those countries without any voice in major 'defense' decisions have never been adequately informed or given the 'right of refusal'.

Physicians have a responsibility to use appropriate diagnostic tests and to interpret them well. If a doctor makes a misdiagnosis on the basis of negligence, he is liable for malpractice. If the diagnosis of the leaders of the great powers is incorrect, and if the 60,000 nuclear weapons ultimately prove catastrophic to the Northern Hemisphere, there is no court of law in which they can be tried.

Are Nuclear Weapons and Nuclear War Inherently Evil?

Evil—the antithesis of good—may characterize the individual, the group, the society, and their actions. When evil is socialized, individual responsibility dissolves, and we join together in the common effort to destroy. Invariably, we do this with the rationale that good will come of it. Mixing in equal parts wickedness, villainy, decadence, and immorality, the only certainty of evil is that suffering is its inevitable product.

Can weapons be designated as evil? When they threaten to destroy much of the population of the Northern Hemisphere, they cannot be viewed simply as a better alternative to tyranny. We obscure the situation by couching it in terms of the 'better dead than red' construct. The philosopher, Sidney Hook, has attacked the assumption that "the current situation, because of the possibility of a nuclear holocaust, is absolutely unique . . . There is an undoubted element of continuity between nuclear war and World War II." "It is the sheerest dogmatism," says Hook, "to predict that all life and civilization will necessarily be destroyed."[33] How about 50 percent? Or 80 percent? Or 95 percent?

Hook is joined by those who believe we can win or prevail, or even survive. But what is the 'survival' they talk about? Edward

Teller has provided us an explanation. In a recent book, he assailed the "myth of the apocalypse", the myth that a full-scale nuclear war would wipe out mankind.[34] He described the invasion of Persia in 1219 by the armies of Genghis Khan, intent on killing everyone they could find. "Perhaps", he said, "there is no example of greater havoc in human history. Yet at least 10 percent of the Persian population survived." For Teller, the death of 90 percent of the inhabitants of Persia represented "survival". Presumably he would use the same word to describe the extinction of 90 percent of the population of the Northern Hemisphere in a nuclear war.

Of course survival is possible. In a literal sense, the human race, unlike the dinosaurs, will probably inhabit the planet over the next few millennia. In Teller's lexicon, to *survive* is to remain alive. Its meaning is confined to the metabolic life process. The word speaks to duration, to time, but avoids the fabric of living.[35] Species survival does not imply political, social, economic, or psychological survival as we know it today.

When Hook reminds us that "mankind has often paid a heavy cost in defense of freedom," he is talking about the 'just war', which in Augustinian terms, is really the defense of the innocent. But such a war must respect the principles of *proportionality* (no greater force than that required for defense) and *discrimination* (the sparing of the uninvolved, the noncombatants). The use of nuclear weapons, by their very level of destructive power, violates 'just war' principles. The force contained in the arsenals of the nuclear powers today is the equivalent of two thousand pounds of TNT for every man, woman, and child on the planet. Proportionality is thrown out the window. A single megaton bomb can destroy an entire city in seconds to minutes. Discrimination is a mockery. Soldiers may suffer less than the women, children, and all civilians who are the very innocents supposedly being defended.

IS NUCLEAR DETERRENCE MORALLY ACCEPTABLE?

Nuclear war, because it can in no way achieve national objectives, cannot be considered a rational extension of national policy. Nevertheless, as Walzer has pointed out, "we threaten evil in order not to do it, and the doing of it would be so terrible that the threat seems in comparison to be morally defensible."[36] In the dispassionate language of the nuclear strategist, "The purpose of [deterrence] is not, in fact, to destroy the Soviet Union, but rather to avoid the destruction of the United States by having an assured *capability* to destroy the Soviet Union."[37] The same argument is thereby used both to criticize and to defend deterrence. Implicit in this argument is the claim that nuclear deterrence cannot be immoral or evil because the possession of nuclear weapons has kept the peace for 30 to 40 years. Axinn has said that this assertion is as persuasive as holding that if playing Russian roulette thirty times has allowed us to remain in good health, we should continue it.[38]

In fact, the nuclear era has been characterized by some of the bloodiest wars in history, with over a hundred major conflicts since 1945. 'Keeping the peace' really alludes to the absence of direct major hostilities between Russia and the United States during the past 40 years—hardly a persuasive argument, since these two countries have not been adversaries in a major war for hundreds of years. The contention that nuclear weapons have prevented a world war for 40 years implies that the 'normal' interval is 20 years, as between World Wars I and II. But the average time between world wars in the last three hundred and fifty years has been 50 years, without nuclear weapons to keep the peace.[39] Over 1,500 arms races have occurred between 600 B.C.E. and 1960 C.E., and all but ten have led to war. The effectiveness of deterrence as a justification for the massive stockpiles is manifestly an article of faith—neither provable nor disprovable.

The discussion of deterrence is consistently blurred by the confusion of 'moralism' with 'morality'. In distinguishing between the two, Thompson points out that

> Moralism is the tendency to make one moral value supreme and to apply it indiscriminately without regard to time and place. Morality by comparison is the endless quest for what is right amidst the complexity of competing and sometimes conflicting, sometimes compatible moral ends.[40]

Moralism provides the framework for the Cold War: we are the 'shining city on a hill'; they are the 'evil empire'. Deterrence threatens to *punish*, thereby defining the problem as one of good and evil, policeman and law-breaker, rather than one of conflicting ideologies and interests.[41] Deterrence requires a high level of moralism. The potential consequences of 60,000 nuclear weapons can only be justified, in a breath-taking mirror image, by evoking an immutable threat to one's absolute goodness.

The moral question then becomes whether the threat to retaliate constitutes a 'conditional intention' to do so. The credibility of deterrence depends on the willingness to use nuclear weapons. Nevertheless, it is contended that a threat does not imply an intention. In other words, deterrence is just a bluff. A further step in the argument suggests that if deterrence fails, nuclear war can be controlled so that nuclear weapons use might be neither immoral nor evil, because gains would outweigh losses. Using the 'just war' principle of proportionality, maintaining democracy can then be 'appropriately' weighed against the deaths of tens of millions of noncombatants. But once the wall that separates nuclear from conventional weapons is breached, no one can predict the magnitude of the nuclear exchange that will follow. Those who believe that deterrence is a morally sound posture must provide a moral justification for nuclear retaliation.

If the major risk is accidental or inadvertent nuclear war, then the concept and the reality of 'deterrence' obscure the understanding that the annihilatory weapons controlled by complex and fallible systems are the primary adversary. If this combined Soviet-American system is likely to erupt because of the interactions with explosive situations, it should be attacked without regard for the spurious arguments that we must continue to design more lethal and sophisticated components in order to deter.

ARE WE PREPARED TO USE WEAPONS OF ANNIHILATION?

Nuclear weapons, it is said, serve only to deter; they cannot and must not be used, according to some civilian and military authorities. Others see it differently. On November 30, 1950, President Harry Truman, when asked during the Korean War about use of the atomic bomb, replied, "There has always been active consideration of its use."[42] General

Russell Dougherty, commander-in-chief of the Strategic Air Command from 1974 to 1977, stated recently that should "the use of nuclear weapons become necessary to forestall defeat in a vital area, the Command's plans, effectiveness, diversity, and command and control must permit it both to apply decisive weapons to the point where defenses are failing and to be prepared to broaden the conflict against a far wider range of targets."[43]

Is it possible that military personnel might resist orders to unleash weapons of annihilation? Dougherty has said that "the inherent discipline of senior military commanders and nuclear weapons crews is strong enough to ensure their execution of any nuclear launch order."[44] Clearly this is not a discussion of a 'nonusable' and purely 'deterrent' force but rather an acceptance of nuclear weapons as potentially important elements in the military hardware. Policy makers have confirmed this view. "The United States has asserted its willingness to be the first—has indeed made plans to be the first, if necessary—to use nuclear weapons to defend against aggressors in Europe."[45]

We have agreed with Hook that the prediction that *all* life and civilization will *necessarily* be destroyed is unwarranted. But if nuclear winter and nuclear famine combine to cause many billions of deaths, then at least the *possibility* of extinction may warrant consideration. Kateb has argued that any use of nuclear weapons contains the possibility of extinction because it may lead to escalation, or provide precedents for future use. He considers any use a declaration of war against humanity, whether first use or retaliatory. Any use is criminal. He advocates the policy of 'no use'. If those who use nuclear weapons are criminals, Kateb would contend that those who contemplate their use are guilty of criminal intent.[46]

How Did We Get Where We Are?

We must ask ourselves, finally, how did we get here? Was it evil for Fermi and Szilard to work on the nuclear chain reaction, for Oppenheimer and his colleagues at Los Alamos to develop the bomb? Scientific discovery and understanding of natural phenomena have been twin goals of human progress. The bomb was produced in an atmosphere in which the country had been attacked and the Western world was threatened. It was possible, therefore, to argue that under the 'just war' theory the United States moved ahead with the development of the A bomb in self-defense—hence, the act was said to be moral. But with the end of the war, the effort to fabricate even more destructive weapons could not possibly be considered moral.

Questions must be asked of the scientists and engineers who use their brilliance to create biologic weapons, chemical weapons, and new generations of nuclear weapons. Can moral issues be reduced to the matter of 'exciting technical challenges'? Or of 'making a living'? Is that all it is? If the Northern Hemisphere goes up in smoke, who will have been responsible for this irreparable evil? Archbishop Hunthausen of Seattle would say that those of us who paid our taxes to support the production of the weapons were at fault. Bishop Matthiesen of Amarillo, Texas, would say that those who worked in the factories constructing the Trident missiles were engaged in immoral acts.

Where were the rest of us as the nuclear arms race intensified and our countries produced thousands of portable holocausts targeted at our adversaries? We skied in the Rockies. We listened to rock and roll. We read the Bible and *Sophie's Choice*. We pursued the many acts that comprise the garbage of existence: we paid our bills, filled the gas tank, fixed the refrigerator. When did we have time to consider our own complicity in the preparation for annihilation?

Most of us, U.S. and Soviet citizens alike, are following the course of the German people who sat passively by under Hitler or even helped on a journey to oblivion. "Not to act is to act; not to resist is to participate."[47] Can we state unequivocally that indifference to evil—passivity—is evil? Is it more or less evil than active evil? These are questions that we must ask ourselves and we must answer for ourselves.

How did it happen? It happened because we let it happen. Can we prevent the ultimate use of these weapons? Only if we try.

In 1923, a great Czechoslovak playwright—Karel Capek—wrote a prophetic play called *RUR*[m] 'Rossum's Universal Robots'. At some time in the future, the Rossum Factory had manufactured hundreds of thousands, even millions, of "living automats, without soul, desires, feelings, good for nothing but work". Ultimately, a world revolt of robots took place, with the death of all but one of their human masters. Man's creation—the machine—had destroyed and replaced man.

Capek, broadcasting on Czech radio at the time of the Nazi invasion of Czechoslovakia, shot and killed himself as the robotic tanks moved across the border, and the Germans used the technology they had created to overrun his beloved homeland. The nuclear weapons that we have designed and built on the basis of our scientific brilliance and technologic innovation threaten to accomplish in life what Rossum's robots were able to do in theater.

The religious among us might hold that nuclear war would represent the final sacrilege, the most vicious attack on God's creation, man. This small planet in the vastness of the universe—perhaps the only one that supports life as we know it—is uniquely threatened.

A great American, himself a central progenitor of modern technology, once said, "There will one day spring from the brain of science a machine or force so fearful in its potentialities, so absolutely terrifying that even man the fighter, who will dare torture and death in order to inflict torture and death, will be appalled, and so will abandon war altogether. What man's mind can create, man's character can control."

Was Thomas Alva Edison expressing an authentic conviction, or a groundless wish?

RESPONSE TO HERBERT ABRAMS

Frank Vandiver

Frank E. Vandiver was the nineteenth president of Texas A&M University at the time of the symposium. He is now Director of the Mosher Institute for Defense Studies. A Ph.D. graduate of Tulane University, he has been a Rockefeller and a Guggenheim fellow. He is a member of the Secretary of the Navy's Advisory Board on Education and Technology and of the Board of Visitors of the

U.S. Air Force Air University. He has been a professor of history at Washington University (St. Louis, Missouri), Rice University, Oxford University, and the United States Military Academy (West Point, New York). He has been provost, vice-president, and acting president of Rice University, and president of North Texas State University. Vandiver has been president of the Southern Historical Association, Texas Institute of Letters, Philosophical Society of Texas, and Bicentennial Association of Texas. Among his books are *Mighty Stonewall, Their Tattered Flags: The Epic of the Confederacy*, and *Black Jack: The Life and Times of John J. Pershing*.

"War *is* Hell", as Herbert Abrams has so eloquently reminded us. William Tecumseh Sherman made that observation during a graduation address at Michigan Military Academy.[48] Abrams's writings, from both a professional and a political viewpoint, graphically detail the particular horrors of nuclear war.

The photographs and, of course, the statistics from Hiroshima and Nagasaki have had profound effects on the collective psyche of much of the world's population. I submit that likewise the photographs, and yes the statistics, of the Holocaust, shamed the civilized world.

General Sherman was right. War is Hell. From Mycenae to My Lai, human beings have committed unspeakable evils on one another in the name of war. Yes, the instruments of war have changed dramatically through the ages, but the purpose of those instruments has changed very little. For support of this construct, I would call on no less an authority than Plato, who believed that change is characteristic only of the physical world—in the world of ideas, all things remain eternally the same.

It is, of course, true that a person is no less dead if he is disembowelled by a spear than if he happens to be in the wrong place when his ship takes a direct hit from a Silkworm missile.

Wars have been fought for varied reasons—for freedom, for religion, for territory, for honor, for revenge, for survival (which, on the surface, appears to be an oxymoron), for riches, for glory, and by mistake. For whatever reason, the act of making war somehow unleashes a primeval urge not only to kill, but also to kill in ways that are particularly brutal. It is as if the act of declaring war somehow grants a license to behave in a manner contrary to what we all believe is civilized. People go to war with the authority of their country behind them, and in the heat of the moment, violate what they thought were firmly held values. As history goes, it is only fairly recently that common folk have been involved in warfare. Wars formerly were waged by the aristocracy. Honor and custom among gentlemen dictated the rules of war. Today there are laws as well as customs for waging war. Trials for war crimes are almost entirely a product of the twentieth century.

Yet I think we can all agree that some causes are noble, worth giving freely of our own blood. Through the ages, we would defend the morality of doing battle to protect our families, our homes, and those beliefs and values that we hold inviolate. To be a bit more specific, we are here today in Salado, Texas, because wars were thought to be worth fighting in Trenton, at San Jacinto, and perhaps at Guadalcanal and Argonne.

Is the concept of *justum bellum*, or 'just war', valid? My American and Texan heritage tells me that it is just for a people to go to war for the right to decide their own destiny. I believe it is just for a country to defend its borders and people as the United States did in the Pacific during World War II.

The 'just war' theory has Augustinian origins. As restated in 1983 by the United States Catholic bishops, a 'just war' must meet several criteria: be absolutely necessary, waged by a competent authority, use comparative justice (that is, only such force as is necessary), fought with the right intentions, begun only after peaceful means of settlement have been exhausted, have some probability of success, and the costs incurred be proportionate to the expected good.[49] Catholic tradition has also affirmed the solidarity of the family of nations—that is, the obligation for the nations as a whole to fulfill their duty not to abandon a nation that is attacked.

That, my friends, is an extensive and exacting list. I suggest that the United States War of Independence and Worlds Wars I and II meet these criteria. Our wars against the Indian nations of our own continent do not. The Indian wars were waged by a competent authority and, with regard to the military aspect, had a high probability of success. But who among us would dare defend, on any grounds whatsoever, the intentional use of germ warfare—in this case, pox-infected blankets—against native Americans?

As examples of 'just wars', one might mention some of the small wars or conflicts of Queen Victoria's reign; however, since these wars were colonial, examples from that era would meet the proportionality criterion only in the short run.

As an academic exercise, one could examine the annals of war through the ages, placing the combatants on either side of a demarcation line with one side labeled 'just' and the other 'unjust'. Presumably, the wars waged by Nazis and Spartans, who had much in common, would be considered among the unjust.

Abrams's writings have focused on future wars. He concludes (and although this is my interpretation, I have no doubt he would agree) that present war instruments dictate that no war employing these instruments can ever be considered 'just'. That is a subject of considerable discussion among philosophers on the one hand, and an international political debate on the other.

The announced subject of this conference, however, is understanding evil. If we can all accept the premiss that evil can be perpetrated both against individuals as well as against humanity in the abstract, allow me to offer a historical example.

Between 1600 and 1200 B.C.E., the city of Mycenae flourished in Greece. The Mycenaeans were accomplished and enterprising. They were the descendants of the Minoans, whose homes had plumbing—even flush toilets. The Mycenaeans themselves were spectacular builders. They were immensely wealthy and their goldsmiths were superb. Their society included shipwrights and surgeons, bakers and bureaucrats. They developed a script writing, known today by archaeologists as Linear B.

A principal Mycenaean business seems to have been war. Their civilization ended when they were obliterated by successive invasions of Dorians. The few Mycenaeans who lived were driven out of their city and scattered. The Dorians occupied burned-out Mycenae, but they did not rebuild the city; rather, they lived as squatters. The civilization vanished, and the art of writing disappeared. The Dark Age of Greece that followed lasted for several hundred years. As described by Hesiod, who lived at the end of the Dark Age, it was a time of violence and brutality, intolerance and indifference, stealing, cheating, and lying.[50] In short, what was left of society was evil. We can perhaps take some comfort from our knowledge of what followed.

I offer this not as a justification of Evil, but rather as historical evidence that humankind eventually rises above it. Is war evil? Sometimes. Is war ever justified? Of course. Are evil acts committed, even in a just war? Certainly. So, where does this leave us? We have come full circle, back to General Sherman. "War is Hell."

NOTES

[1] Herbert L. Abrams, 'The Problem of Accidental or Inadvertent Nuclear War', *Preventive Medicine*, 16 (1987), 319–333. p. 319.

[2] Richard Halloran, 'U.S. Discloses 5 Accidents Involving Nuclear Weapons', *New York Times* (May 26, 1981).

[3] Milton Leitenberg, 'Accidents of Nuclear Weapons Systems', In: Stockholm International Peace Research Institute (Ed.), *SIPRI Yearbook of World Armaments and Disarmament, 1977* (Cambridge, Mass,: MIT Press, 1977), p. 53.

[4] Stephen Talbot, 'The H-Bomb Next Door', *The Nation* (February 7, 1981), p. 147.

[5] Herbert L. Abrams, 'The Problem of Accidental or Inadvertent Nuclear War', *Maintain Life on Earth!*, documentation of the Sixth World Congress of the International Physicians for the Prevention of Nuclear War in Cologne, May 29 to June 1, 1986. K. Bonhoeffer and D. Gerecke (eds.) Jungjohann Verlagsgesellschaft Neckarsulm und Müchen, West Germany, 1987), pp. 180–183.

[6] Daniel Frei, *Risks of Unintentional Nuclear War* (Totowa, NJ: Rowan and Allenheld, 1983), pp. 161–163.

[7] Lloyd Dumas, 'National Insecurity in the Nuclear Age', *Bulletin of the Atomic Scientists*, 32 (May 1976), pp. 24–35. p. 28.

[8] U.S. Congress, House. 1982. *Drug Abuse in the Military*. Department of Defense Appropriations for 1983. Hearing before the Subcommittee on Appropriations. Part 3. 97th Congress, 2nd session, pp. 253–444. April 1, 1984 (Washington, D.C.: U.S. Government Printing Office), p. 281.

[9] Herbert L. Abrams, 'Sources of Human Instability in the Handling of Nuclear Weapons', *The Medical Implications of Nuclear War*. Institute of Medicine-National Academy of Sciences (Washington, D.C.: National Academy Press, 1986). pp. 520–522.

[10] Herbert L. Abrams, 'Who's Minding the Missiles?' *The Sciences*, 26 (July–August 1986), pp. 22–28. p. 24.

[11] Department of Defense, Office of the Secretary of Defense. Calendar Year Ending December 31, 1975, 1976, 1977. Annual Disqualification Report, Nuclear Weapons Personnel Reliability Program. RCS DD-COMP(A) 1403. Washington, DC; and Department of Defense, Office of the Secretary of Defense. Calendar Year Ending December 31, 1978, 1979, 1980, 1981, 1982, 1983, 1984. Annual Status Report, Nuclear Weapons Personnel Reliability Program. RCS DD-POL(A) 1403. Washington, D.C.

[12] Marvin R. Burt, 'Prevalence and Consequences of Drug Abuse Among U.S. Military Personnel: 1980', *American Journal of Drug and Alcohol Abuse*, 8.4 (1981–82), 419–439. p. 425.

[13] *Ibid*, p. 431.

[14] Herbert L. Abrams, 'Human Instability and Nuclear Weapons', *Bulletin of the Atomic Scientists*, 43.1 (January-February 1987), pp. 34–39.

[15] Jerome D. Frank, *Sanity & Survival: Psychological Aspects of War and Peace* (New York: Random House, 1967), p. 61.

[16] Dwight D. Eisenhower, *The White House Years: Mandate for Change, 1953–1956*. (Garden City, NY: Doubleday, 1963), p. 545.

[17] U.S. Congress, Senate Committee on Armed Services. 'Recent False Alerts From the Nation's Missile Attack Warning System.' Report prepared by Senators Barry Goldwater and Gary Hart (Washington, D.C.: U.S. Government Printing Office, October 9, 1980), pp. 4, 5.

[18] Philip C. Bobbitt, 'Communications Failures: Discussion', Hilliard Roderick, (Ed.) in *Avoiding Inadvertent War: Crisis Management* (The Lyndon B. Johnson School of Public Affairs, University of Texas, 1983), p. 51.

[19] Charles Perrow, *Normal Accidents: Living with High Risk Technologies* (New York: Basic Books, 1984), p. 62–100.

[20] Paul Bracken, *The Command and Control of Nuclear Forces* (New Haven: Yale University Press, 1983), p. 54.

[21] Walter Pincus, 'Congress and Tactical Nukes', *New Republic* (October 12, 1974), pp. 19–20.

[22] 'Demonstrators Criticize Security at Missile Plant', *New York Times* (April 24, 1984).

[23] Nuclear Control Institute. Issue Brief. 'The Use of Atom Bomb Material in Civilian Research Reactors' (February 1984).

[24] U.S. Congress. Office of Technology Assessment. *Nuclear Proliferation and Safeguards* (New York: Praeger, 1977).

[25] Alexander L. George, 'The Impact of Crisis-Induced Stress on Decision Making', *The Medical Implications of Nuclear War*. Institute of

Medicine-National Academy of Sciences (Washington D.C.: National Academy Press, 1986), pp. 529–552.

[26] Irving L. Janis, *Groupthink: Psychological Studies of Policy Decisions and Fiascoes*, 2nd edition (Boston: Houghton Mifflin, 1983).

[27] Herbert L. Abrams, 'Summary and Perspective: With Some Observations on Informed Consent', *The Medical Implications of Nuclear War*. Institute of Medicine-National Academy of Sciences (Washington, D.C.: National Academy Press, 1986), pp. 583–588.

[28] Herbert L. Abrams, 'Chernobyl: How Radiation Victims Suffer', *Bulletin of the Atomic Scientists*, 43.1 (August–September 1986), pp. 13–17.

[29] Herbert L. Abrams, 'The Fire Next Time', *The Rotarian*, 141.5 (November 1982), pp. 14–15.

[30] Herbert L. Abrams and William E. Von Kaenel, 'Medical Problems of Survivors of Nuclear War: Infection and the Spread of Communicable Disease', *New England Journal of Medicine*, 305 (1981), pp. 1230–1231. See also Herbert L. Abrams, 'Infection and Communicable Diseases', in Ruth Adams and Susan Cullen (eds.), *The Final Epidemic: Physicians and Scientists on Nuclear War* (Chicago: Educational Foundation for Nuclear Science, 1981), pp. 192–218; and Herbert L. Abrams, 'Survivors of Nuclear War: Infection and the Spread of Disease', in Eric Chivian *et al.* (eds.), *Last Aid: The Medical Dimensions of Nuclear War*. (San Francisco: W.H. Freeman, 1982), pp. 211–233.

[31] Herbert L. Abrams, 'Medical Resources After Nuclear War: Availability vs. Need', *Journal of the American Medical Association*, 252 (1984), pp. 653–658.

[32] David S. Greer and Lawrence S. Rifkin, 'The Immunological Impact of Nuclear Warfare', *The Medical Implications of Nuclear War*. Institute of Medicine-National Academy of Sciences (Washington, D.C.: National Academy Press, 1986), pp. 317–328.

[33] Sidney Hook, *Out of Step: An Unquiet Life in the 20th Century/Sidney Hook* (New York: Harper & Row, 1987), p. 576.

[34] Edward Teller, *The Pursuit of Simplicity* (Malibu, CA: Pepperdine University Press, 1980), p. 136.

[35] Herbert L. Abrams, 'Surviving a Nuclear War is Hardly Surviving', *The New York Times* (February 27, 1983), p. E 18.

[36] Michael Walzer, *Just and Unjust Wars: A Moral Argument with Historical Allusions* (New York: Basic Books, 1977), p. 274.

[37] Richard Garwin, 'Launch Under Attack to Redress Minuteman Vulnerability?' *International Security*, 4.3 (Winter 1979), pp. 117–139, p. 118.

[38] Sidney Axinn, 'Honor, Patriotism, and Ultimate Loyalty', Avner Cohen and Steven Lee (eds.), *Nuclear Weapons and the Future of Humanity: The Fundamental Questions*. (Totowa, N.J.: Rowman and Allanheld, 1986), p. 286.

[39] Gwynn Dwyer, 'The Nuclear Dilemma', Paper presented at the Seventh Annual Congress of International Physicians for the Prevention of Nuclear War in Moscow, May 26–June 1, 1987.

[40] Kenneth W. Thompson, *Moralism and Morality in Politics and Diplomacy* (New York: University Press of America, 1985), p. 5.

[41] Michael MacGuire, 'The Insidious Dogma of Deterrence', *Bulletin of the Atomic Scientists*, 42.10 (December 1986), pp. 24–29.

[42] Harry S. Truman, *Public Papers of the Presidents of the United States: Harry Truman, 1950* (Washington, D.C.: Office of the Federal Register, National Archives and Records Service, 1965), p. 727. For news account, see 'Truman Gives Aim', *New York Times* (Dec. 1, 1950), p. 1.

[43] Russell E. Dougherty, 'The Psychological Climate of Nuclear Command', in Ashton B. Carter, John D. Steinbruner, and Charles A. Zraket (eds.), *Managing Nuclear Operations* (Washington, D.C.: The Brookings Institution, 1987), p. 418.

[44] *Ibid.*, p. 417.

[45] McGeorge Bundy, George F. Kennan, Robert S. McNamara, and Gerard Smith, 'Nuclear Weapons and the Atlantic Alliance', *Foreign Affairs*, 60.4 (Spring 1982), pp. 753–768, p. 754, 757.

[46] George Kateb, 'Nuclear Weapons and Individual Rights', *Dissent* 33.2 (Spring 1986), pp. 161–172.

[47] Hartmut M. Hanauske-Abel, 'From Nazi Holocaust to Nuclear Holocaust: A Lesson to Learn', *The Lancet* (2 August 1986), pp. 271–273.

[48] William Tecumseh Sherman, attributed to a graduation address at Michigan Military Academy, in Emily Morison Bech *et. al.*, (eds.), *Familiar Quotations, John Bartlett* (Boston: Little Brown 1980), p. 579.

[49] National Conference of Catholic Bishops, 'Challenge of Peace: God's Promise and Our Response. A Pastoral Letter on War and Peace' (Washington, D.C., U.S. Catholic Conference, 1983).

[50] Hesiod. *Works and Days*, lines 172 ff.

PART III

THE PARADOX OF HOPE

1

TAI JI

Chungliang Al Huang

Chungliang Al Huang is founder-president of the Living Tao Foundation in Urbana, Illinois, and in Basel, Switzerland; he is also the director of the Lan Ting Institute, an international cross-cultural, interdisciplinary study and conference center (at Wu Yi Mountain in the People's Republic of China). He is a Tai Ji master, brush calligraphic painter, and bamboo flute player. He was a Ford Foundation research scholar, a visiting professor at the College of Chinese Culture, a doctoral research fellow at the Academia Sinica, and a fellow of the World Academy of Arts and Sciences. He is author of *Embrace Tiger, Return to Mountain: The Essence of Tai Ji, Living Tao: Still Visions and Dancing Brushes, Tao: The Watercourse Way* (with Alan Watts), and *Quantum Soup: A Philosophical Entertainment*.

[Chungliang Al Huang's presentation combined flute playing, Tai Ji dancing and a great deal of body movement and facial expressions. The words we have transcribed here are only a partial statement of his contribution to the symposium.]

I think many of you probably feel as I do now—almost on the verge of tears. Our first instinct is to control the tears, to try to think through our emotions, to be logical and to overcome this feeling—but I refuse to suppress this human spontaneity. I will stay with my feeling and I will continue with the natural process of my feeling.

I was devastated by the picture Herbert Abrams painted in his talk. I was even more devastated later. I was outraged, because I wanted this Earth to stay beautiful for us. I love this Earth. I love all the people on this Earth. And inside of me is this rage that something's happening that we are not stopping. We are ignoring the 'evil' of destruction. I also think it is important for all of us to deal with what Maya Angelou was talking about: 'the big bugaboo'—death. And there is no exit or escape.

Perhaps I can make a small contribution to all these concerns. I grew up in China. China is my motherland. My thoughts, my thinking, my being is basically Chinese, even though I've lived in America and all over Europe for the past 30 years. I am Chinese. China is me. I have been going back and forth from China in the past seven years since China opened her doors to the West. And since I represent the minority in this conference, I feel almost responsible to share with you some of China and the essence of the East.

I think it is very important to realize that so often we talk about opposition, dualism: black and white, love and hate, good and evil. I am now trying to communicate with you in English; it is something very strange to me still when I use English to talk about dualism, because in Chinese we don't really have duality. All of you know the words *yin* and *yang*. The 'and' has been put in by translation. In Chinese we only say *yinyang*, as one complete unified expression. There is no such thing as 'and' in between. The language itself combines, and is constructed with, wholeness in mind. Chinese is a picture language, a language of process, of the unconscious, a language about being.

I feel the Chinese language is more universal than any other language, and it is not as difficult as some of you think. I will show you why. The only trouble for many of you who try to learn Chinese is that you try to translate it into your language. And the minute you make the translation you put the 'and' in, and you create dualism. Suddenly it is no longer Chinese.

A perfect example is the word, *hsing*. We only have one word for both mind and heart, rather than two separate words. Hsing is both heart and mind. I have been listening to all of us talking together in English. Mostly we say 'I think', 'you think', 'we think'. Maybe it is the word 'think' that we associate with the mind—that's the small mind. The big 'M' Mind must combine with the heart. As we think, if we include 'we feel', 'we sense', 'we live', 'we rage', and 'we are', then we are thinking in Tai Ji. Perhaps Tai Ji is not the answer, but definitely an alternative to all the confused thoughts.

I would like to show you Tai Ji. I was fortunate enough as a child in China every morning simply going out of the house waking up with other Chinese, to learn Tai Ji through osmosis.

One of the sights those of you who have travelled to China will probably never forget, is witnessing hundreds of people doing Tai Ji on the street, everywhere. Every morning, everybody is out there doing something physical in nature, and spiritually doing something relating to other than the small 'little me' ego. You see people in the park circling their arms, meditating in front of the trees, feeling the juice of life going through their bodies just like trees. You see people feeling their whole bodies vibrating, waking up with nature, with life all round. Very simple philosophy. Chinese are pragmatic. When you get up in the morning—*wake up*. Otherwise, don't bother.

One of my Zen poet friends in San Francisco used to tell me that every morning when he woke up he would look into the bathroom mirror and say, "I don't know who you are, but I'm going to shave you!" We spend so much time each day fixing ourselves up. Men shave. Women put on makeup. We worry about fixing ourselves up externally, but we don't take enough time to really wake up, to find out what's inside of this face, this body, because we think we have no time for it. We've got to rush to work. But we are not awake. We end up wasting a lot of time. It's a whole nonsense of imbalance. We separate work and play, we separate inside and outside, we separate light and dark, sky and earth, outer space and home. We do too much of that.

We forget that the body is wise and is continually enlightened, if we trust it. Instead, we pump up muscles for more power and control. We learn superimposed 'fancy steps', going to endless lessons to end up looking more unnatural and awkward. We don't trust simple, organic, everyday movement—which can be so beautiful—because we are out of touch with this simple beauty. I hope you will trust me, to experience with me, to regain your own trust in yourself, and regain the dance in all of you. In my view, a big evil is to stop utilizing our full human potential—our creativity, our beauty and our bodily aliveness. That's a shame; that's an evil.

Try this. Reach up and down with alternating arms. You can introduce heaven and earth together inside your body. And when you realize heaven and earth take a fancy with each other and decide it's a nice marriage—love at the first sight—that's when Tai Ji happens inside you. When you bring the two primal forces together, a real unifying dance begins within. You have the fire of life. You begin to dance.

And try this. Cross and open your arms in front of you. We open our eyes and we enlarge our vision. A very simple gesture. Every child does that. Peek-a-boo! Surprise! Now you see it. Now you don't. Now you see it again—a different sight. Delightful surprise.

Truth often hides within us. We are often looking in the wrong place where we miss the truth right under our nose. Open our arms, open our hearts and minds. Look one more time. But, often people say, 'just another lousy sunset. I have seen it. No. You again. I know you . . . ' No more surprises. Our heart closes, our mind closes. We become small human beings. And when an individual becomes internally small, he or she turns evil. But when we continue to open our eyes, open our spirit, there is no chance evil can breed. We can also influence others to open up. Let's all open. This time, let's say 'another lousy sunset in paradise!' Of course you have seen a sunset, but this time it is different. It is always different.

Sir Laurens van der Post talked about people "running amok" out of a sense of meaninglessness, a sense of despair. We can take care of that through spending more time to nurture beauty, and this excitement of being alive, or being who I am and who you are. It is such a shame that we spend too much time worrying about meaningless rhetorics—the dry and abstract philosophy of cerebral questions floating in the stratosphere. We need to come down to earth, to this earthbody and come to our good commonsenses.

True Tai Ji dancing is the aliveness of your spirit, your life's daily practice. And all variations are accepted and encouraged, depending on who you are and how you wish to begin. You will get better and better. And you will enjoy Tai Ji more and more and more. And you will finally, truly, totally and completely believe that you are a Tai Ji dancer. So, make that promise not only to me, which is a nice honor, but to yourself. Yes?

Finally I would like to share with you something quite uplifting. I won't have time to go into details about my China experiences. It's wonderful. It has been my homecoming. And the more I return to China, the more I feel I belong to the world. There is so much to do, to bring the essence of China to all of you in the world.

Last year being the International Year of the Peace, the popular Chinese singers, one hundred and eight of them, came together to record a song in Beijing, inspired by the American song, 'We Are the World'. It was the Chinese singers' gift to world peace. It became the sensational hit of the season. It still is. No wonder; the title of the song is 'Let the World Be Filled With Love'. In the introduction of the song, we hear this:

> This world does not lack sunshine and fresh air.
> The good earth with wind and rain.
> So many years we have searched
> painstakingly for genuine fellowship
> Love and faith in one another.
> Where is the goodwill?
> Hiding in our hearts and our minds?
> We, one hundred and eight of us
> coming from every corner of this vast
> continent of China, together
> we offer you this strong voice.
> A song deals with our blood and tears.
> We wish to penetrate into your hearts
> and circulate our warm love in your very veins.
> We wish you warmth, we wish you love.
> Come, let us join in to sing together as
> we walk into the sunshine, into the future . . .

[As the song was being played, Chungliang Al Huang invited all of the conference participants to dance with him. Everyone joined in the celebration of joy and peace on earth.]

2

COMMENTARY:
THE GUISES OF EVIL

Betty Sue Flowers

Betty Sue Flowers is associate professor of English and director of the Plan II Liberal Arts Honors Program at the University of Texas at Austin. A Ph.D. of the University of London, she has worked in public relations and as a TV announcer. In 1982, she participated in the PBS series *Six Great Ideas*. She won the Holloway Teaching Award at the University of Texas in 1983. She is author of *Browning and the Modern Tradition*, co-author of *Four Shields of Power*, editor of *The Power of Myth*, and co-editor of *Daughters and Fathers*.

When I came to Salado on Friday, I wondered when the subject of evil would first come up, when I would hear the first mention of it—in what context? I didn't have long to wait. At dinner, Jane Wilmer said, "The telephone is the invention of the Devil." The seminar had started. Gathered together here as we try to understand evil, the Stagecoach Inn marquee proclaims to passers-by: "Understanding Evil".

I keep thinking about that telephone—technology, distance, our dependence on machines. During Herbert Abrams's thoughtful and sobering lecture, there flashed on the screen that image of the malfunctioning computer chip—no bigger than a dime—that could very nearly have caused World War III. I wondered, could the Hitler of the twenty-first century be a chip? I know we're told that chips don't kill people; people kill people, or perhaps indifference or inattention do. But Evil often comes in the guise of the ordinary. When the telephone rang in the midst of Jeffrey Russell's sensitive talk about the Evil One, I thought, "Isn't that just like the Devil, to come unexpectedly in the guise of the ordinary, of the banal, in the banality of an Eichmann, (as Hannah Arendt might say)?"

Thomas Merton said that what worried him about Eichmann was not Eichmann's banality but his sanity. The psychologists found Eichmann to be a very sane man. I think of those fifty thousand nuclear weapons workers relieved of their duties for being unfit. But what about the rest: the ones that are still there—the sane ones? In his 'Devout Meditation on the Memory of Adolf Eichmann', Merton says, "We rely on the sane people of the world to preserve it from barbarism, madness, destruction. And now it begins to dawn on us that it is precisely the *sane* ones who are the most dangerous. . ."[1]

What makes us so sure, after all, that the danger comes from a psychotic getting into a position to fire the first shot in a nuclear war? Psychotics will be suspect. The sane ones will keep them far from the button. No one suspects the sane, and the sane ones will have *perfectly good reasons*, logical, well-adjusted reasons, for firing the shot. They will be obeying sane orders that have come sanely down the chain of command. . . We can no longer assume that because a man is 'sane' he is therefore in his 'right mind'. The whole concept of sanity in a society where spiritual values have lost their meaning is itself meaningless. "Resist not evil", we are told, "but overcome evil with good."

But, says Philip Hallie, Hitler could not have been overcome by good, only by force—only by our becoming murderers ourselves, "decent murderers". I think to myself, however, what if all the villages of Europe had disarmed the Nazis with love?

It was too late for Hitler, says Hallie; maybe if his mother or father had loved him. The sins of the fathers and mothers are visited upon the children, even unto the ninth generation. Man's inhumanity to man arises in part from man's inhumanity to children, and to women.

Man, woman; white, black; good, evil—we Westerners tend to think in terms of these dichotomies, these dualisms. When you have duality, you also have, or tend to have, hierarchy. Male over female; White over Black; Good over Evil—and the lower, inferior ones can be banished to the unconscious, to the neglected and despised shadow side of our life in the sun. When we have become conscious of this shadow side of ourselves, when we have given it a local habitation and a name—maybe even personified it as the Devil—then we can begin to understand it.

Could it be that we have something to learn from the Devil? In the *Book of Job*, even God listens to the Devil; and in doing so, Jung suggests that God is listening to himself. *Devil* and *Divine* come from the same root word after all: *deva*—God.

The poet William Blake wrote a marvelous book called *The Marriage of Heaven and Hell*. I'll read what the Devil says in it: As you listen, think of Philip Hallie talking about the importance of the concrete and think, too, of all the bodies whose lives we're prepared to sacrifice for ideals. Here is the voice of the Devil from Blake's *Marriage of Heaven and Hell*:

> All Bibles or sacred codes have been the causes of the following errors:—
>
> 1. That Man has two real existing principles—viz. a Body and a Soul.
> 2. That Energy, call'd Evil, is alone from the Body; and that Reason, call'd Good, is alone from the Soul.
> 3. That God will torment Man in Eternity for following his Energies.
>
> But the following Contraries to these are True:—
>
> 1. Man has no Body distinct from his Soul; for that call'd Body is a portion of Soul discern'd by the five Senses, the chief inlets of Soul in this age.
> 2. Energy is the only life, and is from the Body, and Reason is the bound or outward circumference of Energy.
> 3. Energy is Eternal Delight.[2]

I think back to my arrival on Friday, and I'm astounded now on Sunday morning to realize how much of our talk has been about joy, courage, creativity, love. Scott Peck defines 'love' as the will to extend oneself for the purpose of nurturing one's own, or another's, spiritual growth. I think Peck is right about that definition as he is about so much else in *The Road Less Traveled*.[3] After this book, he wrote *People of the Lie* which has a very thought-provoking chapter on the massacre at My Lai.[4] Recently he's written a book about community.[5] Love, evil, community—there's a progression there worth paying attention to.

Let me end by telling you about a young woman who came up to me after class one day. We had read Peck's chapter on My

Lai, we'd studied Stanley Milgrim's devastating experiment on obedience (in which people give electrical shocks to each other in obedience to orders)[6] and we'd just seen a film called the 'The War Game'. This young woman came up to me with tears in her eyes and she said, "Why have you told me about these things? You have destroyed my happiness. You had no right to do that."

Well, maybe she had a point. The attempt to understand evil does destroy a certain kind of innocent happiness because it's true, I think, that not only is evil within us, but we are also vulnerable to the evil in others. In this age now, it is literally the case that we must "love one another or die". In *The Courage to Create*, Rollo May quotes part of a wonderful poem by Marianne Moore, which begins:

> What is our innocence,
> what is our guilt? All are
>   naked, none is safe. And whence
> is courage?

Moore ends the poem with this image:

> The very bird,
>   grown taller as he sings,
> steels his form straight up. Though he is captive,
> his mighty singing
> says, 'Satisfaction is a lowly
> thing, how pure a thing is joy.
>   This is mortality,
>   this eternity.'[7]

NOTES

[1] Thomas Merton, 'A Devout Meditation in Memory of Adolf Eichmann', *Raids on the Unspeakable* (New York: New Directions, 1966), pp. 45–49.

[2] William Blake, 'The Voice of the Devil', *The Marriage of Heaven and Hell* (1790). In *The Poetical Works of William Blake*. London: Oxford University Press, 1913, p. 248.

[3] M. Scott Peck, *The Road Less Traveled* (New York: Simon & Schuster, 1980).

[4] M. Scott Peck, *People of the Lie: The Hope for Healing Human Evil* (New York: Simon & Schuster, 1983).

[5] M. Scott Peck, *A Different Drum: Community Making and Peace* (New York: Simon & Schuster, 1987).

[6] Stanley Milgrim, 'Behavioral Study of Obedience', *Journal of Abnormal and Social Psychology*, 67.4 (1963), pp. 371–78.

[7] Marianne Moore, *The Complete Poems of Marianne Moore* (New York: Macmillan, 1967), p. 95.

3

HEALING INSTITUTIONAL EVIL

M. Scott Peck

M. Scott Peck is a psychotherapist, author, and lecturer. He received the 1984 Kaleidoscope Award for peacemaking given by Creative Ministry Associates of Durham, North Carolina. He earned his M.D. from Case Western Reserve University. He is the author of *The Road Less Traveled*, *People of the Lie: The Hope for Healing Human Evil*, *What Return Can I Make? The Dimensions of the Christian Experience*, and *The Different Drum: Community Making and Peace*.

The subject of Evil is huge, difficult to come to grips with, and almost impossible. It is inherent in the nature of Evil that it is a many-headed kind of monster. The process of dealing with it will be like peace keeping: an ongoing one, forever and ever dealing with all the different heads.

What I'm going to talk about is the healing of corporate evil in the United States. Because the subject is so large I'm not going to talk about individual evil; I'm going to restrict myself to corporate evil. By *corporate*, I do not mean a business corporation, I mean a body—the evil that occurs in bodies of human beings in institutions. I think this problem of corporate evil is far greater than the problem of individual evil. As the Berrigans have said, perhaps the greatest problem that we have is to figure out, somehow, how to exorcise our institutions. It is this bland, nameless institutional evil that I am talking about.

I am talking about it in the United States, for several reasons. One is that I do not know enough about other cultures to be able to talk about evil in those cultures. I know only in depth about my own. I do this also because, as Tolkien said, "It is our task to till the fields that we know." Healing, like the charity it requires, begins at home. And so it begins with the United States, and it begins here in this room. As so many speakers before me have continually tried to point out—the solution resides with us. After some two-and-a-half years working in Washington, I can tell you that the world is one whole hell of a lot more likely to be saved from Salado than it is from Washington. It's not going to come down from there; it's going to come up from here.

As Herbert Abrams pointed out, we are all involved, all of us, in the arms race, in the evil of that arms race, and, yes, in the insanity of that arms race. (The arms race is insane. Should we have time in the question-and-answer period, I would be happy to document it. Just let me say that as a psychiatrist, I have the credentials to make that diagnosis—it is insane.) We all participate in it, not only with our taxes, but also with our naiveté. We think that the people in Washington know what they are doing. They do not know what they're doing. In our naiveté, we think that Americans are well-meaning people, when the fact of the matter is that there are hundreds of thousands, perhaps even millions, of Americans who want war. They don't necessarily want a nuclear war. They don't necessarily want to lose their lives. But they like war for one reason or another, including the fact that they profit economically from it. There are huge lobbies in this country that want to maintain the arms race. And it's not just the arms race. Of course, this many-headed monster can pop up all over and there are so many aspects to it. One that was just touched upon was this reactive kind of self-defense.

Evil is a disease. As an old priest friend of mine said, it is the ultimate disease. To treat a disease, we have to understand its causes. There are evil people, but they are in a very small minority. We're talking about perhaps no more than one percent of the population, if that. People get confused about the difference between sin and evil. We are all sinners. In fact, the only prerequisite I know for membership in the true Christian church is that you be a sinner. If you're not a sinner, you ought to leave and come back when you realize that you are one. We are all sinners. However, all sins are redeemable except the sin of refusing to acknowledge that you can make a sin. That is what evil is. Evil is not simply sin. At its root is the sin of refusing to acknowledge that you've sinned.

In talking about corporate evil, institutional evil, I am talking about the evil not that one percent of the people cause, but in which 100 percent of us ordinary sinners participate through our everyday sins. In coming to terms with the causes of evil, we must ask: what are those sins? They are so many that I can't even begin to go through all of them. One we've just mentioned, this instinctive kind of thoughtless self-defense: animalistic self-defense that we have not overcome.

Running quickly through some others, you may remember that in 1978, Aleksandr Solzhenitsyn was invited to give the commencement address at Harvard.[1] To everybody's dismay, instead of poking the finger at Russia, he poked the finger at the United States. He listed six or more very telling sins of the American public. One he referred to as legalism: If it's legal, it's okay—go ahead and do it. Forget about whether it's ethical or nice; if it's legal, go ahead and do it. Another that he pointed to is the failure of courage on the part of the American people. This failure relates also to the whole self-defense issue: that we don't have the courage sometimes to drop our defenses.

Another sin is politeness. I told Maya Angelou, "I'm glad you're gonna keep us honest here" when she said, "Bring it back in the room. Don't talk about the Holocaust. Bring it in here."

I said, "It's easier for you to do that because you're Black, Maya, and everybody knows that you've got reasons to be angry and enraged. You've got a kind of right to speak up. You're a minority anyway; we'll forgive you for all that."

But for us WASPs, that's a much different thing. We're raised to be polite, even if we might stab people in the back. I'm not arguing that no politeness is called for in the world. But how much politeness is dictated by a fear of being unpopular? How much politeness is related to our being unable to say that the emperor has no clothes, when the emperor obviously has no clothes? Yet everybody's going around talking about his clothes.

Another sin is specialization—the potential for evil that resides in excessive specialization in our culture. I talked about this in *People of the Lie*: Large institutions develop departments and subdepartments, and the conscience of the institution becomes so fragmented and diluted as to be virtually nonexistent.[2]

I could go on and on and on with causes and causes of this many-headed monster, but I'm just going to focus on one, after having gotten across the point that there are so many causes. The one that I would like to focus on is 'Good Old American Rugged Individualism'. In 1830, Alexis de Tocqueville, a Frenchman, came to these shores. After traveling around for three-and-a-half years, he returned to France and wrote a book entitled *Democracy in America*, which remains today the classic work on the American character. In that book, he talked about the American character being made up of certain mores, or what he called "habits of the heart". The one that he talked about the most—indeed, that he admired a great deal—was the individualism in the American character. As I say, he admired it; he wished he could take some of it back to Europe.

In that book, however, he also warned that if the individualism in the American character failed to be counterbalanced by other social forces and other habits of the heart it would inevitably lead to fragmentation of American society and isolation of its citizens, one from another. That was 1835. One hundred and fifty years later, in 1985, esteemed sociologist Robert Bellah and his colleagues published a book entitled *Habits of the Heart* based on that de Tocqueville phrase and subtitled *Individualism and Commitment in American Life.*[3] What that book does, based on considerable soft sociological research, is to proclaim that de Tocqueville's warning has come precisely true. The individualism in the American character has failed to be counterbalanced by other social forces and other habits of the heart. It has led to just exactly what de Tocqueville predicted—namely, fragmentation of American society and isolation of its citizens, one from another.

That isolation is very real. When I give a day-long string of lectures, as I quite often do, I ask my audience please not to ask me questions during the break times because I need those times to get my heads together. (I'm a Gemini.) Actually I say this because invariably the questions they ask are very good questions. They represent concerns that other people in the group have. But just as invariably, somebody will come up to me during the break and ask me a question.

I'll say, "Well, I thought I requested you not to."

They'll say, "Yes, but Dr. Peck, this is terribly important to me and I can't talk about this in the group because some of the members of my church are here."

Now, I would like to say that's not an exception. There are a few exceptions, very few. What I'm talking about is the norm—the normal level of vulnerability, of intimacy, of community that exists even in those places where we might like to find it, in our churches. This is due to the great American ethic of rugged individualism and the fallacy of it. Like most of the Devil's lies, it is a half-truth. It runs with just one side of the paradox.

What that ethic says is that we are called to become individuals. That is correct; God calls us to become individuals. Jung said that the whole goal of psychospiritual growth was individuation, which most of us failed to complete. Most of us remain tied to the apron strings of our parents—if not financially, at least intellectually and emotionally. We never really learn to think for ourselves, to become full individuals. So it's true; God calls us to become individuals.

The ethic of rugged individualism also says that we are called to autonomy. We are called to responsibility. We are called to become captains of our own ships, if not masters of our own destiny. We are called to stand on our own two feet as best we can. All of that's true; but the problem with the ethic of rugged individualism is that it neglects the other side of the coin, the rest of the truth, which is that we are also called to come to terms with our own brokenness. We are also called to come to terms with our own sin and meanness and smallness, and our own inadequacy and inevitable mutual interdependence.

The problem, you see, with the ethic of rugged individualism is that it runs with just a half-truth—the one side that we have to try to get it all together. What we do is, we go around pretending that we've got it all together, denying the other side—our sin and our brokenness. And so it is possible that we can sit in our churches together, hidden behind our masks of composure, separated from the person in the pew next to us.

I would like to focus on one particular part of that rugged individualism that relates to evil—and that is the lack of the sense of corporate responsibility that most Americans have, the lack of a sense of corporate sin or shame or guilt. The audiences that come to hear me are not necessarily a cross-section of Americans. For one thing, the average American probably doesn't even really read very much. They're a cut above average and they're very interested in their spiritual growth. But what has struck me over the years is that, while these people have a sense of their individual sin and imperfection in the sense that they need to go someplace and they are concerned with their own development, they are generally lacking in concern for society's development or the health of the institutions to which they belong.

Were I to go into a city in which I had never spoken before, let's say Kansas City, and were it advertised that Scott Peck would be talking about spiritual growth and family life, I can guarantee you that a thousand people would come to hear me. Now were it put out that Scott Peck was coming to talk about the arms race I can guarantee you that it probably wouldn't get over 150 people to come hear me.

Nowhere was that lack of concern with institutional corporate sin more clear than in a workshop I did about six months ago in Chicago. When I got there, I found out to my surprise that they had given me only one topic, which I usually talk about for an hour and then have a question-and-answer period. But they had devoted a whole day for five hundred people to listen to me talk about that one topic, which was 'Self-Love versus Self-Esteem', a talk I give that has to do with issues of guilt, sin, remorse, and contrition. I usually talk about these at an individual level.

It seemed to me it would be boring to have a whole day of questions and answers, so I decided to spend the morning of the symposium focusing on issues of individual guilt, remorse, and contrition. Then the afternoon would focus on issues of group guilt, remorse, and contrition. The morning went very well indeed. In the afternoon, however, as we began to focus on notions of corporate guilt, sin, contrition, and remorse, the spirit went out of the group. It got lower and heavier and heavier and heavier.

I said, 'My God, something's gone radically wrong. I'm going to have to do something.'

It was taken care of for me when a woman got up and said, "Dr. Peck, I am seriously concerned about the way that you have been blessing the sexual behavior of Jimmy Bakker and Gary Hart today." A third of the people clapped. I recovered myself as quickly as I could and said, "I'm very glad that you made that statement, because if you have been hearing me as blessing the sexual behavior of Gary Hart and Jimmy Bakker you've not been hearing me correctly. Or, more likely I haven't been saying to you what I wanted to say. All that I have said in regard to this is not to bless their behavior but to wonder (as I have wondered with you) why we are so concerned with the sexual behavior of these individuals, these hero figures we put up there, for which we have no responsibility, whereas we have virtually no concern with such things as the pornography of our unbalanced budget and the insanity of the arms race for which we do have some responsibility." It didn't help much.

Just as the causes of corporate evil are multitudinous, so the healing of corporate evil must be multidimensional, must proceed on many fronts. But before I get into that kind of feeling, which calls for what Barbara Jordan referred to as orchestration of good in people and Philip Hallie called *nurture engineering*, I need to give you a kind of talk within a talk (or a lecture within a lecture) on the subject of grace.

As many of you know, because I'm a scientist I had to give *grace* another name. I referred to it as *serendipity* in *The Road Less Traveled*. Sometimes in question-and-answer periods when I talk, people ask me, "Well, Dr. Peck, since you wrote *The Road Less Traveled*[4] ten years ago, have you had any more examples of grace?" They don't seem to know that grace just goes on and on and on.

It is hardly the most recent example, but this is the most appropriate. About two years ago, I was going to a speaking engagement in Minneapolis. I get to do all my writing on planes these days, so it's very precious time for me. I always carry my yellow pad with me. I don't like to talk to the person next to me. I'm a shy person. Because I'm a smoker, I sit in the smoking section and he's usually intoxicated. You've all had that experience. So whether I'm writing or not, I usually protect myself with my yellow pad.

On this particular occasion, I got on the plane in Hartford with a man about my own age, who was quite sober. I gave him my usual nonverbal messages that I didn't want to talk with him and I was delighted to see him give me equally strong nonverbal messages that he was not the least bit interested in talking with me either. And so we sat there in silence together, him reading a novel, me with my yellow pad for the hour-long flight from

Hartford to Buffalo. We sat in silence together for an hour-long layover in the same lounge of the Buffalo airport. Then we got back on the plane in silence together. We continued to sit in silence together until 45 minutes west of Buffalo and 45 minutes east of Minneapolis.

The first words passed between us when out of, literally as well as figuratively, the clear blue sky this man looked up from the novel he was reading and said, "Excuse me, I hate to bother you, but you don't by any chance happen to know the meaning of the word 'serendipity', do you?"

I said that as far as I knew, I was the only person who had written a significant portion of a book on the subject. Perhaps it was serendipity that at the one particular moment in time when he wanted to know the meaning of word 'serendipity', he happened to be sitting in outer space next to the nation's authority on the subject. When that sort of thing happens, sometimes even I have to put down my yellow pad.

We got to talking and he asked me what this book was about. I told him it was about psychology and religion. He said he didn't know about religion any more. He told me that he was an Iowa boy, born and bred—born into the Methodist Church and raised there. He liked the church a great deal, but he had a whole lot of questions. I looked like somebody he could talk to and to be perfectly frank, he wasn't sure he bought this virgin birth business. As a matter of fact, I not only looked like somebody he could talk to, but I also looked like somebody he'd never even have to see again. To be totally honest about it, he wasn't even sure about the Resurrection. He was feeling really bad about it because it looked as if he was going to have to leave the church.

I talked to him about the holiness of doubt and the holiness of skepticism—how it's the beginning of thinking for yourself, searching for what Tillich called "the God beyond God", part of the spiritual maturation. When we parted in the Minneapolis airport, he said, "Well, I don't have the foggiest idea of what all this means, but maybe I don't have to leave the church after all."

Grace is not just some kind of miraculous circumstance; it's also one that has a certain meaning, a certain beneficial healing outcome. The reason I've had to talk to you about grace is that I had a dream Friday afternoon as I was worried about this conference. God gave me a dream, a kind of a Star Trek dream.

I'd been wandering around to different planets, different cultures of extraterrestrials. I had recently come to a planet that had looked extremely good on paper. I really had been looking forward to coming to this planet because I had thought it would be a utopia. When I arrived and walked around this planet, however, I realized that it was just as bad, just as ridden with evil as any other planet. It had its very clear virtues, but on the dark side of that those virtues turned into vices. Even though it had looked so great on paper, it was no better than any other planet.

Angry and upset at being disappointed, I exclaimed, "Well, I thought that, as in all the other planets I had visited, the laws of serendipity would apply here!" What I had found was a culture that looked great on paper, but there was no grace there. And so no matter how great it looked on paper, it didn't work that well.

The moral of this dream, I believe, is that God wants us to work toward Utopia with this social engineering that we're talking about. God calls us to work toward Utopia, but we are going to fail in this work if we fail to rely upon grace, if we think that we can pull it off just by ourselves. We are going to succeed only insofar as we are co-creators with God.

Now with that caveat that we need God's help in this process, let me talk about the multidimensional treatment of corporate evil. Again, just as there are innumerable causes, there must be innumerable kinds of treatments. I can't begin to mention them all. Some of them have already started. In the midst of decay lie the seeds of new life. When an old order is collapsing, under the rubble we often find the new. Despecialization is beginning to happen. We are slowly moving into an age of integration. You see it in such things as the holistic medicine and ecology movements, which are movements of integration.

We need to reward transcendent behavior. This occurs in such things as the Nobel Prize. We need far more of these, however. I think they're coming. Norman Lear is in the process of establishing something called the Claremont Good Business Awards to reward business leaders who do something beyond focusing on the bottom line of profits this quarter.

We need to desecularize our education. We need to introduce ethical teaching into our schools and there is no way that we can do this. You cannot introduce ethics without having a higher power. Right away, you're out of the realm of the secular. Somehow we need to figure out how to do this. If you want a good topic for a 1992 conference, I would suggest it be 'How To Bring the Teaching of Values and Ethics Into Our Schools', so that our children grow up learning that we are *Homo ethicus.* That's what is meant by our being created in God's image—that we have free will and hence the opportunity to be ethical creatures.

Just as there are many causes of corporate evil, there are many things that must be done to combat it, but I am going to focus on one that is relatively new, yet has so much potential that my wife and I have devoted our lives to it in recent years—the development of The Foundation for Community Encouragement. This Foundation seeks to encourage the development of community wherever it does not exist, to encourage existing communities to strengthen themselves in community and relate with other communities without getting into enemy formation.

When we use the word 'community', we do not use it the way it's usually bandied around in the United States—as Morristown, New Jersey, or the Third Presbyterian Church of Morristown is said to be a community, when the people in the church can't even talk to each other about what's most important to them. But rather we refer, not just to a geographical aggregate of people, but also to an aggregate of people who have made some kind of serious ongoing commitment to each other to learn how to communicate—community has something to do with communication—to communicate with each other on an ever deeper, more vulnerable, honest, real, authentic kind of level.

Perhaps the principal way this Foundation works is through holding community-building workshops where we lead groups of people (50 to 60 at a time) out of their usual state that we call 'pseudocommunity' through various difficult stages into 'real community'. This community-building process is described in *The Different Drum.*[5] I don't have the time to cover it, so I very much hope that you will get that book—not to make money (because the money will be given away), but because I think it is a saving book.

What I'd like to focus on is what this community-building process does on a multidimensional front. It teaches people the various things that I have been talking about. One of the things that happens in this process is a process of public confession. We know that the early Christian church had this phenomenal community and then it blew it, and one of the reasons it blew it is that it dropped the policy of public confession. By public confession, I don't mean there is a group of people saying in unison, 'We have done those things that we ought not to have done, and we have left undone those things that we ought to have done.' I mean that the people in the early churches used to get up and say, 'I hit my kid last night. I'm feeling out of control and my mother's dying and my heart's breaking. I lusted after a woman in my heart. As a matter of fact, I did more than lust after her.' Or their joys: 'My wife's pregnant' or 'Baby's okay.'

Public confession is a place where they relinquish their personal defenses. Part of that process is learning how not to talk in abstractions, which has been mentioned here so much. God is in the details, as somebody once said. They learn how to give up politeness. This does not mean they give up respect for each other; to the contrary, one of the things they learn again is respect for each other. They learn how to be honest and authentic with each other. They learn how to diminish their fear. The most common thing people say is that the group has become a safe place. And consequently it is a place where what I call 'soft individualism', instead of rugged individualism, can flourish, where people can really be themselves—but only because they have made a commitment to each other, a commitment to the body, a commitment to hang in there with each other. Only then can it be safe. You can't say what's on your mind if you think that people are going to drive you out or if you're going to drive somebody else out. But when you've made a commitment to hang in there with each other, then it becomes safe. It's a place that becomes despecialized. A true community is a group of all leaders. Because it is a safe place, compulsive leaders will feel free—often for the first time in their lives—not to lead. The shy and reserved will feel free to step forward with their gifts of leadership.

It is a place in which people learn the appreciation of the body—that a body needs different members and unique talents. Even though they're different, they're all required and all valuable. Through this process people learn how to contemplate the body. It is amazing that probably only about one in a thousand Americans has the capacity to look at a group in which she or he is involved and say, 'How's this group doing?' We Americans lack this capacity to contemplate the body, to look at it—but it's something that can be learned. Above all else, it is a place where people come to learn to love one another.

About three years ago in Atlanta, one middle-aged woman said, "You know, Scotty told us that we weren't supposed to drop out. That's part of that commitment. But when my husband and I got home last night, we were seriously considering doing just that. I didn't sleep very well last night, and I almost didn't come back this morning, but you know, something very strange has happened. I don't know how to explain this, but yesterday I was looking at all of you through hard eyes and today for some reason or other I have become soft-eyed, and it feels just wonderful."

This community-building process is an antidote to evil. We have the technology to combat evil. I could guarantee you, for instance, that if we could do a community-building workshop with five Anglos and ten Afrikaaners and thirty Blacks in South Africa, within three days those people would be loving each other—they would love one another. The problem is, of course, how do you get them there? How do you get them past the tremendous resistance to this?

Psychiatrists for 30 to 40 years have known the benefits of therapeutic community, so you would think that our psychiatric wards would be organized into therapeutic communities, would you not? Except, of course, to be organized into therapeutic communities would require that the doctors be vulnerable to the nurses, and that the nurses be vulnerable to the patients—until then it's organized hierarchically where the patients, the ones most in need of self-esteem, are down at the bottom. Nobody is vulnerable to them.

Similarily, I offered to give a community-building workshop for free in my little local church. It wouldn't cost people anything, just a weekend of their time, as long as ten people would show up out of the parish. It's a very small parish—120 adult members. We got three: the minister, his wife, and one other parishioner—and that was for free.

People are smart. They know that this community sounds

awfully nice. But they also think, 'Yeah, we'd like to have more community in our church but—but I might have to cry in front of my fellow parishioners. Thank you, God is calling me to more important things this weekend.'

It's natural to resist this. Every time Lily and I go back into community and do this work, we say, 'Oh God, not again. Not again are we going to have to make ourselves vulnerable and let ourselves in for this.' It is not an easy process to exercise this technology, but we have it; it's guaranteed, if you can get people in. The question is, can we get people in to practice building community, to practice this technology?

Let me bring it back home and ask you: How many of you here would really like to be authentic and real and vulnerable with each other? How many of you would like to become conscious of your own idolatries and addictions—not only to drugs but also to money, to the avoidance of issues, to sex, to popularity, to security, to your own ideas and thoughts? How many of you would like to come to terms with your own addictions and start confessing them? How many of you would pay a little money to break down in front of other people and cry in front of them? How many of you would like to talk about how you'd been molested? And you have been, all of you here have been molested. How many of you would like to talk about your griefs, and your brokenness? And yes, all of you here have griefs. You may not be in touch with them at the moment, but you're likely to become in touch with them. Or to talk about your inadequacies. How many of you would like to be held in the arms of strangers and comforted? How many of you would like to come to love somebody and then come to learn that he or she is homosexual, and has AIDS? How many of you would like to pay this money or spend this time to come and listen to people's pain, helplessly, not only to listen but to be affected?

I don't know how many of you would be willing to do this, but what I can tell you is that there is a way of healing. There is a way of reconciliation. Yes, we have a technology of reconciliation, but it does require that people get down to the level of their real humanity together with each other. There is a way of reconciliation. There is a way out of the arms race. We do not have to listen to this kind of blather that perhaps, just perhaps, like Mycenae three thousand years ago, after eight generations of squalor and chaos we might, maybe, just survive.

There is a way out and that is community. We have the technology for community. Community is the antithesis of evil. Painful, hard work though it is, Lily and I keep coming back to it—back and back—because hard work though it is, it is the only way to the greatest joy there is; the joy of reconciliation.

DIALOGUE
WITH M. SCOTT PECK

JOSEPH WHEELWRIGHT: What about the idea that good can be brought out of evil?

M. SCOTT PECK: I'm glad you raised the issue because that relates to perhaps the only concern that I have had [about what other contributors have said]. I have had some concern about this notion of turning good out of evil, of somehow transforming evil. I know that is a Jungian notion of integration, but I think there are different ways of defining that notion. I do not think that evil within us should be repressed; this is what happens when people refuse to meet their Shadow. I think that it should be suppressed, generally speaking, and not trans-formed.

There is a criminal Scott Peck who at first sign of any significant stress is quite tempted to lie, cheat, and steal. If I repressed him he'd get out of hand. It is only because I can acknowledge him and am aware of him that I'm able to add another cinder block to his cell each week or so. You have to be aware—otherwise you can't lock it up, you can't suppress it.

Now, mind you, you can go home today and you can say you've met the criminal Scott Peck. You've shaken hands with him in between the bars. But I try not to let him get out. He's got a very comfortable cell now. It's got wall-to-wall carpeting and color television. Sometimes in the evening when I am in need of a certain kind of street smarts, I may go down to the dungeon and consult with him in between the bars, although the better part of me makes the decision, I hope. That's what I think is meant by integration—not to kill evil because to do so would be to kill myself.

Some people think that we should loosen up, that we ought just to let it out and somehow it'll turn into flowers. It won't. I think most of the time it needs to be locked up, although we can't lock it up unless we acknowledge it.

WALTER ULMER: I think of that same organization that certainly was responsible for My Lai and for a variety of other things over the last 20 or 30 or 40 years as an institution, as a people, seen by de Tocqueville and others as having remarkable individual strength as well as a sense of community. We have done some rather bizarre and unusual good in the world. I can't imagine anything in history, anything, for example, that compares even remotely to what the United States did as a nation after World War II when we restored our enemies to a very powerful position socially and economically.

As for your comment that there are large numbers of people, or lobbies within this country—I think the term was "huge lobbies that want war"—I guess no one can speak for all the lobbies in the country, but I don't know where they are. My friends and I, who have been in this part of our world for 30 or 40 years, haven't seen that. I'm sure there are people who make money from such things as explosives, but I'm not familiar with those kinds of lobbies and the kinds of people who are doing that.

In Solzhenitsyn's wonderful remarks at Harvard he did mention, of course, the criticism that Western civilization might have as a primary flaw the lack of courage. Didn't he, in fact, say he was concerned that we lacked the courage to face such things as the inappropriate expansionism of the Soviet empire, and that he did not feel that Americans were committed appropriately (nor were Westerners in general) to back the kinds of values that need support—basically, the human spirit? I think he said that too in his wonderful address. I simply wanted to say that it's appropriate for

Americans to keep My Lai in perspective because it was done by Americans. To talk about evil in the world in the last 50 years, however, concentrating on My Lai and leaving out some of the true horrors—the annihilations in Cambodia and a variety of other atrocities currently going on in the world—gives perhaps an inappropriate view of ourselves. We are an imperfect society, but an awful lot of people are trying to do well.

M. Scott Peck: You're quite correct that in the same speech in which Solzhenitsyn talked about our lack of courage he recommended a very hard line against the U.S.S.R.—and that is a point where we differ—but you're quite correct that he said that.

The military is in many ways a wonderful institution. I wouldn't have been able to stay in it for nine-and-a-half years otherwise and be a colonel—ex-colonel. The military has great spirit. Those of us who are in peace work are not trying to get rid of the military. Instead, we talk in terms of conversion or substitution. Partly because the military is such a fine institution, I have very little difficulty in talking to military audiences. I find them quite willing to address and struggle with certain issues. I have enormous difficulty—impossibility—talking to people who are involved in defense-related industries. I have enormous difficulty. And there are a lot of them.

Dolly McPherson: One of the things that we've always been aware of, some of us in the Black community, is the fact that we've never been able really to focus on that thing called 'rugged individualism' because we've always known that what the individual did affected the community at large. One sees a marvellous example of that in Richard Wright's *Black Boy* when he receives a terrible beating by his grandmother because what he has done might cause members of the community to be abused and lynched.[6] Maya Angelou provides a marvelous example of that in *Gather Together in My Name* when she returns to Stamps, Arkansas.[7] She behaves rather arrogantly and perhaps foolishly and her grandmother beats her for the first time.

On the positive side we've seen those marvellous relationships that Black women develop between and amongst each other that we call 'sisterhood' — the community of sisters that serves as a means of encouragement and provides an arena for confession and praise and all the other things of which you speak. I've been moved by that and I would certainly like to become a part of it.

M. Scott Peck: I hope you will become a part of it. One of the greatest problems we have is that it is natural to form community in response to crisis and when people are under crisis. I don't want to say, 'Oh boy, isn't it great the way we treat the Blacks in this country, so that they can have community with each other?' But the terrible danger is that as it becomes perfectly respectable to be Black, you find that you may lose it. Don't lose it. You said it, sister.

Again, you may remember I talked about that wonderful community the early Christian church had. But then, when did it go away? It seems to have gone away just about the time of Constantine, when it became first legal and then official to be a Christian—when it was safe to be a Christian. To be a real Christian is and should still in this world today be a dangerous business. Don't lose it. Keep the crisis. In one sense, what the Foundation for Community Encouragement is trying to do is to teach people how to get into community without having to have a crisis or teach them that they're in crisis anyway, which we are.

William McKay: Is there a genetic potential in people to commit evil, and if there is, how do you deal with this in community or how do you deal with it at all?

M. Scott Peck: The question was addressed in *People of the Lie*, which focuses primarily upon individual evil. The subject of evil is so huge. They're both complex. I just had to choose a part of it, and I think corporate evil is the bigger problem that we have. Most of that book is devoted toward the study of individual evil. The major intellectual chapter is entitled 'Toward a Psychology of Evil' because we do not have a body of scientific knowledge about the subject of human evil worthy of being dignified by the name of a psychology.

There are profound reasons for that because we have defined science, including the science of psychology, as being a value-free kind of activity. To study human evil, you have to make *a priori* value assumptions about what's good and what's evil. That's not allowed under traditional science. Traditionally we've not been allowed to study scientifically the phenomenon of human evil. Nonetheless, I urge strongly in the book that we need to study it. One of the things I suggest is that there may very well be a genetic component to evil.

One editor said, "Surely, Scotty, you can't mean to propose that evil might be biological!"

I said, "How can you say it isn't biological when we haven't even been willing to study it yet?"

This is very much one of the things that ought to be studied. Those of you who've read the book may remember that one of the things that characterized the cases of evil people about whom I talked is that they were all cheap. Bobby's parents gave him his brother's suicide weapon because they couldn't afford a better one. Roger's parents kept looking for the cheapest school, not the best school, although they had plenty of money. Underneath that cheapness, that greed, lies panic for these people. They never feel that there's enough. Maybe that panic is biologically rooted. And maybe there is some kind of medication that could relieve the level of panic sufficiently to allow these people to get beyond the level of reactive self-defense. However, if evil has genetic causes, the treatment is not going to be to quarantine its victims.

CHUNGLIANG AL HUANG: I came to this country without knowing the language, and experienced prejudice and struggled to become a part of America and the world. It's not always that easy. I want also to acknowledge the truth of what you said about the 'rugged' individual. This is a key word that really got to me, because when I first came to this country, being Chinese and being soft, the rugged American individual really bugged me. Because I couldn't reach them. I couldn't put my arms around my roommate. I couldn't feel a part of the jocks, of the male-energy American. I acknowledge the kind of drama and the community that you talk so beautifully about. In order to have peace, we've got to make community.

NOTES

[1] Aleksandr Solzhenitsyn, *A World Split Apart*, Commencement Address at Harvard University, June 8, 1978 (New York: Harper & Row, 1978).

[2] M. Scott Peck, *People of the Lie: The Hope for Healing Human Evil.* (New York: Simon & Schuster, 1983.) See esp. p. 217 on fragmentation, and pp. 212–53 on the My Lai incident.

[3] Robert Bellah, *Habits of the Heart: Individualism & Commitment in American Life* (Berkeley: University of California Press, 1985).

[4] M. Scott Peck, *The Road Less Traveled: A New Psychology of Love, Traditional Values and Spiritual Growth* (New York: Simon & Schuster, 1978).

[5] M. Scott Peck, *The Different Drum: Community Making and Peace* (New York: Simon & Schuster, 1987).

[6] Richard Wright, *Black Boy* (New York: Harper & Row, 1945).

[7] Maya Angelou, *Gather Together in My Name* (New York: Random House, 1974), pp. 92–93.

4

Evil: THE UNFULFILLMENT OF THE GOOD

Samuel D. Proctor

Samuel D. Proctor, Martin Luther King, Jr., professor emeritus of Rutgers State University in New Jersey, is pastor of the Abyssinian Baptist Church of New York City. He began his career as minister of the Pond Street Baptist Church, Providence, Rhode Island. He then joined the faculty of Virginia Union University, where he became dean and later president. Next he became president of North Carolina A&T State University at Greensboro. He has held administrative positions with the Peace Corps in Nigeria and Washington, D.C., the National Council of Churches, the Office of Equal Opportunity, the Institute for Services to Education, and the University of Wisconsin. Dr. Proctor received the Doctor of Theology degree from Boston University. He is author of *Sermons from the Black Pulpit* (with William D. Watley), *The Young Negro in America, 1960–1980*, and *Preaching About Crisis in the Community*.

I make a confession now that I stand in the midstream of Protestant thought and experience in our country. That is my training and my background. My great heroes are people like Harry Emerson Fosdick, Reinhold Niebuhr, Elton Trueblood, and Walter Rauschenbusch. Thereby you may determine where I will end up on this topic, 'Evil: The Unfulfillment of the Good'.

Our experiences—moral, social, and physical—have brought us to a consensual acceptance and an awareness of a set of conditions that we choose to label the 'good' in life. We have had centuries of experimentation and observation with various responses to the most frequent challenges that we must face as humans. There have been many different approaches to the givens among natural phenomena and processes. We have made countless efforts through trial and error at the most effective and satisfactory human social arrangements to preserve best our most cherished values. Generation after generation, we have witnessed the struggle to harness our instincts; to channel our glandular currents; to control our subliminal urges; to restrain our native aggressiveness, our hard-driving pugnacity, and our survival proclivities; to contain our libidinal drives and necessities; and to overcome our moral torpor. Yet we do have before us a general, reasonable, operational consensus concerning the Good in life.

Regardless of our religious affliation (or no affiliation at all) or our political persuasion, not much debate is necessary to affirm that adequate nutritious food, ample clean water, safe shelter, fair and peaceful relations with others, care for children, and protection of the infirm and defenseless are all a part of the Good. Understanding nature's torrents and fury as well as its order and provisions, defense against the ravages of disease, achieving peace and concord among those who differ greatly, and creating an opportunity for intellectual growth and aesthetic delight are all further aspects of the Good. An economy that allows all persons to enjoy at least life's basic necessities is another. A respect and affirmation of the claims of all for protection from abuse and injustice through exploitation and fear, and a guarantee of safety and asylum for poets and artists and dreamers and those who simply await the dawn—these further enhance and embellish our understanding of the Good. Moreover, it is because we do hold and affirm this knowledge of the Good that we are so aware of its antithesis—Evil—the unfulfillment of this Good.

This point is old. It's where the Protestant community has settled down for a very long time. It is much older than that, however. How old I cannot say, but at least as old as Maimonides, a twelfth-century Jewish philosopher. In his *Guide for the Perplexed* he stated:

> Evils are evils only in relation to a certain thing. And that which is evil in reference to a certain existing thing either includes the nonexistence of that thing, or the nonexistence of some of its good

conditions. The proposition has therefore been laid down in the most general terms. All evils are negation. Thus for man, death is evil. Death is his nonexistence. Illness, poverty, and ignorance are evils for man. All of these are privations. If you examine all single cases to which this general proposition applies, you will find that there is not one case in which the proposition is wrong, except in the opinion of those who do not make any distinction between negative and positive properties or between two opposites, or do not know the nature of things—who, for example, do not know that health in general denotes a certain equilibrium and is a relative term.[1]

Whether what we call 'evil' is caused by a world that is wanton and random and capricious, or caused by dualism in the world (two super forces, a force that works for evil with equal authority to one that works for good) or whether what we call 'evil' is caused by a purposive divine Intention that permits evil to exist, the deliberate choice of a supreme eternal and absolute Being who has self-imposed limitations—nevertheless, this evil represents the unfulfillment of our chosen values, the good in life. The absence of this good—often in long-term, inhuman, brutal, and destructive ways—we call evil. While this is called the problem of evil, the presence of the good may be called a problem also. One is as fraught with mystery as the other. While lacking complete empirical data or even a method of absolute proof, we begin our quest for an understanding of evil by examining the postulates that we hold about the good.

Evil is that condition that falls short of the good, that opposes the good, or that defies, threatens, jeopardizes, or defeats the good. It is conflict and war rather than concord and peace. It is racism and xenophobia rather than appreciation and understanding. It is hunger and want rather than adequacy, ignorance, and dullness rather than enlightenment and curiosity. It is the terror and havoc of an earthquake, the destruction and waste of a wild flood, the spread of the AIDS virus, a solemn funeral of a child struck by lightning, or a lynching victim hanging from a tree.

Our understanding of evil is, of course, from our own human viewpoint as well as from our acceptance of certain values and conditions as good, *a priori*. It is clear, however, that much of what we look upon as the source of evil may be the source of a greater, more remote, less obvious good. We're not yet able to judge whether some parasites, for example, that cause human illness and death may have a need to exist in order to satisfy, or may be the absolute concomitant to, a prior or greater good than the one of which we feel deprived.

In another city not long ago, I was awakened in the middle of the night by some banging noise. I was annoyed and angry. But when it ceased, and when morning came, I learned that the noise was caused by an emergency plumbing job to repair a faulty valve in the hot water system. All of the water had to be cut off. Without that repair the dishes would not have been washed; they would have been left dirty and unavailable for breakfast. The linens could not have been laundered and ironed and ready for the next clients coming in. There would have been no shaving or showering, and all water uses (use your imagination) would have been postponed until the repair was completed. So then I reflected that the noise for a few minutes in the middle of the night was a bargain. The defective valve was not defective from the beginning, but it was a normal valve with a normal accumulation of corrosion and rust. While it was the unfulfillment of the immediate good in and of itself, it was not of evil intention or of evil design or ultimately of evil consequence.

It should surprise no one that this is called 'the problem of evil', for as long as we look upon all pain, all suffering, inconvenience, and unhappiness from an anthropocentric point of view, and in purely anthropomorphic terms, it may remain a problem. But the faith proposition of this central Protestant position that I'm presenting to you now, the position of the theist, is that God has purposes at work that are beyond our finite perception. After all, when an elephant sneezes, a flea may call it a hurricane.

Some persons declare that because of hurricanes, floods, and famine and because there are disease and death and genetic flaws, war and racism, that the world is therefore without purpose whatsoever. The idea of God as a loving, intelligent, powerful being is a deceit and a placebo. All theistic sentiment is a bromide. Nevertheless, imagine these same persons all using the complicated larynx with which to speak, a most wonderful piece of acoustical engineering, replicated billions of times through the faithfulness of genetic accuracy. Those persons are also using strength delivered to the muscles by the nurture of the blood—oxygenated by its unfailing route through the lungs, cleansed and inspected by the liver, refueled by the manufacturing perfection of the stomach, the pancreas, and the kidneys, and responding to subtle and swift signals from the brain to fight off alien and vagabond germs, sending its white cells to fight to the death, to lay down their lives so that the person infected might live. My soul, what a catalogue of miracles and of the Good in contrast to what we regard as the inextricable evils in life!

My theistic faith says that I would rather be burdened with trying to live with the riddle of the storms and floods, cancer, diabetes, racism, incest, Wall Street insider trading, and our first child's interventricular septal defect—our first baby boy, a blue baby—I would rather have to struggle with these than to be left with no starting point whatsoever; left denying the goodness of the sun majestically climbing to its zenith every day, the tides ebbing and flowing unerringly every 24 hours, the seasons unfailingly trailing each other in unbroken procession, the immaculate selflessness of a mother's love, the amazing efficiency of the human brain, the martyrdom of Martin Luther King, and the sincerity of Jesus carrying his cross to Golgotha.

There is unquestioned goodness in the world—overwhelming, everywhere—that is just as mysterious to my finite mind as the evil that I encounter. Indeed, it is a value judgment that causes us to label those certain experiences and benefits good that we enjoy, that answer the yearnings of the heart, and that make music in the soul. We bring to this question of evil our package of values, and we label some things and actions good in consequence of our priorities, our valuing process. These hard-won values are etched on the conscience and filed in the brain like computerized, coded and stored data. This is not trifling—this is important. This is where we all begin, with this stored computerized data. Our value system is the thing that causes the conscience to sound alarms, makes chill bumps pop out on us and causes us to sweat with guilt. They're there. In the presence of the Good, we write music and poems, we sing new melodies, and we dance the dance of joy.

When the Good escapes us, when in its place we taste the bitter dregs of undeserved grief and hurt, or endure the tedium of making the best of bad situations, we have our labels ready also from our package of values. We tag these conditions 'evil':

slavery, war, greed, deceit, pain, and suffering. Evil, therefore, is not to be denied or defined out of existence. Pain, hunger, war, racism, and injustice are all real and they're here. They all represent the unfulfillment of the Good.

These can be understood by postulating, on the one hand, a physical world that has its own requirements and its own necessities that we understand only partially now with all of our advancements, but that we understand better with each passing generation. (It costs an awful lot of humility for us to recognize that we still know only a fraction of what we're going to know about the physical order.) It is also, on the other hand, explained by acknowledging the freedom and the mental and emotional capacity of humans, the endowment of God, the total human equipment, loaded with potential for enormous harm or immeasurable good. Ultimately, this view accepts a world created by an intelligent, benevolent God who created free persons for superior moral and spiritual maturity, whose absolute power is limited by the kind of world that God chose to create, and the goals God set for the crowning outcome of creation—*Homo sapiens.*

The corollary to this view is the faith that humans are not left in this world as helpless orphans, but that God is engaged without ceasing in the human enterprise ever since the day of Abraham coming out of Ur of the Chaldees, intuitively revealing new truths to a Moses in Midian and Elijah on Mt. Carmel and Mother Teresa in Calcutta—guiding and directing spiritual growth, providing comfort and nurture when the necessities of the creative order or the perversity of human capacity cause enormous suffering that we call evil.

Professor F. R. Tennant of Cambridge was one of my favorite theologians when I was in the seminary. Here are some lines from him on this subject. Professor Tennant said:

> . . . pain is either a necessary byproduct of an order of things, requisite for the emergence of the higher goods, or an essential instrument to organic evolution, or both. Short of this, we cannot refute the charge that the world is a clumsy arrangement or an imperfectly adjusted mechanism.[2]

Those who deny the existence of an absolute supernatural creator and who view the world as a mysterious physical phenomenon without any intelligent purpose at all, populated by persons who are merely the marvellous outcome of natural selection, may and do experience the same evil privately, corporately, socially that the others of us experience—namely pain, suffering, and numbing destruction. But for them it is not a problem at all. They have a deeper problem—explaining the universe itself. It is simply the blunt, cold reality of our precarious existence on an indifferent, unfathomable, and uncaring planet. One huge, lukewarm cinder whirling in an unmeasured abyss. That's a problem.

Professor Wieman, the very popular humanist many years ago from the University of Chicago, makes this humanistic point in his book, *The Growth of Religion*, conclusively based on the absence of an absolute God, of course:

> All of these philosophers that struggled with the problem of reconciling the goodness of God's controlling power with the patent facts of evil in the universe fall back on the mystery of God's ways on the one hand and the good uses of evil on the other. Always the problem is left unsolved. Essentially, all they succeed in doing is to veil the raw and bloodied face of it. God is somehow good and the ultimate source of all, they aver, and yet evil is here indubitably.[3]

Obviously, such a position leaves us with a Problem of Evil, without any adequate conclusion at all except to give up on God entirely and to begin again with the world without purpose. Perhaps the greatest good lies in the fact that the human spirit rises up to challenge evil from whatever source it may come. The moment arrives when we cease our debate on how evil got here, and we focus on the fact that our growth and spiritual moral maturity will be reckoned on how we approached the evil that is here—cumulative evil, continuing evil. The greatest evil is to allow ignorance, lethargy, indolence, and moral inertia to impede our efforts in pursuit of the fulfillment of the Good, and thereby erase or lessen the effects of evil.

This position does not let us off the hook by simply saying that this is the world of necessity and we've got freedom. There's a corollary to this. It says, 'Stand tall and face the mysteries in the physical order. Stand tall and face the freedom that we've been given. Then start responding as best we can to help lessen the effects, the consequences, of evil.' We're not interested simply in a solution to a kind of a conundrum. That's only amusing. It's a wasteful intellectual exercise. What we do want is a working proposition so that from that moment on we can move and make meaning out of our lives.

The Problem of Evil is a question not only of the source of it but also of its consequences. Here we stand body deep in its consequences—the compounding results of it and the questionable and paltry efforts that are set forth to reduce it. We know that evil is not a static quantity. It is subject to change. Much of the evil known in the nineteenth century is gone, both evil caused by natural forces and evil caused by the misuse of human freedom. You can look at me and tell, at age 66, that I have outlived huge quantities of social evil in my lifetime. This is not the same world into which I was born.

The genetic flaws of nature now are being challenged by recombinant DNA research. I'm not talking about manipulating people in a kind of Skinnerized or E. O. Wilson sort of fashion. I'm talking about finding something that is a genetic change that will help us to get rid of diabetes and certain forms of mental illness. The habits of war and its carnage are challenged by international dialogue and responses to nuclear terror. The ugliness of racism recedes before the growth of understanding and before the persistent legal challenges and equal opportunity. The scourge of hunger is challenged by research in geography, environmentalism, agronomy, and so forth. Illiteracy, overpopulation, epidemics, and depressed physical qualities of life remain a challenge to the compassion, technology, and commitment of those who are not willing to sit down and wrestle with the issue forever, but are willing to stake off some propositions that can be lived with and then move in pursuit of the fulfillment of the Good.

The misuse of human freedom and evil created by our perversity and the evil that we experience resulting from spiritual estrangement—our finite and often alien existence—the transiency and brevity of our days—the fear that all striving is for naught, and that our lives are like a tale that is told by an idiot, signifying nothing, or a brief, brief candle without abiding significance—these are all responded to, not by gritting our teeth and clenching our fists, but by an enlightened faith proposition that we can live with every morning at 6:30, that this vale of soulmaking is the best equipped moral and spiritual arena that could have been designed. Can't prove it, spent enough time trying, given up on all of the available methods of proof, but got to live from day to day. You've got to make it somehow before noon.

This faith proposition asserts further that this world is equipped with enough mystery to cultivate our intelligence, enough pain to make us empathetic, enough discomfort to make us creative, enough freedom to compel sound moral debate and choice, and enough uncertainty every step of the way to induce stronger faith and trust. The Problem of Evil, therefore, is best addressed by earnestly seeking ways of pursuing diligently the fulfillment of the Good. Indeed, if this world is designed to foster moral and spiritual maturity—if that's our working hypothesis, if that's the best answer that we can have operationally to complete our destiny as creatures a little lower than the angels crowned with glory and honor—then we should settle on our faith proposition with humility, but with steadfastness, and move on in pursuit of the fulfillment of the Good.

Here are some examples. We could continue to hurl at length the most profound and penetrating questions about Nature that we can in order to maximize its benefits to humankind and to minimize the suffering from its apparent caprice and randomness. Many persons in this room have no idea how far we've got to go before we can effect some kind of reasonable conciliation in our own country between science and religion.

Do you know that right around us right now there are still debates going on about how to read the book of Genesis? There are many people who are not interested in hearing anything about a God who had to take twenty billion years to build the universe. It's got to be done in seven days, and more than that, a snake has got to learn how to conjugate Hebrew verbs! We are really at the very earliest stages of educating our population. I want to say this without any suggestion of embarrassing anybody or ridiculing any kind of movement, but when you observe in America how many millions of people there are whose only religious outlook is what's fed to them by these electronic churches and these so-called 'Multimillion Dollar Ministries', and when you listen to all that and say 'this is where the American mind is', you know that a whole lot of evil is going unattended to that could be dealt with a lot more intelligently.

There is a wave of anti-intellectualism in this country that we have not dealt with yet. It makes me wonder what has happened in our public schools that this kind of debate could be going on again in the 1980s and going on with vigor, with millions of dollars being spent behind it. So we need to ask of Nature, 'What are those answers to questions that we can find to help us minimize the effects of natural causes of what we call evil?'

My wife reminded me as I was getting ready to leave, just at the very last minute, she said, "Don't forget this. On October 19, 1987, the *Home News Newspaper* of central New Jersey reported that Merck and Company, one of the strongest companies in our country (a big pharmaceutical company in New Jersey, a world leader in pharmaceuticals) announced that they were going to donate their new antibiotic, called *ivermectin* to help prevent river blindness among 85 million of the world's poorest people who are threatened by this parasitic disease. Today 18 million children are already blinded by it—children, fathers, mothers, and street beggars—blinded already without knowing that the parasites have come from the dirty water that they're using.

The drug was first discovered as a veterinary medicine. Incidentally, it was discovered first to help kill heartworms in cute little dogs and cats, thoroughbred pets. You know that old hymn 'God Moves in Mysterious Ways His Wonders to Perform'? This drug was found to kill the parasites in pets in American veterinary hospitals. Now we're going to clean up the parasites that were making people blind—18 million of them around the dirty waters, all around East and West Africa and on the coastlines.

In the language of the theist, by the providence of God and through the skill and genius of Merck's researchers, here all of this terrible blindness that we took for granted, consummate evil if you please, here with one stroke of a pen this big corporation with enormous profits and high stocks is saying, 'We want to enter into this battle and not count all of our profits, but give away enough of this drug to curb a parasite.'

That's what we mean by hurling at Nature the most profound and penetrating questions. This is the answer to the issue of evil, and in order to get to this answer you don't have to answer everything empirically. All you need is a strong working hypothesis like that of the great apostle Paul: "All things work together for good to them that love God" (Romans 8:28).

The next thing I think we've got to do is go further into what I call exotic research, and indulge for a moment in those kinds of questions that are not on the surface of things. We've got to find out how far back we must push this curtain of mystery. I'm an ethicist and a theologian and a preacher in Harlem, but I'm not antiscientific. I want to applaud all the great laboratories around the country that are probing deeply to find out how much caprice there is in the universe.

Hurry and tell me something before I say some silly things. How much randomness is there in the world and how much wantonness is there in Nature? Tell me these deep secrets as fast as you can find them out. I'm going to live on what I've got right now because life must go on. But hurry and find out, with the methods you've got available, with the vocabulary you've got available, with the computers you've got available, with the metaphors, and analogies, and all the analytic techniques you've got—go and press further. Find out how much of this we've got to take on faith and how much we can know about.

I don't want to have faith substitute for facts; I want faith to start where the facts leave off. Listen to what Tennyson sang in his dulcet tones. There's nobody like Tennyson to talk about this.

Our little systems have their day,
They have their day and cease to be.
They are but broken lights of thee
And thou O Lord art more than they.[4]

This is an appeal to invest in what we called exotic research. But what are now called mysteries may one day not be mysteries at all. They may not be any more mysterious than television, laser beams, and nuclear fission were in 1920.

Doubtless there is an impenetrable area out there somewhere that will defy the probing of a mind and we must rely upon the limited scope of the human brain's capacity. But we don't know yet where that is, and I think every sincere preacher of the gospel, every sincere priest and rabbi, ought to be encouraging the scientists to keep on probing—probe for a lifetime, probe for centuries—to help us find out what are the proper uses of faith so that we are not saying to people something in the name of faith that has already been demonstrated factually.

We have only hints that there is a larger cause-and-effect relationship lying out there somewhere that may be learned by humans. The same apparent caprice and randomness of nature that cause mudslides in California, burying million-dollar homes in muck, that shake skyscrapers with frightening earthquakes, that spread river blindness among the helpless, illiterate, impoverished people of the world, that strike down innocent young campers with fatal bolts of lightning—it's also the unseen force that guides the five thousand incredible daily processes of the liver, the magic of the pancreas with all of its little islands and rivers and streams, the amazing functions of the eye, the synergistic rhythm of the heart and the lungs, and that perpetuates all of these wonderful physical endowments by the relentless, faithful, and informed wisdom of DNA and other genetic functions.

If the wild and untouched rain forests of India, Brazil, Bolivia, and sub-Saharan Africa suddenly ceased to produce those complex molecules for our pharmacologists, we might as well turn our hospitals into condominiums. As sophisticated as we are, we are being healed by things that come to us out of these places, these miraculous molecules that treat malaria, leukemia, glaucoma, and a catalog of other diseases. These things are growing from trees and bushes out there among leopards and cobras and screaming monkeys. The same physical processes of nature that destroy us so much are still providing our very sustenance and our healing. Our suspicion is that as we move forward we want to find a billion more secrets yet to be fathomed for the pursuit of the good and the diminution of evil.

Next we must continue to examine human proclivities and propensities to learn the better uses of human freedom. What do we know about people and how their loyalties come about? We need to know a lot more about why human beings behave the way they do. Why would young, well-to-do White boys in a rich little suburban town of Philadelphia, over in south Jersey, put notebooks in front of their faces so that they would not have to look at the picture of Martin Luther King in one of the chapel services where they were having a memorial? What would make somebody 15 or 16 years old be so mean as that? What do we know about that? What would make well-to-do kids on Long Island continue to paint the swastika on Jewish temples and synagogues right now in New York City, with everything going for them?

There's more to be discovered and I don't think we need to go and create the Devil all over again. He's gone. Let him stay where he is. We don't have the time to fool around now with three or four first causes and three or four prime movers in the world. It's enough of a risk to have this monotheistic system with which we try to live.

One of the most serious challenges to the pursuit of the Good is the problem of dealing with the raw survival impulses that lie beneath the thin veneer of civility among humans. We need to learn a lot more about that. How much more do we need to know? You know how I found out about the death of Martin Luther King? I was coming into Dallas on that April day, way back in 1968, to take part in a conference on how to strengthen the faculties of the Black colleges. We had several Black colleges around Dallas.

There I was, coming in with my briefcase. I went outside the airport looking for a taxi and they pointed me to a taxi. A Black fellow was in charge.

"Bbbrrrrp—you want a cab? Here's a cab."

I looked and there was this scrawny, thin White fellow—hair stringing down his back; tatoos crawling up his arm; had a dirty little juicy brown cigarette butt; blackheads all over his face. He looked so grimy and ill-kempt, I started to say, 'Sam! You don't need to get a cab like that, do you?"

There I was standing in my pressed-up blue pinstripe suit; my button-down shirt. I almost waved him along, joining in the whole business of perpetuating prejudice. I started to say, 'Go ahead, fella,' but the Lord wouldn't let me do it.

'Sam, don't do it. Don't join in that. Get in the cab.'

I got in the cab. I didn't know King had been shot. The driver was so quiet.

"Where're you going?"

"Going to the Sheraton downtown." He went on, turning out of that airport—it takes a lot to get out of that airport—and finally he said, "Mister, must be you don't know what done happened today." He could hardly talk—this language.

I said, "What did you say?"

He said, "Must be you don't know what done happened today."

"What happened?" I asked.

I thought first this was some dirty kind of a racial thing he was going to pull off on me. The stereotype was there. He trembled. He shook. I looked in the mirror. His head was hung down over the steering wheel, and in a cracked voice, this fellow whom I'd already learned to discount in the world said, "Somebody killed Martin Luther King today."

That's how I found it out. From a person I least expected to be broken up in tears about it; from a person I least expected would want to tell it to me. He looked so poor, so out of it. He's the one who said that to me. Why is it that my information about human beings did not allow me to be open to that possibility? We don't know enough about the ingredients of community yet and we need to spend an awful lot of time laboring on that. There's an awful lot of evil we're letting slide right in because we've not given enough attention to this.

When I went to Crozer Seminary, I had a nice scholarship and a lot of encouragement. First day, I was there sitting in the chapel with my blue suit on. I was looking nice, scrubbed up, fingernails clean, ready to go to work. I was the only 'colored' boy there. See, we were 'colored' then! I'm so old I've been everything, but we were 'colored' at about that time. I went to chapel because they were passing out jobs. A war was on and all civilians had to have some kind of a job to help the war effort. The seminary students had a deferment to study for the Naval chaplaincy so we were there principally to go to school, but we had to do some kind of work to help the seminary get along. So I signed up. I told them I could type. I could do this, that, and the other. And I sat there.

A Ph.D. in church history from the University of Chicago on the faculty was the chairman of the Student Employment Committee. I'll never forget it as long as I live. He stood there and read off all the job assignments and I was still sitting there. Everybody left the chapel.

Then he said, "Mr. Proctor, would you step here a moment?"

He said to me, smiling as if I were to be complimented, he said, "Mrs. Moitz wants to see you in the kitchen."

I got up and walked out. I must have grown a thousand years between that chapel and Mrs. Moitz. But at the top of the steps as I was about to say, 'I'm going back to Virginia. I'm not going to stay in Pennsylvannia and be insulted like this! Of all the things for him to think of doing, he wanted to perpetuate the whole thing and assign me to the kitchen, and I'm not gonna do it.'

But then strangely, somehow, a voice said to me, 'Sam, be bigger than that. Go on down there and wash the dishes, scrub the pots and pans, convince them that they can't diminish you one whit by sending you to the kitchen. Go down there and scrub the kitchen better than anybody ever scrubbed it before. And let God take care of the residue. All the equations will work out somehow. Go on down there and do it.'

I went down there and this lady came to me and hugged me.

She said, "Did they send you here?" She could hardly talk. She was a Hungarian refugee cook there at the seminary. I said, "Yes, ma'am."

You know, she took that dirty apron, put it up to her face and cried, and she said, "Why did they send you here? They won't let but one colored boy in the school at a time, and they always want him to work down here. They're professors and ministers and theologians and that's the way they think. They do the same way they do downtown."

I said, "Would you mind if I stayed down here with you?"

She said, "Would you stay?"

I said, "You bet I'm gonna stay. I'm gonna stay. Something tells me I'm gonna learn more about Jesus down here with you than I'm gonna learn upstairs with them."

Talking about the ingredients of community, do you know that later on I went downtown and got a haircut, in the same two- or three-day span. I found a nice haircut, in the 'colored' neighborhood downtown in Chester, Pennsylvannia. I came walking back to the campus and all of the fellows were standing out front—all White boys from Southern Baptist institutions like Wake Forest, Mercer, and the University of Richmond, right down the line. They wanted to be trained in a liberal seminary, but they didn't want to go too far. So they crossed the Mason-

Dixon Line to Chester, and that's as far as they wanted to get. My classmates came from Duke and Emory and all down the line. There they were standing. I was the only Black student there. Martin Luther King came eight years later. I was walking up there a total stranger, first-year student. They were all standing by the big columns watching me.

One stepped out in front—a great big fellow, freckle-faced, red-headed fellow:

He said, "Um, where you been Sam?"

I said, "I've been downtown."

"For what?"

"To get a haircut."

He looked down on me (he was huge) and said, "Where did you get the haircut?"

"At a barbershop in the 'colored' neighborhood down in Chester."

He looked at me, and they all heard us. He was doing this for his audience. He said, "I want to tell you something. I'm the barber on this campus. I cut everybody's hair. The president's hair and the janitor's hair and everybody's hair. And I'm gonna cut your hair too, as long as you're here. If I catch you with another haircut from downtown, I'm going to beat your ummmmmm." It wasn't seminary language either!

I said, "Uh, wha, a . . . " I didn't know what to do. This red-headed White boy from down in Fuquay-Varina, North Carolina, right down the road from Raleigh, is gonna be my barber here, and I just left Virginia? I had to go upstairs and get myself together. I looked at my mirror and had one of those frequent and long conversations.

"Sam, you gonna let that guy cut your hair?"

I said, "Yeah, but I'm not gonna let him shave me though!"

I had the biggest decision to make and then came the word—'Sam, you don't know what's happening in his mind. You don't know how ready he is for a brand-new experience. If he says he wants to cut your hair and says it in front of everybody, go on in the room and have him cut your hair.' And for three years we became the best of friends, and are friends today.

How do we know where these openings are for community? We're so bogged down in traditional ways of doing things, we don't know what's buried in the human spirit or how much capacity there is for change. We don't know how much evil we're putting up with that we don't have to put up with at all. I carry with me that simple faith from this tradition in which I stand—that the Earth is the Lord's and the fullness thereof, and that all things do work together for good for them who believe, and who believe enough to be in the pursuit of the good that's in the world.

My daddy lived in the midst of all of that ugly racism down in Virginia. But I remember how he belonged to the Philharmonic Glee Club. Daddy would come home from driving that truck in the Navy yard and put on that stiff-bosomed suit. He looked like he was so happy to break his back putting on his shoes. He would press his pants perfectly. And all 60 Black men—coal trimmers and truck drivers, table waiters, all of these kinds of fellows out there—would sing for the White population in the middle of the 1930s. They would give one concert a year, practicing every Wednesday night, but it was down to perfection. They came marching out there singing. We had to sit on the back row because we were Black. The back row had benches without the backs on them. That was our punishment for showing up—we sat on the row without backs! We had our little tickets. Only a handful of Black folks were allowed to come.

"Daddy, why do you all want to sing for the White folks?"

"They need the experience of having us stand there and sing this music and we gonna keep on singing it until times change down here."

It was sort of a silent kind of continuing testimony to the fact that they were totally human, and that they were not going to succumb and have their hearts eaten out by evil. There's where my Daddy was standing, in this same tradition trying to make all things work together for good. You know the last song they sang every night at that concert? I've never seen it written. I've never heard anybody else sing it, and I haven't heard them sing it for 50 years. But the words will never leave me. There I was, a little fat-faced boy with my legs just swinging; they weren't even long enough to touch the floor.

At the end, they were singing, "Dawn is breaking and a new day is born. The world is singing the song of the dawn. Yesterday the skies were gray, but look, this morning they're blue. The smiling sun tells everyone, 'Come, let's start life anew! Let's all sing hallelujah, for a new day is born.' The world is singing the song of the dawn."

My Daddy died before he ever saw that new day really being born, but he lived with the hope that with faith a new day would be possible.

NOTES

[1] Maimonides (Moses ben Maimon) (1135–1204), *Guide for the Perplexed*, M. Friedlander (tr.), 2nd rev. ed. (N.Y.: Dover, 1956 (orig. 1904)).

[2] F. R. Tennant, *Philosophical Theology* (Cambridge University Press, 1928); Vol. II, 'The Problem of Evil'. Quoted from Bronstein and Schulweis, *Approaches to the Philosophy of Religion* (New York: Prentice Hall, 1954), p. 255.

[3] Henry Nelson Wieman and Walter Marshall Horton, *The Growth of Religion* (New York: Willett, Clark, 1938). Quoted from Part II, 'Approach to God', p. 356.

[4] Alfred Lord Tennyson, 'In Memoriam, Prologue', lines 17–20.

5

REFLECTIONS ON EVIL

Richard W. Lyman

Richard W. Lyman, ninth president of the Rockefeller Foundation, is a member of the Board of Independent Sector, the Council on Foundations, the National Committee on U.S.-China Relations, and the Council on Foreign Relations. He is a director of the International Business Machines Corporation and the Chase Manhattan Bank. A former chairman of the Commission on the Humanities and of the Association of American Universities, he served as vice-chairman of the the National Council for the Humanities. Lyman holds a Ph.D. in history from Harvard University. He has studied at the London School of Economics as a Fulbright fellow. He is a Fellow of the Royal Historical Society and an officer of the (French) Legion of Honor. At Stanford University, he has been professor of history, associate dean of the School of Humanities and Sciences, vice-president and provost, and president. He is currently president emeritus and the J. E. Wallace Sterling professor of humanities emeritus of Stanford. Lyman is co-editor with Lewis W. Spitz of the two-volume *Major Crises in Western Civilization* and author of *The First Labour Government*.

I was on the phone this morning with a friend who knew what I was doing here. As we signed off she said, "Good luck with Evil." I'd like to think she meant that for a lifetime, but I'm afraid she meant it only for this talk; I'm grateful nevertheless.

My knowledge of Evil is neither that of a professional student of the subject nor a therapist accustomed to trying to help victims of it. My perspective is merely that of an amateur observer, and no doubt occasional practitioner.

I do, however, have some observations based on our three days together. Going into the symposium, there seemed to be some uncertainty, perhaps 'ambivalence' would be a better word, as to how to approach the topic. There is a problem in definition, clearly. One can define 'evil' in various ways and the subsequent discussion would be to a great extent determined by the definition chosen. If evil is simply the absence of good, which as we've heard is a traditional Christian view, that's one thing. But if it is an active agent in the world, perhaps aided and abetted by an even more active external agent in the person of the Devil, that's something else again.

Satan seems to be enjoying something of a revival lately, incidentally. Jeffrey Russell seems to be involved in a growth industry. Leaders as diverse as the Ayatollah Khomeini and the Pope have spoken publicly about Satan in recent weeks, although it's not entirely clear they have in mind the same creature.

Confronting the problem of distinguishing evil from mere wrong, we are tempted to make lists to seek a definition by accumulating examples. Failing to keep an appointment with your Jungian analyst is wrong, but few surely would be willing to call it evil. Active participation in the operation of Hitler's gas chambers would appear to satisfy just about anyone's criteria for establishing the presence of Evil. But there's a lot of ground in between.

That point about Hitler's gas chambers brings me to the first of my random observations. As the materials for this symposium made clear, there is in our day a pervasive tendency to bring up one or the other, or both, of the two great twentieth-century examples of Evil incarnate: the Holocaust carried out by the Nazis in the 1940s, and the prospect of thermonuclear war and the consequent devastation of human civilization. The latter is often coupled with affecting accounts of the only uses thus far of nuclear devices—the attacks on Hiroshima and Nagasaki in 1945.

Note, of course, the all but inescapable euphemisms with which we have sought to conceal the unbearable nature of the subject. A 'device' sounds so neutral, so mild—even harmless—more reminiscent of someone's workshop than Armageddon. That's why such terminology is the usage of choice in the Department of Defense—another comforting euphemism—we used to have the War Department. Herbert Abrams introduced us to two more examples: the Pentagon terms 'Broken Arrow' and 'Bent Spear' for accidents involving nuclear weapons. One wonders whether there was conscious irony in establishing those terms in the first place.

This dominance of the Holocaust and nuclear catastrophe is understandable. The two phenomena have done more than anything else to confirm us in the belief that Evil, once widely thought (in the West, at least) to be in full retreat before the forward march of human progress, is not only alive and widespread in our time but also has taken on a potency never before encountered in the long sweep of human history. Massacres and attempts at genocide carried out in previous centuries, and there certainly have been plenty, seem pale by comparison with these twentieth-century developments. We are properly appalled not only by the fact of some six million murders of Jews, but also because they were carried out so dreadfully methodically (as Russell remarked) and by a nation that has given us the music of Beethoven, the poetry of Goethe, the institution of the research university, and countless other hallmarks of advanced civilization (as Rollo May said).

I know these are clichés by now, but they are also a continuing source of puzzlement and they trouble us profoundly and appropriately. We contemplate the horror of Hiroshima and Nagasaki and then consider how limited, almost primitive, were the weapons of mass destruction used on those occasions compared with what would be loosed on the world by the explosion of just one modern H-bomb, let alone the thousands that would be expended in a full-scale exchange between the superpowers. Where are Theodore Roosevelt's evocations of Indian massacres or settlers' vengeance in comparison to such megadisasters?

Yet it does seem to me there are dangers in concentrating so much on these two examples of evil. I am not advocating inattention to these, please understand that. One danger is pretty obvious, however, and has come out from time to time at this symposium—that we may be tempted to brush aside as minor and unworthy of our serious attention a host of other manifestations of evil, including the homely, familiar ones of our own private lives. It is certainly more dramatic and more fascinating to deal with evil at its worst and most extreme than to analyze the relatively trivial nastiness encountered in day-to-day living. But there are powerful reasons for paying attention to the latter.

For one thing, day-to-day nastiness is surely connected with the greatest outbreaks of human cruelty and destructiveness. There must be a continuum from a child pulling the wings off houseflies to Auschwitz and Buchenwald. Understanding as fully as we can the instances of evil that are closest and most accessible to us is probably important to our effort to comprehend how a civilized society could set out to exterminate six million fellow countrymen and women. For another, it has been pointed out repeatedly that focusing on other people's capacity for evil is an awfully convenient way of escaping the need to think about our own. I think Karl Weick is very much on target when he writes, "Crusades have such poor results precisely because crusaders find it harder to deal with their own dark side, but easier to deal with the darkness in others" (p. 88). To paraphrase Mark Twain only slightly: to be good is noble, to show others how to be good is nobler and much less difficult.

Another conceivable risk of excessive focus on the Holocaust and the bomb was suggested recently by Bruno Bettelheim in a review of Robert J. Lifton's latest book, *The Nazi Doctors*[1] (to which Raul Hilberg referred). "Lifton," Bettelheim wrote, "comes dangerously close to the attitude expressed in the French saying: *tout comprendre c'est tout pardonner* (to understand everything is to forgive everything)."[2] I must confess, however, that I don't see this as a major problem. I thus find myself in partial disagreement with Karl Weick when he writes that "the biggest danger of all, and the danger toward which this symposium is dedicated, is indifference. Indifference, understanding, and awareness have a strange relationship to one another; if we understand evil and how it works, then it may be easier for us to dismiss it or become indifferent to it" (p. 89).

My disagreement is not with the assertion that indifference is an enormous danger and is the appropriate target of this symposium; rather it is with the idea that understanding is likely to breed or lead to indifference. I believe that, throughout life, understanding is the sworn and deadly enemy of indifference. Whether we like what we find when we come to understand a person or event or institution or idea, or whether we do not, indifference appears to me to be the least likely outcome of a successful effort to understand.

A particular version of the claim that understanding leads to indifference or to an inapproriate tendency to forgive evil is the criticism of modern behavioral science and its practical consequences in our attitude toward criminal justice, often heard from conservatives who maintain that in our zeal to comprehend the external causes of criminal behavior we risk becoming unable to make any moral judgments at all about its perpetrators. If criminal behavior is seen as stemming from poverty and familial breakdown and bad schools, what is left? Roger Scruton, a British essayist, puts it succinctly: "As we look for the causes of our behavior, so we take attention away from the act itself, fencing it round with excuses, isolating it from judgement and making inaccessible the only ground in which the seeds of morality can be sown: the ground of individual responsibility."[3]

The immediate appeal of this line of thinking is clear enough. We rebel against interpretations of human behavior that emphasize the role of environment whenever we hear specific reports of horrendous actions and callous attitudes: the murder of a child or an old woman for no motive other than seeking thrills, carried out by youths full of bravado who neither feel nor express remorse; or the rampage in which a tormented loner erupts into violence on a mass scale, generally with a gun, killing numbers of individuals he (and it is overwhelmingly males who do these things) has never met, knows nothing of, and whose only offense is to be within his reach.

To react to such depravity by blaming unsympathetic parents, insensitive teachers, or economic hardship in a world of affluence strikes us as somehow woefully inadequate. The popularity of attacks on relativism and of laments for lost moral absolutes—a political stock-in-trade for some (Secretary of Education William Bennett), a path to the best-seller list for others (Allan Bloom)—owes much to this feeling that too much concern for the context of the offense results in letting people quite literally get away with murder.

Yet social and behavioral science, with all its shortcomings, is not nonsense. We cannot brush aside the demonstrated connections between an impoverished or destructive environment and atrocities committed by human beings who, as we say in everyday speech, are the products of their environment. Individual responsibility remains nevertheless. There are, after all, individuals who survive any number of negative influences to lead positive, constructive, and crime-free lives. So when we speak of people being the products of their environment, in short, we only partly mean it. At bottom, to reject that sociology and psychology and history can tell us about conditions that are conducive to evil conduct is a form of anti-intellectualism better suited to the ostrich than to human beings concerned with each other's welfare and that of the species.

Evil has shown itself to be a tough, relentless foe against which we need every weapon we can create or on which we can lay our hands. Knowing that most murders are committed by young males between the ages of eighteen and twenty-four does not suggest that persons who fall in that category of age and sex should be excused, therefore, and left free to kill again. It does tell us where in our society our focus ought to be if we wish seriously to do something to reduce our disgraceful homicide rates. It is tempting, when discussing evil, to veer toward absolutism and even apocalyptic thinking. So serious is our predicament in the late twentieth century that we find it easy to believe that nothing short of a drastic and revolutionary change in our ways of thinking can possibly save us. No less an authority than Albert Einstein is often cited in support of this position.

I'm inclined to view this belief, however, as a counsel of despair. If we must revolutionize human nature to survive, survival is not likely. We are the same species as fifth-century B.C. Athenians who brought upon themselves catastrophe in the Peloponnesian War, of which Thucydides wrote so compellingly. Indeed, the reason we find his account so compelling is that the actors in the tragedy are so recognizable to us. That can only be because they're very much like us.

An alternative approach, one frequently encountered (we heard it from Scott Peck), is epitomized by the title of an article in the *Kennedy School Bulletin* a few years ago, 'The Senseless Arms Race; A Plea for Sanity.' Treating nuclear war and even the nuclear arms race as insanity too readily becomes a way of oversimplifiying the problem because it suggests that all that is necessary to be rid of this nightmare is to put power into the hands of people more rational than those who have been wielding it.

A good case can be made, however, for the proposition that at least in part, war has more often than not been the product of calculation and of thinking that was, by most human standards, extremely rational. Michael Howard, the Regius professor of history at Oxford, made such a case with concise brilliance:

> The conflicts between states, which have usually led to war, have normally arisen not from any irrational and emotive drives but from almost a superabundance of analytic rationality . . . There have certainly been occasions when states have gone to war in a mood of ideological fervor . . ., or of swaggering aggression . . ., or to make more money . . . But in general, men have fought during the past two hundred years neither because they are aggressive nor because they are acquisitive animals, but because they are reasoning ones; because they discern or believe that they can discern dangers before they become immediate, the possiblity of threats before they are made.[4]

I noted that Herbert Abrams, alias Professor Cordova of Buenos Aires, demonstrated this element of rationality—superabundance of rationality, indeed—in his scenario for the coming of World War III. Each step had a logic about it that grew out of the preceding step. Anyone who has studied at all closely the origins of World War I is likely to have shuddered in recognition upon hearing that chilling account.

I do not think I really agree with my old colleague Frank Vandiver that World War I was a *just* war by the criteria set forth by the Catholic bishops. It was a war blundered into, fought at a cost grossly disproportionate to anything gained by it, and in fact it sowed the seeds of World War II in several ways. It was hardly a benefit to humanity, let alone one worth all those tens of millions of lives. But again the statesmen in 1914 thought they had no choice. Indeed, their reasoning in the context of their interests as they perceived them gave them no choice.

I do have a serious bone or two to pick with Herbert Abrams. He argues that the deterrent as a means of preventing war from breaking out between the U.S. and the U.S.S.R. is somehow less necessary because these two powers have never fought one another before and therefore would not have fought even without the deterrent in the time that's passed since World War II (above, p. 162). Technically, to begin with, the facts are wrong. The U.S. joined in the invasion of Russia in support of the Whites at the time of the Bolshevik Revolution, and if we have forgotten this, they have not.

Leaving that aside—and it is a somewhat technical point, I agree—that because we have not gone to war against the Russians we are not likely to do so in the future is, I'm afraid, the kind of highly misleading historical interpretation that can cause the most serious mistakes in policymaking. The principal wars in any era involve the major sovereign powers of that era. In the seventeenth and eighteenth centuries, England and France were as inevitably among the antagonists and on opposite sides in every major conflict (and there were many) as France and Germany seemed to be from the Franco-Prussian War of 1870 through World War II. Yet today, war between either of these two sets of former superpowers is pretty much out of the question. We and the Soviets have moved into the great power slots—each with global interests, each claiming superpower status with all of the irrational trappings that such status has involved throughout history, neither able to accede to the creation of mechanisms for resolving our possible disputes that would in any way diminish our cherished, but I'm afraid in many ways illusory, sovereignty.

I once heard Secretary of Defense Caspar Weinberger maintain that of course the Soviets understood the United States would never launch a pre-emptive strike against them, whereas we could clearly have no similar faith in them. I rose in the question period to ask for a single example from history in which one great power had ever possessed the kind of faith in the good intentions of its principal antagonist that he seemed to imagine characterizes the Soviets' view of us today. To that question, he had no answer.

But I digress. I would urge Abrams to drop this particular argument from his brief. The basic case concerning our danger doesn't need it, and as an argument against the deterrent it is more likely to raise doubts as to the speaker's understanding of how wars come about than to be convincing.

I'm afraid I also find the analogy that he drew between the arms race and the Holocaust seriously flawed. The conscious aim of the deterrent policy, whatever one may think of its soundness or efficacy into the future (and I share many, many of Abrams's worries—indeed all his worries about accidental or unintentional nuclear war), is the avoidance of war and therefore the saving of human lives. The conscious aim of the Holocaust was to wipe out the Jews.

Furthermore, even if one thinks deterrence is a mistaken policy, I think anyone who asserts that owes it to his or her audience to advance an alternative, one that stands a better chance of keeping the peace for the next 42 years and has a reasonable chance of being adopted. It is not enough just to suggest, by quoting Roman Catholic bishops in the states of Washington and Texas, that we should withhold taxes or refuse to work on weapons of mass destruction. Not to act is to act, says Abrams. Of course he is right, but that doctrine by itself sheds no light on what the morally justified and potentially effective actions may be that are open for us to take. The case for unilateral disarmament, if it's to be made, should be made directly and not indirectly by what amounts virtually to innuendo. If you are going to urge people not to work on weapons of mass destruction in this country—and you have absolutely no influence on their working on them in the Soviet Union—you are arguing for unilateral disarmament and you should say so[5]. Then we can have it out.

Indeed, while I've heard much that was wise and humane and informative and thought provoking at this conference—uttered by a series of very powerful and eloquent speakers—it does seem to me that, as is so often and understandably the case, we are longer on diagnosis than on prescribing cures. Several speakers have wound up with eloquent perorations imploring us to find new ways to release the healing power of love to do its beneficent work in the world. While I do not doubt that love can and often has made deliverance from Evil a real possiblility when nothing else could in those specific circumstances, it has not been made clear to me even here just how we are likely to succeed in the more general task—a task to which, after all, Christian churches have been recruiting us with only very mixed success for nearly two thousand years.

Again, many have spoken, as Jeffrey Russell did most succinctly, of the challenge being that of "identifying evil, facing it, and using its energy to achieve good." Perhaps that is as far as we can go. I think it is a good statement.

While listening to Maya Angelou, one certainly felt one's energies being released in the direction of good, whether or not those energies came from the evil that is within us. But a general replicable way to convert evil energies into good I don't think has really been offered to us. Maya Angelou said when she first heard about this symposium and its subject matter she thought that it was a very daring thing to do—full of risk. The ancient Greeks might indeed have accused Harry Wilmer of hubris, that pride and overconfidence they thought had the effect of bringing down the wrath of the gods upon those who exhibited them. Ms. Angelou then went on to say that only the highest standards of honesty with and about ourselves would make possible a successful meeting on this topic. She then gave us a fine example of this herself. She demonstrated what Philip Hallie called "generosity without yielding". No one could accuse her of Uncle Tomming, but her account of that phenomenon as it related to the impossible position of Black Americans before the civil rights movement was sensitive, honest, caring, funny, and deeply sobering all at once.

She also quoted Bob Dylan: "You got to serve somebody." Many years ago, the philosopher William James said, "We are all ready to be savage in some cause. The difference between a good man and a bad one is the choice of cause."[6] Most of us here have, I think, adopted the Jungian view that evil and good co-exist inside each of us. I'm not going to argue with that. Perhaps James was talking about converting the energy deriving from evil for the pursuit of good—at least it sounds that way to me.

What I've been saying is that although Evil has taken on new force and scope in the twentieth century, I question whether it is, therefore, really a new and different phenomenon from ages past. Humanity remains—in its strengths and weaknesses, in its capacity for good and evil (and, let us not forget, for self-delusion—I happen to think hypocrisy is one of the rarest faults in the world because self-delusion is much more common)—strikingly recognizable throughout recorded history. In seeking ways to cope with evil we are also left with our human capacities and limitations. There is no shame in that. As Jeffrey Russell reminded us, the belief that we can build a perfect world leads to fanaticism and therefore disaster. No shame then, merely the need to recognize as fully as we can who we are and what we are equipped to do as we go about the serious business of trying to assure a future for ourselves, our children, and our world.

SUMMARY AND DIALOGUE
Karl Weick

The tone for this last session was set vividly the first night when Gregory Curtis rolled his eyes and said, "Boy, these are awfully deep waters." And it's become deeper ever since. That didn't deter Liz Carpenter, who urged us to clear the debris so the stream can run free and so we can see.

I'd like to take stock and see how we've done in getting clarity on the issues of Evil. I want to develop with you a variety of images about our accomplishment without appearing breezy or disrespectful of the magnitude of these issues. I want to use a variety of images so that we can connect our experiences here with the different kinds of lives to which we're going to return.

Early in our exploration we heard about two musicians humming refrains from Mozart. Rollo May made the important point that those young people had something to love, and that we should keep our eyes and ears open for those kinds of exhibits as counterpoint to Evil.

Other speakers such as Richard Lyman, a former college president, acknowledged a feeling of humbleness in the presence of the issue of Evil. I want to reinstate that feeling of humility, but I want to do so with a light touch that involves both music and college presidents.

This is a true story that reeks of humility. It happened at the University of Buffalo when Warren Bennis was president there. The world-famed violinist Jascha Heifetz was to perform a concert at Kleinhans Auditorium, a facility on the Buffalo campus that seats 4,500 people. Warren Bennis was to introduce Heifetz.

The day of the concert a blizzard hit Buffalo, as is common in January. When Heifetz and Bennis got to the auditorium, exactly six of the seats were filled. Heifetz walked out onto the stage, gazing at the six people and said, "Look, this is silly. Let's go over to my room. I'll serve you all drinks and we'll talk for a while. We don't need to stay here."

One person in the back of the auditorium immediately stood up and said, "Hey, I drove here all the way from Toronto to hear you sing and by God, you're gonna sing!"

I think that's humbling. I also think that kind of feeling is part of what we've felt here. But even though we feel humble, we must not be immobilized by the sorts of issues that we have discussed.

A fascinating incident involving immobilization during military maneuvers was once described by Albert Szent-Gyorgi. During this incident, a young Hungarian lieutenant sent a reconnaissance unit out into the icy wastelands of the Alps. Just after he did so, it began to snow intensely. It snowed continuously for two days and the reconnaissance unit didn't return. The lieutenant suffered, fearing that he had dispatched his own people to death, but on the third day the unit came back. Where had they been and how had they made their way?

"We'd considered ourselves lost," they said. "We waited for the end. Then one of us found the map in his pocket. That calmed us down. We pitched camp and lasted out the snowstorm. Then with the map, we discovered our bearings and here we are."

The lieutenant borrowed this remarkable map and had a good look at it. What he discovered, to his utter amazement, was that it was not a map of the Alps, but a map of the Pyrenees.

Now think about that.

One of the morals of that story is: When you're lost, any old map will do. I think there's a grain of truth to that. A map calms you down, and one of the things that we know about stressed people is that they see less. Perception narrows when you're under stress. Calm down and you'll see a little bit more. We also know that a map gets you moving. One of the interesting things about moving is if you keep your eyes open and stay attentive to what's happening right around you, you learn things, you see things, you observe, and you can take more informed action.

Gregory Bateson was fond of saying that an explorer can never know what he is exploring until it's been explored. We've been exploring for three days. I think it's appropriate for us to look back and see what kinds of things we've discovered. One of the ways we make sense out of the world is by following a recipe that goes, 'How can I know what I think until I see what I say?' First we talk, then we look back over what we have said, and finally we arrive at a set of conclusions about what we thought concerning the topic.

In a sense, we can build a community understanding of where we've been and what it means. All of us, I think, are vitally interested in being able to answer people who come to us tomorrow and say, 'What did you learn at Salado? What's this Evil stuff?' So here's the general question: 'What do you feel is going to stay with you from this symposium?'

RICHARD GONZALEZ: We have had a wonderful introduction to a perspective on the understanding of Evil. For centuries, slavery was accepted throughout the world as a normal thing. Only in fairly recent times have we developed a concept of slavery as evil.

CLAUDIO SEGRÉ: What I got out of the symposium was a sense of the variety of ways in which we can learn about this general Problem of Evil. That is, not only through our minds, of course, but also through theological analysis, our hearts, drama, and folk wisdom. In very traditional ways, I think we dealt with a very traditional problem. I benefited from this in many, many different ways.

Finally, in terms of solutions, what I found in the end, or what has stayed with me most of all (particularly because of my own interest and background in issues of the Holocaust) is that, as Raul Hilberg pointed out so brilliantly, the Holocaust was something that was done one step at a time by relatively ordinary people. What that idea shows to me is that if I reverse it, then we, as ordinary people, if you will put it that way, can also fight evil one step at a time. It's the only way we can do it. That is, we can't take it on. We cannot come out with great overarching solutions. That's not possible. So one step at a time we can fight evil.

Another thing I learned from this conference is that we can
choose the places where we want to fight evil. One place that
I will be doing so is simply by giving out information, by
teaching students, since that's what I do. Secondly, as a
citizen, I can fight evil merely by getting more committed in
something like the antinuclear weapons movement. I was
very moved by Herbert Abrams's presentation. What I
learned is that we must choose. We can't fight evil in a general
sense, but we can fight it quite specifically. It's up to us now,
when we go home, to choose the specific points where we
want to fight it and then do it.

JOSEPH WHEELWRIGHT: I haven't cried so much in a long time as I
have in these last two days. It's principally the fault of Maya
Angelou and Sam Proctor. In any case, I am struck by the fact
that subjectivity has been almost universal among the speakers. I am not a great believer in objectivity. I think it's a
fascinating abstraction, but when the sort of enlightened
subjectivity comes out that we've heard, it has an impact that
just gets you right south of the belly button. I wish there had
been more said about women, because if somebody pushes
that button [of nuclear war], that's the irreversible end of life
on the planet. I really believe the biggest hope we have that
the button won't get pushed is women, because they have a
confrontation with life and death that no man ever had or ever
will have—regardless of whether they have babies or
whether they do not. Having a uterus gives them a commitment to humanity and a nurturing quality that we owe to
them. I just hope to Heaven they get the reins soon enough.

WEICK: Thank you. Let me simply underscore your observation
about enlightened subjectivity showing itself in its best form
here.

PAUL WOODRUFF: I agree. I love to see subjectivity bringing light
into the atmosphere here. There were two things I wanted to
mention, one a cause of despair and one a cause of hope. They
balance each other, and I'm going to carry them out one in
each hand this afternoon. The cause of despair was the
thought which came out of the Holocaust discussion that
there are evils for which there can be no forgiveness. That was
a new thought to me and a very sad one, that an evil can go

on unforgiven. The thought that gives me hope I'm going to carry out in the other hand. That is Maya's Uncle Willie, who gave a gift of good that went on to another generation and is going on right here and will go right on giving. I'm going to hold on to that very tightly.

LUCIA WOODRUFF: Very briefly, I think perhaps the people who are going to save the earth (if anyone is) are the women and the minorities.

UNIDENTIFIED MAN: The language of poetry and politics, as spoken by Maya Angelou and Barbara Jordan is particularly important to me. I remember John Adams, who I think said that we have not inherited this land from our fathers, but rather borrowed it from our children. It is important to keep that in mind, to break the cycles of violence and misunderstanding. The model for me has been that of the Bexar County Child Abuse Council, to understand that however one feels about the evil of the abusing parent, if you can simply come to understand that the person was an abused child, then you won't just react to that evil but rather understand its cycles and somehow interfere in them. That's the understanding I think we're looking for.

HANK WILMER: I had a grandfather who used to tell a wonderful story, the conclusion of which was basically that nothing ever really changes in this world—except every twenty years or so we get a new crop of people. I think more than anything else what I realize as a result of all that we've been through in this symposium is that there is no solution, no real simple destination, but rather the continuing and unending process of trying to understand and deal and develop within—to resolve successfully the issues of evil. There is no simple solution.

WEICK: Let me move toward a resolution. I want to use the Uncle Willie strand because we've talked about the kinds of things that are important for us and I want us to be sure that we converge on the issue of what kinds of things we do next. Paul Woodruff talks about using Uncle Willie as a model and I want to build on that.

Claudio Segré commented on a kind of gradualism, an approach that says, 'Let's take things one step at a time and at least we can choose the domains in which we're going to fight the battles that we do.' Uncle Willie, in a way, is a wonderful example of that. He teaches times tables to a variety of people and, in effect, changes the governance of the state of Arkansas. It's a wonderful example of a small win, of something small that grows large. It's that kind of sensitivity we want to cultivate.

Part of that cultivation requires that we pay close attention to details. As Philip Hallie reminded us, it is in concrete details that we can grasp the force of evil and simultaneously begin to see that we can do something about it—the sooty details of the lynching scene in Maya Angelou's poem, the oven doors of Dachau that jarred Gregory Curtis, the silvery bread that squeezes down into a ball when young Philip Hallie grows tense, the soot and smoke after a nuclear war that Herbert Abrams warned us about.

Those details are vivid. When we're thinking about small wins that gain leverage on problems of evil, it's important to start with those details. When we leave here, it's important that we tell concrete stories about specific evils. The lynching in Detroit is where Philip Hallie's otherwise detached students are forced to abandon the easy answer, 'It all depends on your point of view.' Details undercut their relativity and leniency.

Another lesson is that as much as possible, we need to tell the truth. We've heard over and over that lies get us into trouble. In the beginning, it started out with the Devil lying to Eve. As much as we can infuse truth into issues, and not lie, we're in better shape. Talk to other people about the things you're questioning as well as the things that you know well.

We heard about faith in the power of good, and saw it vividly in the form of a bag of money with 99 dollars and a charge of one dollar for the sack itself. Faith in the power of good—we heard it also from Samuel Proctor. Most of all, we've heard the theme that affirmation can overcome negation—affirmation in the form of love and caring. Richard Lyman was pleased and a little surprised to hear that theme, although he was not too sure it was going to change much of anything. That's okay. It's the fact of affirmation, it's the contagious example of affirmation, that has the power to pull us through. We heard that most clearly when Jeffrey Russell said, "Love pierces the darkness and that's all I know."

That's not a bad place to start.

NOTES

[1] Robert J. Lifton, *The Nazi Doctors: Medical Killing and the Psychology of Genocide* (New York: Basic Books, 1986).

[2] Bruno Bettelheim, Review of Lifton, *New York Times Book Review* (October 5, 1986).

[3] Roger Scruton, *Untimely Tracts* (New York: St. Martin's, 1987), p. 251. Quoted in *The Wall Street Journal* (September 21, 1987).

[4] Michael Howard, 'The Causes of War,' *Encounter*, Vol. 53 (March 1982), pp. 22–30.

[5] Abrams has not explicitly endorsed unilateral disarmament, and the groups with which he is associated have pressed for bilateral or multilateral verifiable arms control agreements on nuclear weapons. Abrams specifies measures designed to reduce the threat of nuclear war in, e.g., his 'Sources of Human Instability in the Handling of Nuclear Weapons,' *The Medical Implications of Nuclear War*. (Institute of Medicine, National Academy of Sciences. Washington, D.C.: National Academy Press, 1986. Pp. 349–80.) —*The Editors*

[6] William James, quoted in John W. Gardner and Francesca Gardner Reese, *Know or Listen to Those Who Know* (New York: W.W. Norton, 1975), p. 109.

Afterword

Harry A. Wilmer

We asked members of our audience what they had learned from the Symposium. Here are some of the many answers we received:

—That there is hope and I feel personally powerful and responsible to confront world issues and to begin this at home in my family and community in a personal way.

—That the human spirit can transform the evil found within and without.

—That there are many people who are concerned with making the world a better place.

—I thought anew about people who have survived evil and come out of it whole and strong.

—I felt that the in-depth presentation of three major 'corporate evils,' without at least taking the time for an overview of other relevant topics, such as sexism, communist enslavement, and drugs, may have left attendees with the impression that by solving these three, we can provide all that is necessary to eliminate evil, or at least to put it in proper relationship with 'good.'

—During the symposium I have become aware more vividly that love has power. I have experienced this many times in my life, but somehow did not appreciate it, [but] accepted it, and survived because of it. Now I want to use my power of love.

—If we were to summarize the conference, we would have to quote a rock group from Austin—Timbuk 3—writing about their marriage: "Before they drop the Big One, let's try to get along." We agree that someone, somewhere, someday, will drop the Big One, that we may not escape the 20th century. *But,* we're not going to get out of here alive anyway. Maya reminded us that no matter what we do, something will take us away from here. Accepting that, we can have the courage to go on and live life with joy and love.

My thoughts at the end of the Symposium were these:

We can hope to find ways as individuals and groups to cope with evil as we see it in our lives and in the world. We can hope to bring light into dark places, to bring hope where there is despair, to bring humor and songs where there is drab emptiness, to bring enlightenment into the shadows and to bring simple understanding into perplexities. We can hope to hear what others say with an open mind, to hear what we do not want to hear and to see what others see with an open heart, to ponder together on awesome powers, and to think more clearly and more simply about this present, this now, this here, this moment. The challenge of obstacles, knowing good by evil and doing something about it—these are the stepping stones in life. Now we have begun our work here, which we will continue in the words of the medieval alchemist, *Deo concedente.*

THINKING ABOUT EVIL: A SELECTION OF TEXTS

A. VIEWS OF THE ANCIENT GREEKS[1]
1. Heraclitus[2]

The most beautiful of apes is ugly in comparison to another race; the wisest of human beings seems an ape in comparison to a god.

Fragment 82

Dogs bark, too, at someone they do not recognize.

Fragment 97

For the god, all things are fine and good and right, but human beings have supposed that some things are wrong and other things right.

Attributed to Heraclitus (*Fragment* 102)

2. Epictetus[3]

Just as a target is not set up to be missed, in the same way nothing bad by nature happens in the world.

Handbook 27

Let death and exile and everything that is terrible appear before your eyes every day, especially death; and you will never have anything contemptible in your thoughts or crave anything excessively.

Handbook 21

When you see someone weeping in grief at the departure of his child or the loss of his property, take care not to be carried away by the appearance that the externals he is involved in are bad, and be ready to say immediately, "What weighs down on this man is not what has happened, . . . but his judgment about it."

Handbook 16

3. Epicurus[4]

Death is nothing to us. For what is dispersed does not perceive, and what is not perceived is nothing to us.

Principal Doctrines §2,

The principal disturbance in human minds is due (1) to the belief that although the heavenly bodies are blessed and immortal, they want and do and cause things that are inconsistent with these attributes; and (2) to the expectation and fear of some eternal evil, as is described in the legends. . . But peace of mind is being released from all these beliefs and remembering always the principal causes of things in general.

Letter to Herodotus 81

B. The Christian Theory of Saint Augustine[5]

1. But I still did not see that the pivot upon which this important matter turns is the fact that it is all of your making, almighty God, for *you do wonderful deeds as none else*. My thoughts ranged only amongst material forms. I defined them in two classes, those which please the eye because they are beautiful in themselves and those which do so because they are properly proportioned in relation to something else. I drew this distinction and illustrated it from material examples. I also gave some thought to the nature of the soul, but my misconception of spiritual things prevented me from seeing the truth, although it forced itself upon my mind if only I would see it. Instead I turned my pulsating mind away from the spiritual

towards the material. I considered line and colour and shape, and since my soul had no such visible qualities, I argued that I could not see it.

I loved the peace that virtue brings and hated the discord that comes of vice. From this I concluded that in goodness there was unity, but in evil disunion of some kind. It seemed to me that this unity was the seat of the rational mind and was the natural state of truth and perfect goodness; whereas the disunion consisted of irrational life, which I thought of as a substance of some kind, and was the natural state of the ultimate evil. I was misguided enough to believe that evil, too, was not only a substance, but itself a form of life, although I did not think it had its origin in you, my God, *who are the origin of all things*. I called the unity a 'monad', a kind of mind without sex, and the disunion a 'dyad', consisting of the anger that leads to crimes of violence and the lust that leads to sins of passion. But I did not know what I was saying, because no one had taught me, and I had not yet found out for myself, that evil is not a substance and man's mind is not the supreme good that does not vary.

Crimes against other men are committed when the emotions, which spur us to action, are corrupt and rise in revolt without control. Sins of self-indulgence are committed when the soul fails to govern the impulses from which it derives bodily pleasure. In the same way, if the rational mind is corrupt, mistaken ideas and false beliefs will poison life. In those days my mind was corrupt. I did not know that if it was to share in the truth, it must be illumined by another light, because the mind itself is not the essence of truth. For *it is you, Lord, that keep the lamp of my hopes still burning and shine on the darkness about me. We have all received something out of your abundance. For you are the true Light which enlightens every soul born into the world,* because *with you there can be no change, no swerving from your course.*

I was struggling to reach you, but you thrust me back so that I knew the taste of death. For *you thwart the proud.* And what greater pride could there be than to assert, as I did in my strange madness, that by nature I was what you are? I was changeable, and I knew it; for if I wanted to be a learned man, it could only mean that I wanted to be better than I was. All the same I preferred to think that you too were changeable rather than suppose that I was not what you are. This was why you thrust me back and crushed my rearing pride, while my imagination continued to play on material forms. Myself a man of flesh and blood I blamed the flesh. I was as fickle as *a breath of wind,* unable to return to you. I drifted on, making my way towards things that had no existence in you or in myself or in the body. They were not created for me by your truth but were the inventions of my own foolish imagination working on material things. Though I did not know it, I was in exile from my place in God's city among his faithful children, my fellow citizens. But I was all words, and stupidly I used to ask them, 'If, as you say, God made the soul, why does it err?' Yet I did not like them to ask me in return, 'If what you say is true, why does God err?' So I used to argue that your unchangeable substance, my God, was forced to err, rather than admit that my own was changeable and erred of its own free will, and that its errors were my punishment.[6]

2. Nevertheless I remained on more familiar terms with the Manichees than with others who did not share their heresy. I no longer advocated their cause with my old enthusiasm, but many of them were to be found in Rome, living unobtrusively, and their friendship made me slow to seek another, especially since I had lost hope of being able to find the truth in your Church, O Lord of heaven and earth, Creator of all things visible and invisible. The Manichees had turned me away from it: at the same time I thought it outrageous to believe that you had the shape of a human body and were limited within the dimensions of limbs like our own. When I tried to think of my God, I could think of him only as a bodily substance, because I could not conceive of the existence of anything else. This was the principal and almost the only cause of the error from which I could not escape.

For the same reason I believed that evil, too, was some similar kind of substance, a shapeless, hideous mass, which might be solid, in which case the Manichees called it earth, or fine and rarefied like air. This they imagine as a kind of evil mind filtering through the substance they call earth. And because such little piety as I had compelled me to believe that God, who is good, could not have created an evil nature, I imagined that there were two antagonistic masses, both of which were infinite, yet the evil in a lesser and the good in a greater degree.

All my other sacrilegious beliefs were the outcome of this first fatal mistake. For when I tried to fall back upon the Catholic faith, my mind recoiled because the Catholic faith was not what I supposed it to be. My theories forced me to admit that you were finite in one point only, in so far as the mass of evil was able to oppose you; but, O my God, whose mercies I now aver, if I believed that you were infinite in all other ways, I thought that this was a more pious belief than to suppose that you were limited, in each and every way, by the outlines of a human body. And it seemed to me better to believe that you had created no evil than to suppose that evil, such as I imagined it to be, had its origin in you. For, ignorant as I was, I thought of evil not simply as some vague substance but as an actual bodily substance, and this was because I could not conceive of mind except as a rarefied body somehow diffused in space. I also thought of our Saviour, your only Son, as somehow extended or projected for our salvation from the mass of your transplendent body, and I was so convinced of this that I could believe nothing about him except such futile dreams as I could picture to myself. I did not believe that a nature such as his could have taken birth from the Virgin Mary unless it were mingled with her flesh; and, if it were such as I imagined it to be, I could not see how it could be mingled with her flesh without being defiled. So I dared not believe in his incarnation, for fear that I should be compelled to believe that the flesh had defiled him.[7]

3. I said to myself, 'Here is God, and here is what he has created. God is good, utterly and entirely better than the things which he has made. But, since he is good, the things that he has made are also good. This is how he contains them all in himself and fills them all with his presence.

'Where then is evil? What is its origin? How did it steal into the world? What is the root or seed from which it grew? Can it be that there simply is no evil? If so, why do we fear and guard against something which is not there? If our fear is unfounded, it is itself an evil, because it stabs and wrings our hearts for nothing. In fact the evil is all the greater if we are afraid when there is nothing to fear. Therefore, either there is evil and we fear it, or the fear itself is evil.

'Where then does evil come from, if God made all things and, because he is good, made them good too? It is true that he is the supreme Good, that he is himself a greater Good than these lesser goods which he created. But the Creator and all his creation are both good. Where then does evil come from?[8]

4. It was made clear to me also that even those things which are subject to decay are good. If they were of the supreme order of goodness, they could not become corrupt; but neither could they become corrupt unless they were in some way good. For if they were supremely good, it would not be possible for them to be corrupted. On the other hand, if they were entirely without good, there would be nothing in them that could become corrupt. For corruption is harmful, but unless it diminished what is good, it could do no harm. The conclusion then must be either that corruption does no harm—which is not possible; or that every-thing which is corrupted is deprived of good—which is beyond doubt. But if they are deprived of all good, they will not exist at all. For if they still exist but can no longer be corrupted, they will be better than they were before, because they now continue their existence in an incorruptible state. But could anything be more preposterous than to say that things are made better by being deprived of all good?

So we must conclude that if things are deprived of all good, they cease altogether to be; and this means that as long as they are, they are good. Therefore, whatever is, is good; and evil, the origin of which I was trying to find, is not a substance, because if it were a substance, it would be good. For either it would be an incorruptible substance of the supreme order of goodness, or it would be a corruptible substance which would not be corruptible unless it were good. So it became obvious to me that all that you have made is good, and that there are no substances whatsoever that were not made by you. And because you did not make them all equal, each single thing is good and collectively they are very good, for our God made his whole creation *very good*.

For you evil does not exist, and not only for you but for the whole of your creation as well, because there is nothing outside it which could invade it and break down the order which you have imposed on it. Yet in the separate parts of your creation there are some things which we think of as evil because they are at variance with other things. But there are other things again with which they are in accord, and then they are good. In themselves, too, they are good. And all these things which are at variance with one another are in accord with the lower part of creation which we call the earth. The sky, which is cloudy and windy, suits the earth to which it belongs. So it would be wrong for me to wish that these earthly things did not exist, for even if I saw nothing but them, I might wish for something better, but still I ought to praise you for them alone.[9]

C. CRITICISM OF THE *PRIVATIO BONI* DOCTRINE

1. Well, the great problem of our time for him [Jung] was man's failure to know himself, to recognize evil and deal with it within himself. That is why he was always at war with a Roman Catholicism which held that evil is only an absence of good. This, Jung thought, was blasphemy because evil to him was real. There were these two great opposites in life, good and evil. How relative they might be to a man's state of awareness, and what they represented, were absolutes on man's pilgrim way. To diminish the stature of evil as a reality in life, therefore, was to make man more vulnerable to evil. As he said in his correspondence with Victor White, 'You can't call Hitler's massacre of the Jews merely an absence of good. Nor can you call Stalin's massacre of the peasants in Russia merely an absence of good. These are evil things and we must call them by their right names. This is a sure fact.' And he said, 'Man is only free insofar as he chooses good rather than evil.'

But didn't Jung believe evil was necessary to good? Like Mephisto to Goethe's Faust?

Yes, I think he fully accepted that evil was part of the reality of the universe and had a very important role in that, in a sense, if man did not have good and evil to choose between, life would lose its meaning. But I think one must be at one's most aware when one speaks of the reality of good and evil and not be over-confident, because the problem of their presence in life is only capable of articulation in part. All we can say with a certain instinctive authority is that consciousness, good and evil, all three, burst into life at once; they are interconnected in the most subtle, mysterious and enigmatic ways. The gift of consciousness compels us to recognize good and evil, however provisionally, and with all the awareness we are capable of we have to choose between them. There lies the greatest freedom conferred on us by consciousness: the freedom to choose between good and evil; and as we choose, so shall we increase or decline.

—Laurens van der Post[10]

2. The Christian answer is that evil is a *privatio boni*. This classic formula robs evil of absolute existence and makes it a shadow that has only a relative existence dependent on light. Good, on the other hand, is credited with a positive substantiality. But, as psychological experience shows, "good" and "evil" are opposite poles of a moral judgment which, as such, originates in man. A judgment can be made about a thing only if its opposite is equally real and possible. The opposite of a seeming evil can only be a seeming good, and an evil that lacks substance can only be contrasted with a good that is equally non-substantial. Although the opposite of "existence" is "non-existence," the opposite of an existing good can never be a non-existing evil, for the latter is a contradiction in terms and opposes to an existing good something incommensurable with it; the opposite of a non-existing (negative) evil can only be a non-existing (negative) good. If, therefore, evil is said to be a mere privation of good, the opposition of good and evil is denied outright. How can one speak of "good" at all if there is no "evil"? Or of "light" if there is no "darkness," or of "above" if there is no "below"? There is no getting round the fact that if you allow substantiality to good, you must also allow it to evil. If evil has no substance, good must remain shadowy, for there is no substantial opponent for it to defend itself against, but only a shadow, a mere privation of good. Such a view can hardly be squared with observed reality. It is difficult to avoid the impression that apotropaic tendencies have had a hand in creating this motion, with the understandable intention of settling the painful problem of evil as optimistically as possible. Often it is just as well that we do not know the danger we escape when we rush in where angels fear to tread.

—C. G. Jung[11]

3. On the practical level the *privatio boni* doctrine is morally dangerous, because it belittles and trivializes Evil and thereby weakens the Good, because it deprives it of its necessary opposite: there is no white without black, no right without left, no above without below, no warm without cold, no truth without error, no light without darkness, etc. If Evil is an illusion, Good is necessarily illusory too. That is the reason why I hold that *privatio boni* is illogical, irrational and even a nonsense. The moral opposites are an epistemological necessity and, when hypostasized, they produce an amoral Yahweh and a Lucifer and a Serpent and sinful Man and a Suffering Creation.

—C. G. Jung[12]

4. It is usual to think of good and evil as two poles, two opposite directions, the two arms of a signpost pointing to right and left; they are understood as belonging to the same plane of being, as the same in nature, but the antithesis to one another. If we are to have in mind, not ethical abstractions, but existent states of human reality, we must begin by doing away with this convention and recognizing the fundamental dissimilarity between the two in nature, structure and dynamics within human reality.

It is advisable to begin with evil, since, as will be shown, at the original stage, with which we shall deal first, the existent state of good in a certain matter presupposes that of evil.

—Martin Buber[13]

D. JUNG ON EVIL

1. Since psychology is not metaphysics, no metaphysical dualism can be derived from, or imputed to, its statements concerning the equivalence of opposites. It knows that equivalent opposites are necessary conditions inherent in the act of cognition, and that without them no discrimination would be possible. It is not exactly probable that anything so intrinsically bound up with the act of cognition should be at the same time a property of the object. It is far easier to suppose that it is primarily our consciousness which names

and evaluates the differences between things, and perhaps even creates distinctions where no differences are discernible.

I have gone into the doctrine of the *pivatio boni* at such length because it is in a sense responsible for a too optimistic conception of the evil in human nature and for a too pessimistic view of the human soul. To offset this, early Christianity, with unerring logic, balanced Christ against an Antichrist. For how can you speak of "high" if there is no "low," or "right" if there is no "left," of "good" if there is no "bad," and the one is as real as the other? Only with Christ did a devil enter the world as the real counterpart of God, and in early Jewish-Christian circles Satan, as already mentioned, was regarded as Christ's elder brother.

—C. G. Jung[14]

2. Evil has become a determinant reality. It can no longer be dismissed from the world by a circumlocution. We must learn how to handle it, since it is here to stay. How we can live with it without terrible consequences cannot for the present be conceived.

In any case, we stand in need of a reorientation, a *metanoia*. Touching evil brings with it the grave peril of succumbing to it. We must, therefore, no longer succumb to anything at all, not even to good. A so-called good to which we succumb loses its ethical character. Not that there is anything bad in it on that score, but to have succumbed to it may breed trouble. Every form of addiction is bad, no matter whether the narcotic be alcohol or morphine or idealism. We must beware of thinking of good and evil as absolute opposites. The criterion of ethical action can no longer consist in the simple view that good has the force of a categorical imperative, while so-called evil can resolutely be shunned. Recognition of the reality of evil necessarily relativizes the good, and the evil likewise, converting both into halves of a paradoxical whole.

In practical terms, this means that good and evil are no longer so self-evident. We have to realize that each represents a *judgment*. In view of the fallibility of all human judgment, we cannot believe that we will always judge rightly. We might so easily be the victims of misjudgment. The ethical problem is affected by this principle only to the extent that we become somewhat uncertain about moral evaluations. Nevertheless we have to make ethical decisions. The relativity of "good" and "evil" by no means signifies that these categories are invalid, or do not exist. Moral judgment is always present and carries with it characteristic psychological consequences. I have pointed out many times that as in the past, so in the future the wrong we have done, thought, or intended will wreak its vengeance on our souls. Only the contents of judgment are subject to the differing conditions of time and place and, therefore, take correspondingly different forms. For moral evaluation is always founded upon the apparent certitudes of a moral code which pretends to know precisely what is good and what evil.

—C. G. Jung[15]

3. Evil needs to be pondered just as much as good, for good and evil are ultimately nothing but ideal extensions and abstractions of doing, and both belong to the chiaroscuro of life. In the last resort there is no good that cannot produce evil and no evil that cannot produce good.

—C. G. Jung[16]

4. Our knowledge of good and evil has dwindled with our mounting knowledge and experience, and will dwindle still more in the future, without our being able to escape the demands of ethics. In this utmost uncertainty we need the illumination of a holy and whole-making spirit—a spirit that can be anything rather than our reason.

—C. G. Jung[17]

5. We need more understanding of human nature, because the only real danger that exists is man himself. He is the great danger, and we are pitifully unaware of it. We know nothing of man, far too little. His psyche should be studied, because we are the origin of all coming evil.

—C. G. Jung[18]

6. But a strong moral disposition is a comparative rarity, so that when the crimes mount up, indignation may easily get

pitched too high, and evil then becomes the order of the day. Everyone harbours his "statistical criminal" in himself, just as he has his own private madman or saint. Owing to this basic peculiarity in our human make-up, a corresponding suggestibility, or susceptibility to infection, exists everywhere. It is our age in particular—the last half century—that has prepared the way for crime. Has it never occurred to anybody, for instance, that the vogue for the thriller has a rather questionable side?

Long before 1933 there was a smell of burning in the air, and people were passionately interested in discovering the locus of the fire and in tracking down the incendiary. And when denser clouds of smoke were seen to gather over Germany, and the burning of the Reichstag gave the signal, then at last there was no mistake where the incendiary, evil in person, dwelt. Terrifying as this discovery was, in time it brought a sense of relief: now we knew for certain where all unrighteousness was to be found, whereas we ourselves were securely entrenched in the opposite camp, among respectable people whose moral indignation could be trusted to rise higher and higher with every fresh sign of guilt on the other side. Even the call for mass executions no longer offended the ears of the righteous, and the saturation bombing of German cities was looked upon as the judgment of God. Hate had found respectable motives and had ceased to be a personal idiosyncrasy, indulged in secret. And all the time the esteemed public had not the faintest idea how closely they themselves were living to evil.

One should not imagine for a moment that anybody could escape this play of opposites. Even a saint would have to pray unceasingly for the souls of Hitler and Himmler, the Gestapo and the S.S., in order to repair without delay the damage done to his own soul. The sight of evil kindles evil in the soul—there is no getting away from this fact. The victim is not the only sufferer; everybody in the vicinity of the crime, including the murderer, suffers with him. Something of the abysmal darkness of the world has broken in on us, poisoning the very air we breathe and befouling the pure water with the stale, nauseating taste of blood.

—C. G. Jung[19]

7. Just think for a moment what anti-Semitism means for the German: he is trying to use others as a scapegoat for his own

greatest fault! This symptom alone should have told him that he had got on to a hopelessly wrong track.

After the last World War the world should have begun to reflect, and above all Germany, which is the nerve-centre of Europe. But the spirit turned negative, neglected the decisive questions, and sought solutions in its own negation. How different it was at the time of the Reformation! Then the spirit of Germany rose manfully to the needs of Christendom, though the answer—as we might expect from the German tension of opposites—was somewhat too extreme. But at least this spirit did not shrink from its own problems. Goethe, too, was a prophet when he held up before his people the example of Faust's pact with the devil and the murder of Philemon and Baucis. If, as Burckhardt says, Faust strikes a chord in every German soul, this chord has certainly gone on ringing. We hear it echoing in Nietzsche's Superman, the amoral worshipper of instinct, whose God is dead, and who presumes to be God himself, or rather a demon "six thousand feet beyond good and evil." And where has the feminine side, the soul, disappeared to in Nietzsche? Helen has vanished in Hades, and Eurydice will never return. Already we behold the fateful travesty of the denied Christ: the sick prophet is himself the Crucified, and, going back still further, the dismembered Dionysus-Zagreus. The raving prophet carries us back to the long-forgotten past: he had heard the call of destiny in the shrill whistling of the hunter, the god of the rustling forests, of drunken ecstasy, and of the berserkers who were possessed by the spirits of wild animals.

While Nietzsche was prophetically responding to the schism of the Christian world with the art of thinking, his brother in spirit, Richard Wagner, was doing the same thing with the art of music. Germanic prehistory comes surging up, thunderous and stupefying, to fill the gaping breach in the Church. Wagner salved his conscience with *Parsifal*, for which Nietzsche could never forgive him, but the Castle of the Grail vanished into an unknown land. The message was not heard and the omen went unheeded. Only the orgiastic frenzy caught on and spread like an epidemic. Wotan the storm-god had conquered. Ernst Jünger sensed that very clearly: in his book *On the Marble Cliffs* a wild huntsman comes into the land, bringing with him a wave of possession greater than anything known even in the Middle

Ages. Nowhere did the European spirit speak more plainly than it did in Germany, and nowhere was it more tragically misunderstood.

Now Germany has suffered the consequences of the pact with the devil, she has experienced madness and is torn in pieces like Zagreus, she has been ravished by the berserkers of her god Wotan, been cheated of her soul for the sake of gold and world-mastery, and defiled by the scum rising from the lowest depths.

The Germans must understand why the whole world is outraged, for our expectations had been so different. Everybody was unanimous in recognizing their gifts and their efficiency, and nobody doubted that they were capable of great things. The disappointment was all the more bitter. But the fate of Germany should not mislead Europeans into nursing the illusion that the whole world's wickedness is localized in Germany. They should realize that the German catastrophe was only one crisis in the general European sickness. Long before the Hitler era, in fact before the first World War, there were symptoms of the mental change taking place in Europe. The medieval picture of the world was breaking up and the metaphysical authority that ruled it was fast disappearing, only to reappear in man. Did not Nietzsche announce that God was dead and that his heir was the Superman, that doomed rope-dancer and fool? It is an immutable psychological law that when a projection has come to an end it always returns to its origin. So when somebody hits on the singular idea that God is dead, or does not exist at all, the psychic God-image, which is a dynamic part of the psyche's structure, finds its way back into the subject and produces a condition of "God-Almightiness," that is to say all those qualities which are peculiar to fools and madmen and therefore lead to catastrophe.

This, then is the great problem that faces the whole of Christianity: where now is the sanction for goodness and justice, which was once anchored in metaphysics? Is it really only brute force that decides everything? Is the ultimate authority only the will of whatever man happens to be in power? Had Germany been victorious, one might almost have believed that this was the last word. But as the "thousand-year Reich" of violence and infamy lasted only a few years before it collapsed in ruins, we might be disposed to learn the lesson that there are other, equally powerful forces at work which in the end destroy all that is violent and unjust, and that consequently it does not pay to build on false principles. But unfortunately, as history shows, things do not always turn out so reasonably in this world of ours.

"God-Almightiness" does not make man divine, it merely fills him with arrogance and arouses everything evil in him. It produces a diabolical caricature of man, and this inhuman mask is so unendurable, such a torture to wear, that he tortures others. He is split in himself, a prey to inexplicable contradictions. Here we have the picture of the hysterical state of mind, of Nietzsche's "pale criminal." Fate has confronted every German with his inner counterpart: Faust is face to face with Mephistopheles and can no longer say, "So that was the essence of the brute!" He must confess instead: "That was my other side, my *alter ego*, my all too palpable shadow which can no longer be denied."

This is not the fate of Germany alone, but of all Europe. We must all open our eyes to the shadow who looms behind contemporary man. We have no need to hold up the devil's mask before the Germans. The facts speak a plainer language, and anyone who does not understand it is simply beyond help. As to what should be done about this terrifying apparition, everyone must work this out for himself. It is indeed no small matter to know of one's own guilt and one's own evil, and there is certainly nothing to be gained by losing sight of one's shadow. When we are conscious of our guilt we are in a more favourable position—we can at least hope to change and improve ourselves. As we know, anything that remains in the unconscious is incorrigible; psychological corrections can be made only in consciousness. Consciousness of guilt can therefore act as a powerful moral stimulus. In every treatment of neurosis the discovery of the shadow is indispensable, otherwise nothing changes. In this respect, I rely on those parts of the German body-politic which have remained sound to draw conclusions from the facts. Without guilt, unfortunately, there can be no psychic maturation and no widening of the spiritual horizon. Was it not Meister Eckhart who said: "For this reason God is willing to bear the brunt of sins and often winks at them, mostly sending them to people for whom he has prepared some high destiny. See! Who was dearer to our Lord or more intimate with him than his apostles? Not one of them but fell into mortal sin, and all were mortal sinners." (*Works*, trans. by Evans, II, pp. 18–19)

Where sin is great, "grace doth much more abound." Such an experience brings about an inner transformation, and this is infinitely more important than political and social reforms which are all valueless in the hands of people who are not at one with themselves. This is a truth which we are forever forgetting, because our eyes are fascinated by the conditions around us and riveted on them instead of examining our own heart and conscience. Every demagogue exploits this human weakness when he points with the greatest possible outcry to all the things that are wrong in the outside world. But the principal and indeed the only thing that is wrong with the world is man.

If the Germans today are having a hard time of it outwardly, fate has at least given them a unique opportunity of turning their eyes inward to the inner man. In this way they might make amends for a sin of omission of which our whole civilization is guilty. Everything possible has been done for the outside world: science has been refined to an unimaginable extent, technical achievement has reached an almost uncanny degree of perfection. But what of man, who is expected to administer all these blessings in a reasonable way? He has simply been taken for granted. No one has stopped to consider that neither morally nor psychologically is he in any way adapted to such changes. As blithely as any child of nature he sets about enjoying these dangerous playthings, completely oblivious of the shadow lurking behind him, ready to seize them in its greedy grasp and turn them against a still infantile and unconscious humanity. And who has had a more immediate experience of this feeling of helplessness and abandonment to the powers of darkness than the German who fell into the clutches of the Germans?

If collective guilt could only be understood and accepted, a great step forward would have been taken. But this alone is no cure, just as no neurotic is cured by mere understanding. The question remains: How am I to live with this shadow? What attitude is required if I am to be able to live in spite of evil? In order to find valid answers to these questions a complete spiritual renewal is needed. And this cannot be given gratis, each man must strive to achieve it for himself. Neither can old formulas which once had a value be brought into force again. The eternal truths cannot be transmitted mechanically; in every epoch they must be born anew from the human psyche.

—C. G. Jung[20]

E. The Shadow

1. When the medical psychologist takes an interest in symbols, he is primarily concerned with "natural" symbols, as distinct from "cultural" symbols. The former are derived from the unconscious contents of the psyche, and they therefore represent an enormous number of variations on the essential archetypal images. In many cases they can still be traced back to their archaic roots—i.e. to ideas and images that we meet in the most ancient records and in primitive societies. The cultural symbols, on the other hand, are those that have been used to express "eternal truths," and that are still used in many religions. They have gone through many transformations and even a long process of more or less conscious development, and have thus become collective images accepted by civilized societies.

Such cultural symbols nevertheless retain much of their original numinosity or "spell." One is aware that they can evoke a deep emotional response in some individuals, and this psychic change makes them function in much the same way as prejudices. They are a factor with which the psychologist must reckon; it is folly to dismiss them because, in rational terms, they seem to be absurd or irrelevant. They are important constituents of our mental make-up and vital forces in the building up of human society; and they cannot be eradicated without serious loss. Where they are repressed or neglected, their specific energy disappears into the unconscious with unaccountable consequences. The psychic energy that appears to have been lost in this way in fact serves to revive and intensify whatever is uppermost in the unconscious—tendencies, perhaps, that have hitherto had no chance to express themselves or at least have not been allowed an uninhibited existence in our consciousness.

Such tendencies form an ever-present and potentially destructive "shadow" to our conscious mind. Even tendencies that might in some circumstances be able to exert a beneficial influence are transformed into demons when they are repressed. This is why many well-meaning people are understandably afraid of the unconscious, and incidentally of psychology.

Our times have demonstrated what it means for the gates of the underworld to be opened. Things whose enormity nobody could have imagined in the idyllic harmlessness of the first decade of our century have happened and have turned our world upside down. Ever since, the world has remained in a state of schizophrenia. Not only has civilized Germany disgorged its terrible primitivity, but Russia is also ruled by it, and Africa has been set on fire. No wonder that the Western world feels uneasy.

Modern man does not understand how much his "rationalism" (which has destroyed his capacity to respond to numinous symbols and ideas) has put him at the mercy of the psychic "underworld." He has freed himself from "superstition" (or so he believes), but in the process he has lost his spiritual values to a positively dangerous degree. His moral and spiritual tradition has disintegrated, and he is now paying the price for this break-up in world-wide disorientation and dissociation.

—C. G. Jung[21]

2. If the repressed tendencies, the shadow as I call them, were obviously evil, there would be no problem whatever. But the shadow is merely somewhat inferior, primitive, unadapted, and awkward; not wholly bad. It even contains childish or primitive qualities which would in a way vitalize and embellish human existence, but—convention forbids.

—C. G. Jung[22]

3. In reality, the acceptance of the shadow-side of human nature verges on the impossible. Consider for a moment what it means to grant the right of existence to what is unreasonable, senseless, and evil! Yet it is just this that the modern man insists upon. He wants to live with every side of himself—to know what he is. That is why he casts history aside. He wants to break with

tradition so that he can experiment with his life and determine what value and meaning things have in themselves, apart from traditional presuppositions.

—C. G. Jung[23]

4. The dammed-up instinctual forces in civilized man are immensely destructive and far more dangerous than the instincts of the primitive, who in a modest degree is constantly living out his negative instincts. Consequently no war of the historical past can rival in grandiose horror the wars of civilized nations.

—C. G. Jung[24]

5. The daemonism of nature, which man had apparently triumphed over, he has unwittingly swallowed into himself and so become the devil's marionette. This could happen only because he believed he had abolished the daemons by declaring them to be superstition. He overlooked the fact that they were, at bottom, the products of certain factors in the human psyche. When these products were dubbed unreal and illusory, their sources were in no way blocked up or rendered inoperative. On the contrary, after it became impossible for the daemons to inhabit the rocks, woods, mountains, and rivers, they used human beings as much more dangerous dwelling places.

—C. G. Jung[25]

6. Whether the unconscious comes up at first in a helpful or a negative form, after a time the need usually arises to readapt the conscious attitude in a better way to the unconscious factors—therefore to accept what seems to be "criticism" from the unconscious. Through dreams one becomes acquainted with aspects of one's own personality that for various reasons one has preferred not to look at too closely. This is what Jung called "the realization of the shadow." (He used the term "shadow" for this unconscious part of the personality because it actually often appears in dreams in a personified form.)

The shadow is not the whole of the unconscious personality. It represents unknown or little-known attributes and qualities of the ego—aspects that mostly belong to the personal sphere and that could just as well be conscious. In some aspects, the shadow can also consist of collective factors that stem from a source outside the individual's personal life.

When an individual makes an attempt to see his shadow, he becomes aware of (and often ashamed of) those qualities and impulses he denies in himself but can plainly see in other people—such things as egotism, mental laziness, and sloppiness; unreal fantasies, schemes, and plots; carelessness and cowardice; inordinate love of money and possessions—in short, all the little sins about which he might previously have told himself: "That doesn't matter; nobody will notice it, and in any case other people do it too."

If you feel an overwhelming rage coming up in you when a friend reproaches you about a fault, you can be fairly sure that at this point you will find a part of your shadow, of which you are unconscious. It is, of course, natural to become annoyed when others who are "no better" criticize you because of shadow faults. But what can you say if your own dreams—an inner judge in your own being—reproach you? That is the moment when the ego gets caught, and the result is usually embarrassed silence. Afterward the painful and lengthy work of self-education begins—a work, we might say, that is the psychological equivalent of the labors of Hercules. This unfortunate hero's first task, you will remember, was to clean up in one day the Augean Stables, in which hundreds of cattle had dropped their dung for many decades—a task so enormous that the ordinary mortal would be overcome by discouragement at the mere thought of it.

The shadow does not consist only of omissions. It shows up just as often in an impulsive or inadvertent act. Before one has time to think, the evil remark pops out, the plot is hatched, the wrong decision is made, and one is confronted with results that were never intended or consciously wanted. Furthermore, the shadow is exposed to collective infections to a much greater extent than is the conscious personality. When a man is alone, for instance, he feels relatively all right; but as soon as "the others" do dark, primitive things, he begins to fear that if he doesn't join in, he will be considered a fool. Thus he gives way to impulses that do not really belong to him at all. It is particularly in contacts with people of the same sex that one stumbles over both one's own shadow and those of other people. Although we do see the shadow in a person of the opposite sex, we are usually much less annoyed by it and can more easily pardon it.

In dreams and myths, therefore, the shadow appears as a person of the same sex as that of the dreamer.

—M. L. von Franz[26]

7. Since everybody is blindly convinced that he is nothing more than his own extremely unassuming and insignificant conscious self, which performs its duties decently and earns a moderate living, nobody is aware that this whole rationalistically organized conglomeration we call a state of a nation is driven on by seemingly impersonal, invisible but terrifying power which nobody and nothing can check. This ghastly power is mostly explained as fear of the neighboring nation, which is supposed to be possessed by a malevolent fiend. Since nobody is capable of recognizing just where and how much he himself is possessed and unconscious, he simply projects his own condition upon his neighbor, and thus it becomes a sacred duty to have the biggest guns and the most poisonous gas. The worst of it is that he is quite right. All one's neighbors are in the grip of some uncontrolled and uncontrollable fear, just like oneself. In lunatic asylums it is a well-known fact that patients are far more dangerous when suffering from fear than when moved by rage or hatred.

—C. G. Jung[27]

8. The first prison I ever saw had inscribed on it, 'Cease To Do Evil: Learn To Do Well'; but as the inscription was on the outside, the prisoners could not read it. It should have been addressed to the self-righteous spectator in the street and should have read, "All Have Sinned and Fallen Short of the Glory of God.'

—G. B. Shaw[28]

9. Almost everyone has at least one particularly hated person.
    This hated one is a remarkable clue to
    the most unpleasant parts of the hating one.
    Try that one on for size:
    That's your dark twin.

Remember that you have a shadow. When a patient
thinks you are a stupid, greedy, self-centered,
   power-driven
quack, or thinks you are a god who knows everything,
he's put his finger on the healer's shadow.
By the same token the patient has the shadow
of the sick one: helplessness, weakness, and infantile
   insatiability.

The shadow is inexhaustible.
It is advisable to be able to eat your own shadow.
This metaphor always seems odd.
But there is something to it;
if you can stomach your own shadow
you can take on almost any old thing.

One of the problems of recognizing and facing our
   shadow,
owning it, eating it, and withdrawing it from projection
is that the shadow becomes a serious problem to oneself.
Withdrawing and acknowledging our shadow
is only the first step.
Then there is the long painful negotiation with it.
However, it is quite obvious from dreams
that when one faces a shadow which one has denied or run
   from
it diminishes in power, and size,
and ultimately becomes a positive force.

Our friends show us what we can do,
our enemies teach us what we must do. (Goethe)

The first view of any monster is apt to be
the most unnerving.
When we finally bring ourselves to see the shadow
we project as our own,
we are literally appalled and overwhelmed by the shadow,
the evil out there so plain to see.
At the moment of taking it back within ourselves

we are apt to be filled with self-recrimination,
guilt, and depression.
Little wonder we want to leave it out there
hanging on someone or something or some other
    whatever.

Repeat: We perceive the shadow as if it belongs to the
    other.
We withdraw our projection and our own shadow becomes
    enormous.
After prolonged negotiation we are able to befriend the
    shadow.
But even then it is not over because
the shadow will always be there, always be a part of our
    psyche.
We had best make a truce with it,
for the shadow
alerts us to particular kinds of danger or evil.
                                —Harry A. Wilmer[29]

10. If only it was all so simple! If only there were evil people
somewhere insidiously committing evil deeds, and it were
necessary only to separate them from the rest of us and destroy
them. But the line dividing good and evil cuts through the heart
of every human being. And who is willing to destroy a part of his
own heart?

During the life of any heart this line keeps changing place:
sometimes it is squeezed one way to exuberant evil and sometimes it shifts to allow enough space for good to flourish. One and
the same human being is, at various ages, under various
circumstances, a totally different human being. At times he is
close to being a devil, at times to sainthood. But his name doesn't
change and to that name we ascribe the whole lot, good and evil.

Socrates taught us: *Know thyself!*

Confronted by the pit into which we are about to toss those
who have done us harm, we halt, stricken dumb: it is after all only
because of the way things worked out that they were the
executioners and we weren't.
                                —Solzhenitsyn[30]

NOTES

[1] The texts printed in this section are from three ancient thinkers who represent different points of view. Heraclitus (6th–5th century B.C.E.) was an early Greek philosopher who stressed the difference between appearance and reality. Epictetus (50?–130 C.E.) was a late spokesman for the most popular philosophy of ancient times, Stoicism, which held that the universe is guided in all things by a wise and good Providence. Epicurus (342?–270 B.C.E.) was a materialist and an early advocate of atomic theory. On his view, what we call evil is due to the impersonal laws that govern the motion and combination of atoms; there is no evil power for us to fear.

[2] Translations of Heraclitus were prepared for this volume by Paul Woodruff.

[3] Translations of Epictetus are from Nicholas White, *The Handbook of Epictetus*. Indianapolis: Hackett Publishing Co., 1983.

[4] Translations of Epicurus were prepared for this volume by Paul Woodruff.

[5] In his youth, Augustine had been tempted to join the Manichaeans, a heretical sect who believed that the principle of good was matched by an equally substantial power of evil. Augustine felt that this un-Christian theory was the source of many errors. For a thorough discussion of Augustine's theory of evil, see G. R. Evans, *Augustine on Evil*, Cambridge: Cambridge University Press, 1982.

The theory that evil is not substantially real, but is instead a privation or distancing from God *(privatio boni)* was discussed in the Symposium on Understanding Evil. Russell (p. 67) and Hallie (p. 119) attacked the theory; Proctor defended it in the main part of his paper.

[6] *Saint Augustine: Confessions*. Trans. by R. S. Pine-Coffin. Harmondsworth: Penguin, 1961. Book IV, 15, pp. 85–87.

[7] *Ibid.*, Book V 10, pp. 104–5.

[8] *Ibid.*, Book VII 5, p. 138.

[9] *Ibid.*, Book VII 12–13, pp. 148–49.

[10] Laurens van der Post (in conversation with Jean-Marc Pottiez), *A Walk with a White Bushman*. London: Chatto & Windus, 1986, pp. 45–46.

[11] C. G. Jung, *The Collected Works of C. G. Jung*. 2d Ed. Volume 11. Princeton: Princeton University Press, 1969, p. 168.

[12] C. G. Jung, *Letters*, Volume II. Princeton: Princeton University Press, 1975, p. 61.

[13] Martin Buber, *Good and Evil: Two Interpretations*. New York: Charles Scribner's Sons, 1953, p. 121.

[14] C. G. Jung, *The Collected Works of C. G. Jung*. 2d Ed. Volume. 9.2. Princeton: Princeton University Press, 1970, p. 61.

[15] C. G. Jung, *Memories, Dreams, Reflections*. New York: Random House, 1961, p. 329.

[16] C. G. Jung, *Collected Works*. 2d Ed. Volume 12. Princeton: Princeton University Press, 1970, p. 31.

[17] C. G. Jung, *Collected Works*. 2d Ed. Volume 11. Princeton: Princeton University Press, 1969, p. 180.

[18] W. McGuire and R. F. C. Hull, eds, *C. G. Jung Speaking: Interviews and Encounters*. Princeton: Princeton University Press, 1977, p. 436. From a 1959 BBC interview.

[19] C. G. Jung, *Collected Works*. 2d Ed. Volume 10. Princeton: Princeton University Press, 1970, p. 199.

[20] *Ibid.*, pp. 213–17.

[21] C. G. Jung, *Man and His Symbols*. Garden City, NY: Doubleday, 1964, pp. 93–94.

[22] C. G. Jung, *Psychological Reflections: A New Anthology of His Writings*. Ed. by Jolande Jacobi. Princeton: Princeton University Press, 1978, p. 242.

[23] *Ibid.*, p. 242.

[24] *Ibid.*, p. 232.

[25] *Ibid.*, p. 232.

[26] M. L. von Franz, from C. G. Jung. *Man and His Symbols*, pp. 168–69.

[27] C. G. Jung, *Collected Works*, Volume II, p. 48.

[28] G. B. Shaw, *The Crime of Imprisonment*. New York: Philosophical Library, 1946, p. 70.

[29] Harry A. Wilmer, *Practical Jung: Nuts and Bolts of Jungian Psychotherapy*. Wilmette, Illinois: Chiron Publications, 1987, pp. 98–103.

[30] Aleksandr I. Solzhenitsyn, *The Gulag Archipelago: 1918–1956*. New York: Harper & Row, 1974, p. 168.

ANNOTATED BIBLIOGRAPHY

Jeffrey Burton Russell

The literature on Evil—philosophical, theological, historical, psychological, literary, sociological, artistic, political, experiential —is enormous: it is one of the great problems of human history and human existence. This is therefore only a very select bibliography of some of the most helpful and most recent books on the subject. Most of the books listed below contain bibliographies of their own for further investigation.

Abrahamson, Irving, ed. *Against Silence: The Voice and Vision of Elie Wiesel.* New York: Schocken Books, 1986.
A biographical and analytical account of the courageous and dedicated life and thought of the most influential living survivor of the Nazi death camps.

Abzug, Robert. *Inside the Vicious Heart: Americans and the Liberation of Nazi Concentration Camps.* New York: Oxford University Press, 1985.
A discussion of the liberation of the camps and the effect that it has had upon American political, ethical, and religious attitudes.

Becker, Ernest. *The Structure of Evil.* New York: Free Press, 1968.
A deeply personal, thoughtful, sometimes pessimistic, but always profound reflection upon the human experience of evil.

———. *Escape from Evil.* New York: Free Press, 1975.
Becker's answer to his own pessimism: humans can socially and institutionally, but above all personally, make choices that reduce suffering.

Buber, Martin. *Good and Evil*. New York: Scribner's Sons, 1952.
Perhaps the greatest Jewish theologian and moralist of this century, Buber defines the nature of Good and Evil in Biblical, rabbinic, and philosophical terms: the answer to evil lies in God's empowerment of humans for good.

Carus, Paul. *The History of the Devil and the Idea of Evil*. La Salle, Ill.: Open Court, 1974.

Davis, Stephen, ed., *Encountering Evil*. Atlanta: John Knox Press, 1981.
A collection of deeply thoughtful essays on Evil combined with the authors' critiques of one another. Many major modern theological ideas of evil are here presented with both their defenses and their weaknesses revealed.

Doob, Leonard. *Panorama of Evil: Insights for the Behavioral Sciences*. Westport, Conn.: Greenwood Press, 1978.
A serious approach to the problem quite distinct from traditional philosophical and religious approaches. Evil is seen in its social dimensions of violence and aggression.

Evans, Gillian R. *Augustine on Evil*. Cambridge: Cambridge University Press, 1982.
A masterfully clear discussion of the views of the single most influential Christian theologian of all time, the fifth-century bishop of Hippo whose ideas formed the basis of both Catholic and Protestant teaching.

Evil. Curatorium of the C. G. Jung Institute of Zurich. Evanston, Ill.: Northwestern University Press, 1967.
Essays by a number of Jungian analysts expounding the great psychologist's views on Evil, the Shadow, archetypes, and the coincidence of opposites.

Ford, Franklin. *Political Murder: From Tyrannicide to Terrorism*. Cambridge, Mass.: Harvard University Press, 1985.
A discussion of political morality both national and international: Ford's discussion shows the place that Evil plays in practice in human community and the mechanisms and

institutions by which destructive political forces gain and remain in control.

Forsyth, Neil. *Satan and the Combat Myth*. Princeton: Princeton University Press, 1987.
A deeply learned literary analysis of the origins of the idea of the Devil in the mythology of spiritual combat between opposing spiritual forces. Forsyth shows how Near Eastern mythological motifs influenced the development of the Judeo-Christian literature about the Devil.

Frankl, Viktor. *From Death Camp to Existentialism*. Boston: Beacon, 1959. Expanded edition: *Man's Search for Meaning*. New York: Knopf, 1963.
Frankl describes how he survived the Nazi death camps by finding meaning in life and argues that individual humans and humanity as a whole can be wholly healthy and complete only when they have, or create for themselves, ultimate values. He creates a therapeutical psychology called 'logotherapy' aimed at helping patients establish a sense of absolute meaning in their lives.

Fromm, Erich. *The Anatomy of Human Destructiveness*. New York: Holt, Rinehart & Winston, 1973.
The great psychologist analyzes evil in individuals and in society; he points out the glamour and attractiveness of evil as expressed in the lives of destructive charismatic leaders such as Hitler.

―――. *The Heart of Man: Its Genius for Good and Evil*. New York: Harper & Row, 1980.
A more optimistic or perhaps more practical view than the previous book: by recognizing its tendencies to destructiveness, humans can construct behavior patterns that minimize suffering.

Geach, Peter. *Providence and Evil*. Cambridge: Cambridge University Press, 1977.
One of the most influential recent books exploring the traditional problem of theodicy: how can the idea of a good

and omnipotent God be reconciled with the existence of evil in the cosmos?

Hallie, Philip. *Lest Innocent Blood Be Shed*. New York: Harper & Row, 1979.
This gripping historical account by the philosopher Philip Hallie probes personal and communal courage and will to goodness acting against the weight of an evil political system when the inhabitants of a French village risked their lives to save refugees from the Nazis.

————. *The Paradox of Cruelty*. Middletown, Conn.: Wesleyan University Press, 1969.
A humane and impassioned study of the paradox of the human race inclined to cruelty yet longing for good, and an assertion of our ability to choose kindness over anger.

Hebblethwaite, Brian. *Evil, Suffering, and Religion*. New York: Hawthorne Books, 1976.
A classical account of the paradox of the Judeo-Christian-Muslim God's omnipotence in a world full of suffering, along with a sympathetic but critical view of religion's effort to elucidate the problem.

Hick, John. *Evil and the God of Love*. New York: Harper & Row, 1966.
Hick's classical argument deriving (in theory) from the church father Irenaeus that evil is necessary for "soul-building." Without a choice between true good and evil we would be as children incapable of any mature love or altruism .

Hilberg, Raul. *The Destruction of the European Jews*. 2d. ed. Chicago: University of Chicago Press, 3 vols., 1985.
The most complete and thoroughly documented account of the Holocaust. Hilberg argues that the Holocaust occurred as a result of moral choices for evil on the part not only of Hitler but of authorities throughout the Nazi system over a period of years.

Keen, Sam. *Faces of the Enemy: Reflections of the Hostile Imagination*. New York: Harper & Row, 1986.
A strikingly illustrated book showing how racial, religious, political, and economic propaganda has demonized groups perceived as the enemy so that their destruction or exploitation could be justified.

Kelsey, Morton. *Discernment*. New York: Paulist Press, 1978.

Laqueur, Walter. *The Terrible Secret*. Boston: Little, Brown, 1981.
The great historian reveals and analyzes the systematic suppression of information about Hitler's plans for the extermination of the Jews and its bureaucratic implementation.

Lifton, Robert Jay. *Death in Life: Survivors of Hiroshima*. New York: Basic Books, 1967.
One of America's most prominent writers on public ethics and responsibility, Lifton presents the evidence for the permanent physical, psychological, and social effects of the use of nuclear weapons against civilian targets; the conclusion is inescapable that evil affects the perpetrators as well as the victims.

————. *The Nazi Doctors: Medical Killing and the Psychology of Genocide*. New York: Basic Books, 1986.
Twenty years after his shattering discussion of Hiroshima, Lifton turns his attention to the Holocaust, the even darker symbol of genocide in the twentieth century. He comes as close as anyone has ever done in searching into the psychology and social psychology of educated, responsible humans participating in atrocities against humanity.

May, Rollo. *Power and Innocence: A Search for the Sources of Violence*. New York: W.W. Norton, 1972.
Written during a period when broad and wrenching changes were occurring around the world in such diverse societies as America, France, and China, the great contemporary psychologist addresses the roots of violence and aggression in the individual and the danger of power whether in the hands of oppressors or of revolutionaries.

Moorish, Ivor. *The Dark Twin: A Study of Evil and Good.* Romford, Eng.: L.N. Fowler, 1980.
A Jungian analysis of the 'coincidence of opposites', 'doublets', or 'twins', within the human psyche. The tension between opposites can be destructive; when reconciled and integrated, the tension can produce an energized, creative, good.

O'Flaherty, Wendy D. *The Origins of Evil in Hindu Mythology.* Berkeley: University of California Press, 1976.
A cosmos composed of and populated by billions of gods is a cosmos in which destructiveness acts powerfully yet is also part of a larger pattern of creative energy. O'Flaherty shows how the Hindus cope with the problem of evil through narrative and myth.

Olson, Alan M., ed. *Disguises of the Demonic: Contemporary Perspectives on the Power of Evil.* New York: Association Press, 1975.
A collection of essays dealing with the problem of evil from the point of view of sociology and social psychology; some are specific to the problems of the 1960s and 1970s; more are of enduring value.

Parkin, David. *The Anthropology of Evil.* Oxford: Basic Blackwell, 1985.
Recently many of the most important and influential new methodologies for the human sciences have come from anthropology; here a specifically anthropological approach uses such new methods in approaching evil in a cross-cultural study.

Peck, M. Scott. *People of the Lie: The Hope for Healing Human Evil.* New York: Simon & Schuster, 1983.
Using striking examples, Peck argues from his own practical experience as a psychiatrist as well as from historical and contemporary evidence that evil is an identifiable psychological disorder and that there are some people who, disguising and rationalizing their true motivations, actually give themselves over to this evil.

Philip, Howard. *Jung and the Problem of Evil.* London: Rockeiff, 1958.
A penetrating analysis of Jung's views on the Shadow and on Evil. Evil arises in part from repressions by each human individual; it also arises in part from the collective unconscious of the entire human race, which exerts active though hidden influence in each human psyche.

Reichenbach, Bruce. *Evil and a Good God.* New York: Fordham University Press, 1982.
A recent and up-to-date analysis of theodicy, the problem of reconciling the existence of Evil with that of a good God.

Ricoeur, Paul. *The Symbolism of Evil.* Boston: Harper & Row, 1967.
A philosopher's view of evil. Ricoeur examines philosophical, theological, literary, artistic, psychological, and social expressions of evil and investigates how they may be understood through linguistic analysis.

Rudwin, Maximilian. *The Devil in Legend and Literature.* La Salle, Ill.: Open Court, 1931, 1959.

Russell, Jeffrey B. *The Devil.* Ithaca, N.Y.: Cornell University Press, 1977.
A history of the concept of the personification of evil in cultures round the world but especially in ancient Hebrew and in New Testament thought.

———. *Satan.* Ithaca: Cornell University Press, 1981.
Continues the history of the personification of evil through early Christian theology.

———. *Lucifer.* Ithaca: Cornell University Press, 1984.
The personification of evil in the literature, folklore, and theology of medieval Christianity, Judaism, and Islam.

———. *Mephistopheles.* Ithaca: Cornell University Press, 1986.
The diversification of the personification of evil in modern thought, showing the influence of the Reformation, the Enlightenment, and historical and scientific thought on the subject, as well as its treatment in modern literature.

————. *The Prince of Darkness: Radical Evil and the Power of Good in History.* Ithaca: Cornell University Press, 1988.
A briefer study of the personification of evil from earliest times to the present.

Sanford, John A. *Evil: The Shadow Side of Reality.* New York: Crossroad, 1981.
A contemporary view of evil from a Jungian standpoint, the book offers not only a clear view of the traditional Jungian view but also persuasively argues Sanford's view that evil arises less from the Shadow than from the conscious. Distortions introduced by bad choices and false perceptions made by the ego cause destructive elements to develop in the Shadow.

————. *The Strange Trial of Mr. Hyde: A New Look at the Nature of Human Evil.* San Francisco: Harper & Row, 1987.
A powerful and creative investigation of the coincidence of opposites of good and evil in the human psyche, including a dramatized fictional account of a trial of Stevenson's famous Jekyll/Hyde character.

Sanford, Nevitt, and Craig Comstock, eds., *Sanctions for Evil: The Sources of Social Destructiveness.* Boston: Beacon, 1971.
A collection of essays on social aggression and violence from writers in a variety of disciplines.

Surin, Kenneth. *Theology and the Problem of Evil.* New York and Oxford: Blackwell, 1986.
A critical study of the efforts of theology to understand the origin and nature of evil in a cosmos created by a good God, including a study of the meaning of the term 'good' applied to God.

Von Franz, Marie Louise. *The Shadow and Evil in Fairy Tales.* Zurich: Spring Publications, 1974.
A creative and learned analysis of archetypes in European 'fairy tales' (better 'folk tales'), showing particularly the action of frightening, destructive, and negatively numinous elements.

Wiesel, Elie. *Night*. London: Maegibbon & Kee, 1960, New York: Hill & Wang, 1960.
Perhaps the most penetrating and insightful and disturbing account, by a survivor of the Nazi death camps, of the effects of this most dramatic of human evils upon its victims, it also offers hope to humanity in the courage and dignity that arose even in the worst of circumstances.

Index